# Innovation, Creativity, and Discovery in Modern Organizations

# Innovation, Creativity, and Discovery in Modern Organizations

## WAYNE M. BUNDY

Q

QUORUM BOOKS
Westport, Connecticut • London

Library of Congress Cataloging-in-Publication Data

Bundy, Wayne Miley, 1924–
    Innovation, creativity, and discovery in modern organizations / Wayne M. Bundy.
      p.  cm.
    Includes bibliographical references and index.
    ISBN 1–56720–569–0 (alk. paper)
    1. Creative ability in business.  2. Creative ability in technology.  3. Technological
innovations—Management.  4. Business enterprises—Technological innovations.
5. Industrial organization.  I. Title.
    HD53.B86  2002
    658.5'14—dc21      2001058937

British Library Cataloguing in Publication Data is available.

Library of Congress Catalog Card Number: 2001058937
ISBN: 1–56720–569–0

First published in 2002

Quorum Books, 88 Post Road West, Westport, CT 06881
An imprint of Greenwood Publishing Group, Inc.
www.quorumbooks.com

Printed in the United States of America

The paper used in this book complies with the
Permanent Paper Standard issued by the National
Information Standards Organization (Z39.48–1984).

10 9 8 7 6 5 4 3 2 1
JK

**Copyright Acknowledgments**

The author and publisher are grateful for permission to reproduce material from the
following copyrighted sources:

Figures 6.1, 8.2, 9.1, 10.1, 13.1, 15.1, 17.1, 18.2, and 19.1 from Wayne M. Bundy,
*The Art of Discovery: Fueling Innovation for Company Growth* (Menlo Park, CA:
Crisp Publications, 1997). Copyright © 1997 Crisp Publications, Inc.

Figure 8.2 from David Bloor, *Knowledge and Social Imagery* (Chicago: University of
Chicago Press, 1991).

*For Lorraine, Mark, Janet, and Michael*

# Contents

# Figures

# Preface

From my earliest experience in industrial research management to the day of my retirement, I felt intense pressure to develop ideas that would assist company success. I am keenly aware of the great stress involved in attempting to satisfy managers whose dominant concern is short-term profit. As my employment stability was dependent on creative contributions, this Damocles' sword motivated me to develop a philosophy of discovery and innovation that would dissuade this persistent menace.

After 34 years of technology management, I felt compelled to record what my experience had taught me and to attempt to put it in convincing form. Richly deserving of analysis, finding pathways to discovery is a conundrum of universal concern. To that end, I wanted to offer a guideline that would vitalize technical people to discover and commercialize.

Borrowing from author and physicist C. P. Snow,[1] the two cultures that he described—the literary intellectuals and the scientists—can be extended to a society having multilayered cultures, most not privy to the ways of science. Lack of empathy for science often results in fear of anything technical, distorted beliefs about the environment, and superstition about the nature of our existence and the universe. And it precludes an understanding of the vital relationship between the technical world and a successful economic system in which innovation is a prime driving force. Such a setting is particularly unfit for a representative government whose proficiency depends to a large extent on some knowledge of subjects that play a critical role in society.

Through an understanding of discovery processes, business managers become more efficient in promoting innovation. Such knowledge greatly reduces obstacles to discovery inadvertently imposed and relieves the tension that often exists between technologists and business managers. It promotes understanding between academic researchers and the business world as well. By helping the general public understand the logic, the great power, and the limitations of research, rational government support of science and technology can be enhanced.

Perhaps my most important motivation for writing this book was to emphasize the importance of rationalism, not just in the technical world but throughout society. This motivation can be viewed as a profound concern for the Enlightenment concept of history—the belief that history is driven by the expansion of knowledge and the consequent power over nature. *Innovation, Creativity, and Discovery in Modern Organizations*, then, is a clarion call to eradicate ignorance and mysticism and to support science and technology—tempered by the imperative to balance technological gain with the well-being of nature.

# Acknowledgments

I extend thanks to former leaders of the company where I worked, Dr. Haydn H. Murray, Mr. Edward Engel, and Dr. Jean-Paul Richard. Without their support I doubt that I would have had the motivation to embark on an effort of this magnitude.

Additional thanks are extended to colleagues who have reviewed and commented on this book. They include Dr. Haydn H. Murray, Professor Emeritus, Indiana University, who has been my mentor throughout my career; Dr. Tom Dombrowski, who worked for me for a short period; and Dr. Jack Harrison, retired from my former company, and his wife, Velma Harrison, who gave invaluable suggestions. Dr. Frederick A. Mumpton, Professor Emeritus, State University of New York at Brockport, contributed notable editorial help. I extend my gratitude to Mr. Edward Engel, former owner and president of the company where I worked, for his kindness and his moral support of my in-depth probe into the nature of discovery and invention.

I extend special thanks to Dr. Jean-Paul Richard, who was president of the company where I worked during the latter part of my career. He was the fire, the annoyance, and the inexhaustible pressure that culminated my interest in developing a philosophy of discovery. I thank William F. Christopher, president of the Management Innovations Group, not only for editorial help but for his untiring assistance in finding a publisher and for general advice along the way. Of special importance, I thank my wife, Lorraine, for her patience and support of my long efforts in writing this book. All anecdotes and references to people in this book are general and not specific to any company.

Thanks are extended to Joseph Andrade and Kent de Gruyter for preparation of illustrations in this book.

# Innovation, Creativity, and Discovery in Modern Organizations

# Chapter 1

# The Lure, Some Obstacles, and the Enchantment of Discovery

Before delving into the structure of presentation, a few broad generalities may be of help in understanding the underlying philosophy of this book. These include excitement and challenge, aesthetics, personal benefits, seeds of discovery, strategic research, the best wisdom for achieving discovery, business management obstacles, and consilience (defined by biologist E.O. Wilson as "a 'jumping together' of knowledge by the linking of facts and fact-based theory across disciplines to create a common groundwork of explanation."

Doing exploratory science in a quest for discovery and then changing discovery into innovation rank among the most exhilarating endeavors ever envisioned by the human mind. Similarly, the quest for new knowledge and its application embody an effort that is both noble and essential for the advancement of civilization. It is this kind of excitement and challenge that can hone the researcher's analytical and creative abilities to the most perceptive edge and is an underlying theme of this book. Psychologist Rollo May[1] contended that from rebellion against inevitable death comes creativity, which, indeed, is a marvelously renewing and exciting pursuit.

Aesthetics, therefore, is a major parameter of discovery and creativity—an essential stimulus that procreates the insatiable will to discover. This contention is in accord with the recognition that intrinsic motivation, pure curiosity, is a critical if not essential parameter of creativity. Though not a definitive discussion of aesthetics, this discourse is, in part, concerned with the highlights of the personal, abstract benefits derived from discovery. Stemming from the Orphic tradition of ancient Greece,[2] a passionate search for truth and beauty is important to creativity and discovery.

The "flow experience" as characterized by psychologist Mihály Csikszentmihályi[3] is the perfect example of an aesthetic. It is the experience that one has at the moment of recognition of a problem solution or of a discovery. This is existentialism at its best, by which individuals feel that their aliveness has been fully realized in a "peak experience." These experiences of discovery are conveyed through the media of visual images, visceral feelings, and metaphors, which can create a heightened awareness for greater thought penetration. They are observed through such things as elegant simplicity, symmetry, harmony, asymmetry and even chaos. These exotic feelings stemming from discovery are often the consequence of good science and technology, which this book is designed to promote.

Although this book is specifically directed toward science and technology, such a quest can be in any field of endeavor: all professions or life generally. Principles used for discovery in technical areas are generally applicable to the pursuit of the most effective life. The more that people learn about themselves and their relationship to the world, the more control they can have over their lives. Unforeseen events are continuously chipping away at our well-being, but to the extent that we have some control over our destiny, the good life can be a reality. This quest for understanding and some semblance of control is a primary process interwoven into each chapter—knowledge gain, creativity, and logic in action—always searching for the closest approximation of holistic truth and humanity that can be achieved.

In recent years psychologists, sociologists, anthropologists, and creative scientists in general have shed considerable light on the nature of creativity. Neuroscientists have made notable strides in their understanding of how the brain functions. A few significant commonalities of person and action attendant with creativity have been detected that can be helpful to the promotion of the creative enterprise. These are the seeds of understanding. Pursued with passionate abandon, these seeds, the fundamental basis of this book, offer significant hope for increasing the probability of discovery.

Sometimes there seems to be a yawning gap between pure science and pure technology. But in truth, a close relationship exists, a symbiosis, which helps both to grow to higher levels. Probing the continuum between pure science and pure technology can ease evolution of new science and new technology. Occasionally, innovative advances are made in companies without the benefit of scientific research. Most major advances in technology, however, could not occur without this quest for new knowledge. Such advances are commonly closely related to a leading edge of science. Although some companies exclude it from the technology agenda, basic research, focused on the strategic plan, is important to the cause of innovation. This contention is firmly interwoven throughout each chapter.

Conflicts in style and method often exist between management of a company and management of its technical division. One example is outlined below and, along with others, is alluded to throughout the book.

An important aspect of the business world that can inhibit discovery relates to the concept of the stages of maturity of companies. In the parlance of the business world, many companies are considered to be in the mature stage of business development. It follows that in those companies most of the appropriate research has been done, most potential new products have been developed, and research expenditures are reduced accordingly. This concept seems valid, but often there is a chasm between its perception and its reality.

Because in youthful companies new products are usually easier to conceive and develop, strategic basic research is often relegated to the background. Somewhere in an industry's evolution most of the obvious new products have been developed. Strategic basic research becomes essential to the development of new knowledge so that new products will continue to emerge. As many companies have not established a system of continuous knowledge gain, this is where they begin to get in trouble. They then erroneously conclude that they are in the mature stage of the business cycle. Following from the theory, management makes the tacit assumption that less opportunity for growth via new products is possible. As this conclusion is commonly mistaken, at this stage it seems fair to invoke communications theorist and educator Marshal McLuhan and to emphasize that the media, too easily, can become the message.

An influx of stimulating new approaches is often needed to revitalize a mature company. Little, if anything, is more stimulating to innovators than new knowledge. Strategic research is one of the best ways to develop new knowledge for new products. Not until a company has become fully committed to creativity, discovery, and entrepreneurship, can valid judgment be passed on a company's business potential. This lack of recognition may be one of the most common reasons why technology groups fail and companies fade into obscurity.

Biologist E.O. Wilson's notable work, *Consilience*,[4] expounds a philosophy for the unity of knowledge. In particular this would entail the integration of knowledge from the natural sciences with the humanities and the social sciences. Indeed, more knowledge must be gained to do a creditable job with consilience. Enough is known now, however, to make a significant start. New understanding at the interface between disciplines is the most productive area for discovery and can be one of the most exciting areas in which to work. Creativity and major problem solution occur by the interaction of different knowledge patterns, as in consilience, and this theme is laced throughout the present book.

To address these problems and others, this book has been divided into three sections: "Some Background for Creativity and Discovery," "A New Model for Creativity," and "Making Creativity and Discovery a Reality." Part I, Chapters 2 and 3 give a brief account, ranging from about 40,000 years ago to the present, of the relation between invention and the evolution of civilization. Particular emphasis is placed on the social stimuli that provided the environment and the motivation for invention. The nature of the conflict between technocracy and antitechnology is interwoven throughout much of those chapters. Chapters 4 and 5 are a discussion of the nature of science, innovation, discovery, and creativity. They describe how these phenomena may be driven by the complexity of individuals and culture over the dimensions of time and geography. Working hypotheses for mechanisms and models of creativity are presented in Chapter 6.

Chapters 7 through 17 in Part II are a description of a new model for creativity and how each stage of the model can be critical to the achievement of useful novelty. This approach to creativity was outlined briefly in an earlier monograph, *The Art of Discovery: Fueling Innovation for Company Growth.*[5] In this new book, the subject has been further developed with greater reference to science and creative mechanisms. The classical components of models for creativity have included four stages: preparation, incubation, illumination, and verification. To this model has been added knowledge gain, prior to preparation, and stimulation coactive with incubation.

In the knowledge gain and preparation chapters, among other things, methods are described for generating viable new product concepts: technological market surveys, discovery directed algorithms, and a research method for deriving new product ideas through an in-depth understanding of how products interact in systems of application. Under the heading of stimulation are six chapters giving particular attention to thought processes that are a fundamental basis of discovery. Chapter 17 is a review of obstacles and aids to the achievement of an *aha!*, and the ultimate goal, commercialization of discovery.

Chapter 18 in Part III is a summary of critical steps that can increase the probability of creativity and discovery. Because strict adherence to the scientific method can inhibit creativity, these steps can be considered as ways to facilitate novel thought. Emphasized is the relationship connecting academic and industrial research, discovery, innovation, and the resultant economic wealth necessary to perpetuate the system. An algorithm for discovery is described.

Chapter 19 is an essay on management practices that can encourage discovery and ideas for new products. Chapter 20 emphasizes the critical need for a delicate balance between cooperation and individualism for innovation to occur. Chapter 21 is a concise review of the current status of the technical, creative enterprise in the United States, followed by a broad speculation on the ideal environment and the ideal company for achieving innovation.

This book is dedicated to the advancement of science and technology, which are at least as limited as they are powerful. Nevertheless, the scientific method is the only way of establishing reliable knowledge. The ensuing chapters are an attempt to fathom the art of great achievement.

*Part I*

# Some Background for Creativity and Discovery

# Chapter 2

# Creativity in the Ancient World and the Middle Ages

An incisive down-to-earth comment on the nature of an invention purportedly came from Abraham Lincoln.[1] While he was president, a man who invented a mousetrap believed that his fortune could be realized if he could gain Lincoln's recommendation. After a long and determined effort, he received an audience with the president, who provided an unquestionable recommendation. "For the sort of people who want this sort of thing, this is the sort of thing that that sort of people will want." And the sort of thing to be discussed in this and the next chapter is the sort of generality that may be most useful to those who want to invent.

Before launching into the nature of creativity and its use, it may be helpful to gain some perception of invention history. Knowledge of some of the social and environmental influences on science and technology through history can be helpful in understanding today's environment for creativity. The change in thought processes that catapulted discovery into the twentieth century gives emphasis to the need to think in diverse ways. Awareness of some of the variables that influence the willingness of society to support the good and the bad of technology can be helpful to those involved in a technical, creative enterprise.

Defying Zeus, Prometheus gave us technology. In keeping with its mythical origin, invention technology is equally defiant; it challenges convention, disturbs the status quo, and increases the complexity of society. Just as Prometheus was fettered to a mountain peak where his ever renewing liver was pecked away endlessly by a ravenous bird, technology is both renewing and destructive. It is this ambivalence that beguiles the future of technology and is the fuel for both the technocrats and the antitechnologists. Technology is at once a source of hope and a source of fear; it begets prosperity and defiles the environment. Technology's ambivalence is the prize and the despair of civilization. This catch-22 is a major consideration for the entrepreneur and the creator.

Before philosophy and science came technology, which developed much earlier than science. Philosopher Emmanuel Mesthene[2] described technology as "the organization of knowledge for practical purposes." Invention, the most important component of technology, has been perforce coexistent with survival and the development of civilization. From archaic man to the present, *Homo sapiens* have been intensely cognizant of their limitations. Philosopher Alfred Adler believed that it was this heightened awareness of limitations in the struggle for survival that has led to our abundance of technologic achievements and the evolution of our intelligence.[3]

Technologic innovations, often, have been a matter of common sense evolving pragmatically rather than with the greater clarity of scientific method. Survival frequently has been the consequence of invention to satisfy a critical need. Fire in cold climates was clearly a necessity. Discovery of how to start and control fire did not require a scientific explanation of cause and effect. Its warmth did not depend on a detailed understanding of the oxidation of organic matter. More sophisticated technologic developments (as, for example, nuclear fission) do require scientific understanding if there is to be any control over subatomic events. This knowledge requirement is becoming increasingly critical to modern industry. Opposed to serendipity alone, the greater reliability of understanding is often the basis of discovery. Additionally, if new products are understood from the standpoint of their mechanisms of interaction with applications, the fundamental basis of process control and product improvement, or even other new products, has been established.

According to neuropsychologist Richard L. Gregory,[4] it was, perhaps, technology that freed at least some of society from the most progress-inhibiting myths. Under human initiative, tools were shown more potent than the gods. With tools, society worked miracles of greater import and reliability than the presumed miracles of the gods. Tools are extensions of the limbs, the senses, and the mind. Essentially, invention is about tools, which are the foundation of industry, and "tool" is the Anglo-Saxon word for technology.[5] In this context, Mesthene considered tools to mean, in addition to machines, linguistic and intellectual methods and analytical and mathematical techniques. Bringing the first permanent settlements, the Neolithic revolution, for example, not only had its beginning in refined stone tools but in the cultivation of plants and the domestication of animals, all of which can be considered as tools.[6]

It was the artist and the artisan who first observed many subtleties of materials and exploited their properties.[7] They have alerted scientists and technologists to many aspects of matter that might have gone unnoticed without such provocation. This is exemplified by the etching of metals in the Middle Ages, such as decor for swords, which reflected an internal structure characteristic of alloys that have cooled slowly from high temperatures. The circuitous route from the sensory experience of materials, conveyed by the work of artists, to the theoretical and the practical, carried out by scientists and technologists, calls attention to the interactive nature of progress. Often leading to connections of great utility, different disciplines and crafts may eventually interact to produce a new order.

Isaac Asimov,[8] biochemist and science fiction writer, observed that there is only one scientific endeavor, which is the pursuit of knowledge and understanding. In this sense, all of the subdivisions of science and technology are simply "man-made ways of obscuring that fundamental truth." Science and technology, indeed, are interdependent and merge imperceptibly, from fundamental to applied science, in the eternal search for knowledge and the good life.

## ANCIENT CREATIVITY

Toward the end of the Stone Age, about 40,000 years ago during the Upper Paleolithic period, a critical event in human history invigorated the Cro-Magnon culture of *Homo sapiens*.[9, 10] Art (cave paintings, jewelry, carvings, and general decoration), music, dance, ritual, and culture abruptly came into being. Technology, as innovation, had taken shape as a vital part of social well-being. Tool technology, using new kinds of materials such as bone and ivory, and mass big game hunting were greatly enhanced. Elaborate burials of the dead and the development of ritual were early stages of religious philosophy. Building new kinds of houses, developing new kinds of fire hearths, and tailoring exquisite clothing, they were warmed from the harsh climate of the ice ages.

After more than 1 million years of *Homo*, it does, indeed, seem strange that this creative explosion should have occurred at this time. The human brain had reached its modern large size and was anatomically fully formed close to 60,000 years prior to this creative explosion. So what prevented progress that our brain size and, possibly, brain structure might have enabled long before?

Primates have developed large brains in contrast to other animals, and this seems to be related to complex social environments. Both primates and carnivores show a striking and compelling correlation between brain size and social group.[11] The bigger and more complex a society in which an individual lives, the more developed its neocortex relative to the rest of its brain. From the white lies of daily existence to Machiavellian conspiracy, human life is a continuous struggle to conquer and survive such intrigue. These intricacies of social relationships impose huge demands on human thought.

An intriguing suggestion for the original enlargement of the hominid brain has been that the first use of fire followed by the cooking of food played a role in the evolution of the brain.[12] Although evidence is not found for the ability to start and use fires until a hundred thousand years ago, natural fires had been exploited for nearly one and a half million years. Reducing the necessity of great digestive abilities, cooking makes food easier to digest. By this means, energy was made available to promote the growth and intricacy of the human brain. Indeed, the human digestive system is relatively small and the neocortex relatively large in contrast to other animals. Furthermore, the cooking of food promotes division of labor, different methods of preparation, diverse tastes, and more socialization. As a by-product of fire, socialization promoted the growth of the brain as well.

Change in behavior was so abrupt in the Upper Paleolithic that its causes have been the source of considerable research and speculation. Perhaps the most compelling explanation has been the increased socialization and cooperation that developed among the Cro-Magnon in response to the harsh climate and the dispersal and reduction of resources during the Pleistocene continental glaciation. It was seemingly the pressure of increasing population and climatic change that lead to the understanding that harmonious social relations and cooperation were the keys to survival. These intense social demands may have been a primary driving force for the evolution of the human brain to its current complexity.

Around this time modern speech appeared among the Cro-Magnon, but not the Neanderthal. This development may be another major reason Cro-Magnon flourished and Neanderthal became extinct. Indicated by skeletal remains, the throat and base of the Cro-Magnon skull had developed such that vocal sounds necessary for speech were possible. Language then became possible, which was essential to growth of intelligence and the many advances of modern civilization. Philosophy and science were the intellectual consequences of this monumental adaptation by *Homo sapiens*.[13]

Ethologist Richard Dawkins suggested four potential mechanisms by which the human brain may have enlarged.[14] Both language and semantics, the meanings of words, may have played major roles. Even before language, the development of tracking skills and the maps and pictures that may have ensued could have furthered brain development. Natural selection probably favored those that were most adept at language skills and other methods of communication. Conceivably, throwing a spear at a target where several timing circuits must have been operating in parallel to achieve the right arch and intensity, could have been the beginning of foresight. Dawkins also suggested that memes, anything that replicates itself from brain to brain and spreads itself by imitation, as tunes, refrains, ideas, and so on, could be another important cause of brain enlargement. Fishing for termites by poking a stick into a mound is a meme imitated by other chimpanzees. The acquisition of memes provides a fertile basis for the development of other memes, and the consequent increase in brain capability.

Small bands of people were characteristic of archaic man, and reciprocity within the band must have been essential to survival. Their life was much like the bee or the ant that could not survive without cooperative specialization. Working together in the hunt to enhance efficiency, the sharing of food, mutual protection, and dividing work enabled Cro-Magnons to survive. The absence of the cooperative advantage, perhaps, led to the extinction of the Neanderthal. Some anthropologists believe that the Neanderthal merged into the Cro-Magnon population, but the cause of their demise as a unique society is in great contention.

Probably arising from play and experimentation, art was established seemingly as a form of communication and ceremony, both integral to social harmony. It was this working together in a highly cooperative and interactive environment that seems to have fueled the explosion in creativity—a critical component of enduring life. Emphasized throughout this book, cooperation seems to be an essential key to innovation. Culture, therefore, is a dominant force in the way we think and the evolution of brain structure.

Technology had, perhaps, its most important impetus with the advent of food production.[15] Plants were cultivated for the first time about 8,500 years ago and animals about 8,000 years ago in the Fertile Crescent in Southwest Asia. Food production, derived from the domestication of both plants and animals, permitted hunter-gatherer societies to become sedentary and to accumulate nonportable goods. Pottery making and weaving were dependent on stability, precluding the troublesome transport of pots and looms. Population density increased as food production increased. When food production became sufficiently great for the initiation of non-food-producing specialists, craftsmen of various sorts came into being. These craftsmen then had the opportunity to develop new tools and methods for a more complicated and efficient lifestyle. Technology grew by local invention and by diffusion of invention from other societies. Large, productive, competing populations were catalysts for invention.

From two areas in China where domestication of plants and animals also arose independently about 7500 B.C. and from the Fertile Crescent, inventions spread with relative rapidity after the ice ages. This was made possible by a common latitude along the 8,000 mile east-west axis of Eurasia from the Atlantic coast of Ireland to the Pacific coast of Japan, where day length and seasonal variations are similar. This precluded the necessity of extensive adaptation by domesticated plants. Similarly, there were relatively few ecological barriers to inhibit spread of food production. Along this axis, civilization spread earlier and in greater profusion than on any other continent.

Many inventions spread rapidly along this Eurasian axis by copying, with the wheel being a prime example. Its first known occurrence was near the Black Sea around 3400 B.C. and within a few centuries spread over Europe and Asia. That there were not other independent inventions of the wheel in Eurasia is attested by similar design: three planks fastened together in a solid wooden circle. As with many inventions, writing spread by blueprint copying and by idea diffusion, but was never developed by hunter-gatherer societies. Left to food producing societies with surplus to feed scribes, writing was first developed in about 3200 B.C. by the Sumerians. Writing played a central role in promoting rational thought and the consequent development of science, innovation, and intellectual activity in general.

Because of ecological naivete and low rainfall, the center of food production moved westward from the Fertile Crescent into Europe. Large areas of the Fertile Crescent today have been transformed into desert, and semi-desert, and are heavily eroded or salinized. Beginning in ancient times, its woodlands were cleared for agriculture and other purposes. Regrowth has been inhibited by low rainfall and overgrazing. Consequent increase in erosion led to the heavy silting of valleys, and irrigation agriculture led to salt accumulation in the soils. These injuries to the ecology in the Fertile Crescent have continued to the present time, which is a reminder to the modern world as to its potential fate without ecological sophistication. As a consequence of becoming a center for food production, Europe then became a center for technological development.

## MIDDLE AGES (FIFTH TO FIFTEENTH CENTURIES)

With the demise of the Roman Empire in the fifth century, the Middle Ages, formerly known as the Dark Ages, had its inception. With Constantinople its capital, the Byzantine Empire was the successor to the Roman Empire. Largely without technological invention, Constantinople was highly creative in theology and the arts throughout its 1,000 years of existence.[16] Only when seized by the Turks did its rein of creativity come to an abrupt end.

Indifferent to technology, the Byzantines relied on other peoples to supply their technological needs. Literature, philosophy, religion, and the visual arts to a large extent came to the Western world by way of the ancient Greeks, the Hebrews, the Romans, and the Latin Middle Ages. In contrast, economics, social structures, and most of the basic skills of technology arose with the people of the European Middle Ages. They, in turn, obtained many of their technological skills from China.

### The Chinese Enigma

The first civilization to exploit the depths of its inventive genius was the Chinese. This came about largely because China developed food production independently about 7,500 years ago, close to the same time that food production was developed in the Fertile Crescent.[17] Less ecologically fragile than the Fertile Crescent, China's environment offered many advantages including ecological diversity enabling a wide variety of domesticated crops and animals, more rainfall, and a huge productive area with the largest population in the world. Because of these advantages, China became the invention center of the world from the time of Christ to the mid-fourteenth century,

Despite these environmental advantages, China has had the great disadvantage of unity. In contrast, Europe has a much longer history of densely populated, interacting, and competing societies, which promotes technologic development. While Europe is divided into political units by high mountains, China is divided by a more moderate topography. China is traversed by two long, navigable east-west river systems with rich alluvial valleys. They are connected easily from north to south and have been linked by canals. Easy connectivity has enabled China to be unified for most of the centuries between 221 B.C. and the present. The environmental advantages of China enabled her to be advanced technologically for many centuries, but her extreme unity and consequent lack of interaction and competition among diversity laid the groundwork for her eventual demise as a technologic capital.

Robert Temple, in his book *The Genius of China*,[18] pointed out that most basic inventions and discoveries, which are the foundation of the Western world, came from China. It was the Chinese who invented movable type, not Gutenberg; similarly, the Chinese discovered the circulation of the blood, not William Harvey. Perhaps, most surprising is that the Chinese, not Sir Isaac Newton, discovered the First Law of Motion. It was Newton, however, who developed a quantitative formulation for the laws of motion.

Despite the inventive genius of the Chinese, they did not invent science. Historians are uncertain as to why this development did not occur in China.[19] The religion of the West, in contrast to China, pivoted on a God who made laws for human behavior. Perhaps this law-giving God equated naturally with nature's laws for the unique development of science in the West.

The Chinese approach to science was influenced by Confucianism, which was holistic, the study of the whole as opposed to the parts, and in this fashion they were prevented from understanding the whole.[20] Although holistic approaches to problems can be beneficial and creative, the parts must be understood before the whole can be analyzed successfully. This failure by the Chinese to understand the parts before studying the whole may be a primary reason for their failure to develop science. It was not until the Enlightenment of the eighteenth century in Europe that reductionism, study of the parts individually, took its proper place in the study of technical problems.

The extensive bureaucracy of Chinese civil service probably played a significant role in inhibiting science development as well. Early in the history of China, the people developed vast irrigation systems. The huge civil service that grew to control the system was overseen by strong centralized authority.[21] Guarding its powerful position against change, the civil service encouraged the development of a severely stratified society that precluded movement to a higher class level. Thus, efforts of people to rise to the highest levels of achievement were discouraged.

Although the Chinese invented movable type, they did not cultivate its use. Consisting of thousands of ideograms, the written language of the Chinese precluded development of advanced printing methods.[22] A picture system often with many superimposed concepts, ideographic writing is in stark contrast to lettering systems, which are abstract art forms. Because of their sequential nature, lettering systems impose causality on the thought process. This facilitated abstract thinking among the ancient Greeks.[23] The ideographic barrier to a widespread dialectic and abstract thinking among the Chinese undoubtedly played a major role in preserving their status quo. It was Gutenberg's development of movable type printing and its expedition using the twenty-six letters of the Roman alphabet that promoted the great communication. This stimulated a rapid evolution of science in Europe.

In contrast to the West, innovations were not permitted by the Chinese to effect social change. They honored literary feats but failed to honor entrepreneurship. Significantly, technology thrived, but theory was of little interest in China. In ancient Greece theory dominated. Historians point out that this difference may relate to the occurrence of slavery in Europe and its comparative absence in China. By virtue of slaves, labor-saving methods were of less need in Europe.

Mystical thought and inflexible tradition have hindered intellectual and creative thinking in most societies. In China, *I Ching* apparently played this insidious role. Probably originating in China between the seventh and third centuries B.C., *I Ching* was a philosophy that greatly influenced the Chinese until about a century ago. Up to that time, they believed that truths concerning light, heat, and electricity were held in the hexagrams of the *I Ching*. This philosophy was embodied by sixty-four hexagrams, which were believed to have symbolic significance. Sacrosanct, this well-established philosophy precluded rationalism and is believed by physicists Tony Rothman and George Sudarshan to be an important reason why science did not develop in China.[24]

China's demise as the invention capital and its failure to develop science was reinforced by its withdrawal from the world in the fifteenth century.[25] Not only did the Chinese withdraw from the world, they suppressed the dialectic. The Chinese had constructed huge boats with which they had extensive contact with countries of the Eastern world. But in the fifteenth century all contact with the outside world was terminated by its bureaucrats, and Western knowledge was spurned. With emphasis on the ancient texts, the spirit of enquiry was discouraged. Social conditions that can pique the intellect to the level of science seem to be unique. The conditions that existed in ancient Greece were favorable to the development of science (Chapter 5), but such conditions generally did not exist in China.

Thus, in China reliance on ancient, mystical texts, suppression of a general dialectic (greatly aided by a difficult written language), holistic approaches to problems, and ultraconservative society lacking interaction with diversity seem to explain the demise of its technology and its exclusion of science. Its failure to develop science must have played an important role as well in the demise of its technological superiority. Each of these parameters, which seemed to have subdued intellectual development in China, are a reminder that may help preclude a similar fate in modern societies.

### The Little Ice Ages

The little ice ages occurred in much of the world from the thirteenth through the nineteenth centuries.[26] Throughout this time, colder weather alternated with warmer periods at different times and in different places. The medieval warm period in Europe lasted from about A.D. 900 to 1300. This warm period was a primary reason why the Norse were able to establish a colony in Greenland. In the latter part of the thirteenth century the Norse in Greenland were the first to notice the onset of colder weather by way of sea ice choking formerly ice-free shipping lanes. By the mid-fourteenth century, Greenland was largely uninhabitable, and the island was totally vacated by 1500.

In this same time frame, the weather in northern Europe was slowly getting colder as well. Widespread changes in living style were stimulated by the onset of colder temperatures.[27] Up to this time, the hearth had been located in the center of a building, and smoke was emitted through a central hole in the roof, similar to the Navajo hogan. The beginning of colder weather necessitated more efficient ways of heating. Chimneys were invented to accommodate this need, and they had a profound effect on the cultural and economic life of Europe.

Introduction of the chimney lead to the addition of new rooms, greater privacy, lead pipes to carry water to bathrooms, more frequent bathing, and the resultant increase in birth rate. Permitting more office work, the greater warmth of separate rooms promoted an increased rate of economic growth of Europe. Using imagination, it seems that the extent of the influence of the chimney on society beyond these things has been monumental. This exponential effect is characteristic of the influence of a significant innovation.

Complexologist Stuart Kauffman[28] saw an analogy between the explosion of life during the Cambrian period of geologic history, circa 550 million years ago, and the evolution of invention. Competing with other forms of life, only the most efficient ones have survived. Each new life form, however, has influenced competing life forms to evolve further in a competitive struggle. It has been estimated that between 99% and 99.9% of all species that have existed on earth are now extinct.[29] Currently, there are somewhere between 10 million and 100 million living species. This clearly illustrates the astronomical number of species that have come and gone.

Similarly, as with the bicycle and most important inventions, many different variations enter the scene before the spectrum of possibilities converges on the most efficient systems. As with life's evolution, inventions become extinct and new ones continue to evolve. Each new invention is an attempt to seek a higher level of efficiency and utility to fit a changing environment. In both biological and technological evolution, adaptations promote surges of speciation and extinction.

### Anti-Intellectualism

Of great moment to the history of civilization and discovery, the library of Museion in Alexandria was burned sometime between the fourth and seventh centuries A.D.[30] Having in excess of 700,000 manuscripts, it was a place where the greatest writers and teachers gathered to ply their skills. Subjects studied and taught included mathematics, astronomy, philosophy, medicine, geography, theology, and astrology. It is not known who caused the burning, but the event was an intellectual catastrophe that set back the advance of civilization.

Intellectual destruction was not limited to Alexandria but occurred throughout the Greco-Roman world.[31] In the early centuries of the medieval period, Christians were determined to destroy every work of art, physics, and thought reflecting pagan gods or beliefs alien to their creed. The destruction of past contributions provided the backdrop for the Dark Ages. Although some learned contributions were made and there were numerous inventions, for the most part the Dark Ages represent 1,000 years of intellectual suppression and devastation.

The historian of science and technology, Arnold Pacey,[32] described the people of the Middle Ages as viewing human destiny in the literal terms of the Bible. This was at a time when the modern idea of progress had not been envisioned. It would not be until the sixteenth century that technology would be appreciated in the humanistic sense—for the good of humanity. The final book of the Bible, the Revelation (Apocalypse) of St. John the Divine was interpreted to prophesy the end of the world which would be preceded by a period of evil and corruption.

Although the Franciscan friar Roger Bacon believed that the end would come soon, he nevertheless advocated technical progress. With the end of the world in the offing, such progress in the minds of many was an empty and futile endeavor. Bacon countered this despondency by the belief that the practical arts would be necessary to combat the threat of evil and the Antichrist. Furthermore, knowledge would help people to resist corruption.

## Medieval Inventiveness

By the middle of the thirteenth century, Europeans had become prolific inventors. The inventiveness of medieval Europe seemed to stem, besides religious influences, from their ability to take imported ideas and to develop them in novel ways. Gunpowder invented in China, for example, was used by the Europeans to invent muskets and cannons. New devices for spinning and weaving and the weight-driven clock were some other important contributions.

Conceived as a scaled-down model of heaven, people designed the cathedrals of the time in the image of the New Jerusalem. Similarly, they designed clocks as a scaled-down model of the visible cosmos. They derived both approaches from religious convictions, which served as the prime motivation for creating novelty. By such means the people believed that man might be closer to God. The symbolism of cathedrals and clocks, the influx of ideas from Greek thought, and the technical knowledge from Islam and the East stimulated the imagination of the Europeans. These diverse sources of knowledge aroused the impetus for technical improvement.[33]

One of the more important inventions that promoted the evolution of science occurred in the fourteenth century. Nichole d'Oresme, a medieval scholastic, introduced graphic representation, using two intersecting coordinates, the abscissa and the ordinate.[34] It permitted visual expression of motion, time, and space, and was indispensable in representing and understanding the significance of experimental data. Visualization of phenomena is one of the main features of science that has promoted greater understanding and progress.

Historian Lynn White[35] cited four reasons to account for medieval inventiveness. The first relates to an agricultural revolution that began in northern Europe. Until the sixth century, people used a scratch plow for cultivation, which had major limitations for the comminution of soil. This was replaced by "a heavy wheeled plow having a knife to cut the furrow, a share to cut beneath the sod, and a moldboard to turn over the earth." By using this new plow and replacing oxen with much faster horses, the people greatly enhanced their productivity. Consequently, surplus food supply led to increased population in the cities. Enhanced purchasing power promoted the growth of industry and inventiveness. Urbanization was critical to an increased rate of innovation.

Change in philosophical beliefs is the second reason for the transition to inventiveness. In the Greco-Roman empires people believed in a god for almost every object. In their interaction with nature they were continuously attempting to appease vengeful gods. Christianity liberated people such that they were permitted to interfere with nature almost as they chose. The church considered the world to exist solely for man's use. Along with agricultural advances, this view of the church created conditions conducive to invention.

The third reason described by White relates to a second major philosophical change that was impressed on the populace—the work ethic. Prior to the third century before Christ, the upper classes held manual labor in great contempt. In contrast, among the Jews, the rabbis contended that Yahweh had commanded that people must work six days and rest on the seventh. Even the rabbis worked as craftsmen.

In the third century after Christ, the church was growing so rapidly that many people could not be satisfactorily indoctrinated. Concern for corrupting influences led to a return to the primitive church when it was still essentially Jewish. Monasticism was the result, and the rabbinical equation that work equals worship became the accepted practice. This was the beginning of the sanctity of the work ethic, and it has persisted to the present. Without it, technology would have developed sluggishly, and our society could not have advanced to anything like its present complexity.

The fourth reason for inventiveness in the Middle Ages relates to the proclamation by Western Christianity that technology embodies God's moral expectation of man. Emphasized by White,[36] religious motivations are not prerequisite to technology and can also act to inhibit progress. China and the Hellenistic Age progressed in technology without the aid of the gospel. On the other hand, Eastern Orthodox Christians were often contemptuous of machines and would not allow pipe organs in their churches. The difference in character between Christian Oriental and Christian Occidental beliefs has significantly affected progress in technology. Largely because of its strong support by the spiritual views, invention has made outstanding progress in the Western world.

Physicist Freeman Dyson alluded to Max Weber's book, *The Protestant Ethic and the Spirit of Capitalism*, in which Weber argued that the Protestant ethic came before and influenced capitalistic enterprise and technologic innovation.[37] Indeed, as already described, religious revolutions have played a critical role in the growth of invention. In contrast, both Dyson and the historian Richard Tawney contend that technology has influenced religion as much as religion has influenced technology. For example, printing technology gave a great boost to the rise of the Protestant ethic. Thus, it seems that an interdependency exists between technology and philosophical growth with their influence working in both directions. Dyson believed that technologic revolutions to enable cheap solar energy, genetic engineering of industrial crops, and universal access to the Internet would result in a worldwide social revolution. Each of these technologies then may play an important role in modifying or even in establishing new paradigms of philosophical belief.

The next chapter continues the history of invention through the Renaissance and the emergence of modern technology. These were the ages of great intellectual revolution: the Enlightenment, new economic theory, the birth of modern science, and the transition from reductionism to holism.

*Chapter 3*

# Creativity in the Renaissance and the Emergence of Modern Technology

With the creativity contributed by ancient people, a platform had been established for an increased rate of invention in the Middle Ages. Even before this latter time, around the age of Christ, the Chinese were the supreme inventors of the world and continued to be so until the mid-fourteenth century. Transmission of knowledge from China ignited the inventive genius of the Europeans in the Middle Ages. Rate of invention, again, increased markedly in Renaissance Europe.

## RENAISSANCE (FOURTEENTH TO MID-SEVENTEENTH CENTURIES)

Having destroyed most of the artifacts of intellectual accomplishment of the ancient Greek world, Christianity became the unlikely avenue for the reinstatement of this ancient heritage. Of great import to humanity, the world of Islam had preserved much of the ancient Greek knowledge. As observed by surgeon Leonard Shlain,[1] it was an ironic twist of fate that the Crusades (eleventh and thirteenth centuries) were the agents for the return of Greek knowledge to Europe. This knowledge was a boon to the Renaissance that would begin 200 years later.

Early in the Renaissance, Johannes Gutenberg introduced printing with movable type. It is a superb example of the autocatalytic nature of invention—each new invention may catalyze other new inventions.[2] The more that is known, the more that can be known. Autocatalysis in invention comes about for two reasons. First, invention necessitates mastery of simpler problems, which can lead then to inventions of greater complexity and efficiency. For example, stone tools were replaced by copper and bronze, which, in turn, were replaced by iron. This process of improvement in toolmaking took several thousand years of trial and error and the gradual recognition of new more viable materials and processes.

The second reason is that recombination of two or more technologic advances can be interacted to create a distinctly new invention. Printing came about by virtue of at least six technologic developments:

1. Papermaking, invented in China and transmitted to Europe via medieval Islam in the eighth century A.D.
2. Movable type, invented in China but greatly improved by Gutenberg.
3. Typecasting of metal dyes, developed by Gutenberg.
4. Improved oil-based printer's ink, developed by Gutenberg.
5. Presses derived from screw presses used in making wine and olive oil.
6. Alphabetic scripts, derived from three millennia of alphabet development, which required only a relatively small number of letters that could be easily adapted to movable type. This is in sharp contrast to the thousands of signs needed for Chinese printing.

Considered by historians to be one of the three most important inventions (the other two are the discovery of America and man's walk on the moon), printing led to the mass production of books and paved the way for even more diverse inventions that distinguishes the Renaissance.[3] Without this efficient and low-cost means of communication to the masses, science and technology would have been subdued greatly. Thus, invention thrives on itself and seems to have unending possibilities.

Although the Chinese invented movable type and many aspects of printing were used before Gutenberg, the idea that he was the unique inventor of printing was a product of the attitudes of the fifteenth century.[4] People of that time believed that great artists, poets, and inventors were able to create by a special talent of divine origin. Formerly believed to be the prerogative of God, people of this time saw creativity as an esoteric gift. Rather than a product of evolution and the participation of many different people as is recognized today, invention was viewed as arising from a single creative genius. This attitude was characteristic of Renaissance art and technology.

Printing spread rapidly in medieval Europe after Gutenberg printed the Bible in 1455. As a consequence of widespread printing and publication of scientific work, in particular Copernicus' heliocentric theory of planetary motion, a belief developed among a select few that individuals could make judgements independent of authority. Promoting self-confidence and rationalism, this newly found freedom of thought gave rise to a new philosophy, humanism,[5] which focused on human values and capabilities and rejected medieval, religious authority.

A pioneer of Renaissance architecture, Filippo Brunelleschi in 1421 was honored for his inventions and was granted a patent of monopoly for a three-year period. It was the first known patented invention. Adopted in Venice in 1474 and in England in 1623, patents aroused the interest of all inventors. As Pacey described,[6] writers frequently published lists of patented inventions, which became symbolic of technical progress. Stimulated by the wide availability of publications and achieving prominence during the Renaissance, invention became established as an ideal of accomplishment.

Copernicus, who developed the heliocentric theory, Galileo's break with the physics of Aristotle, Kepler's elliptical orbits of the planets, Newton's universal law of gravitation and his three laws of motion, are but a few of the tradition-shattering events of the Renaissance. Francis Bacon's empirical school of inductive reasoning awoke society to the great power of experiment and observation. These contributions helped alter primitive thought processes to a more rational approach to nature.

Although Aristotle had used inductive reasoning, involving observation and classification, its true value was not realized until its revival by Francis Bacon. Creating a new kind of scientist, the research scientist, Bacon named him the "Merchant of Light."[7] By inductive reasoning, science has shed light on countless phenomena. Bacon stated his scientific method with an incisive metaphor, "Nature shows her true nature only when we twist her tail."[8] Thus arose experimental science.

Near the beginning of the sixteenth century, science was beginning to be used to help technological invention.[9] Galileo believed that the motion of a clock could be greatly improved if it were to be regulated by a pendulum. Its practical application did not come until the 1650s. At this time Christian Huygens, a mathematician, and Samuel Coster, a clockmaker, successfully produced a pendulum clock. In England, the scientist Robert Hooke and a clockmaker, Thomas Tompion, worked on the use of a balance wheel moving against a spiral spring instead of a pendulum. Such interaction between scientist and technician had a considerable influence on the advance of technology. Exemplified by the development of the steam engine in 1712, having its foundation in the work of Hero of Alexandria, second century A.D., the influence of the ancient Greeks on invention in the Renaissance was widespread.

## EMERGENCE OF MODERN TECHNOLOGY

In the relatively short time of four centuries, 1600 to 2000 A.D., the technoscientific age was launched. Observed by biologist E.O. Wilson, this was too short a time for genetic evolution, and such technical potential was possessed seemingly by the brains of our Neolithic ancestors. Because natural selection does not anticipate future needs, it is curious that humans possessed powers for civilization before its existence. This enigma is described by Wilson as the great mystery of human evolution.[10]

One potential explanation for this rapid change may be that we possess qualities that are by-products of adaptations—latent abilities requiring the appropriate environment for full expression. The brain was not evolved to compose music nor were the hand and mouth evolved to play musical instruments, but some people can cultivate and use such genetic talents to become virtuosos. Hence, many of our mental abilities could be indirect results of natural selection.[11] Studies by psychologist Nicholas Humphrey[12] indicate that monkeys and apes have far more intelligence than is needed for their normal environment. He suggests that this extra intelligence is an evolutionary product acquired for the complex social skills needed to survive in communal groups. An analogous explanation seems appropriate for some of the intelligence of *Homo sapiens* as well.

These latent mental abilities, presumably present in archaic man, could not come to fruition until there was a critical accumulation of knowledge and keystone inventions, an appropriate convergence of social conditions, and when great need arose in changing environments. It seems, therefore, that the exponential growth in the technoscientific age from 1600 to 2000 A.D. may have arisen from the by-products of adaptation and the catalytic effect of ever increasing knowledge. The more that is known, the more that can be known. This catalytic effect was greatly enhanced with the introduction of the printing press in the fifteenth century and the consequent wider distribution of knowledge.

Of great moment to the Industrial Revolution (c.1750–c.1850 in Great Britain), the Scottish chemist, Joseph Black, in 1764 determined the amount of heat required to boil water.[13] Temperature of water rises rapidly as it is heated, but with the onset of boiling large quantities of heat are absorbed without rise in temperature. He recognized that this seemingly mysterious loss of heat was essential for the conversion of water to vapor. This is the "latent heat of evaporation." Steam, therefore, contains far more energy than hot water at the same temperature.

Scottish engineer James Watt, who was acquainted with Black, utilized this new knowledge to improve his steam engine. Duly impressed with this application of his discovery, Black lent Watt money to support him in his work. Crucial to the Industrial Revolution, the steam engine was expedited by the interaction of science and technology. The steam engine along with other new technology led to the factory system, which, in turn, led to dramatic changes and improvements in social and economic structure. Characteristic of new technology, problems were induced as well, such as labor-management conflicts and environmental pollution.

Although modern technology is a product of knowledge built on knowledge through the ages, economic philosophy has also influenced the rate and nature of intellectual growth. Perhaps, the acceptance of self-interest by religion has been one of the most significant stimulants for technological growth. Numerous philosophical approaches, economic and otherwise, have markedly affected industrial growth. Some of these approaches include mechanism and reductionism, the Enlightenment concept of history, theological, existential, technocratic, and antitechnocratic.

### Some Philosophical Approaches That Have Influenced Economic Life

The scientific revolution, occurring in the latter part of the Renaissance in the sixteenth and seventeenth centuries, significantly changed our view of the world. Acquisition of new knowledge and the use of experimental techniques effected great advances in science, but a new philosophy of nature further enhanced progress in understanding.[14] Some believed that the universe was organic in nature to be studied as one would study animals or plants. Others held that nature was occult and could only be understood by the agents of magic or astrology. On the other hand, the scientific revolution led to the universe being viewed as a machine.

The mechanistic view readily extinguished the ideas of the organic or mystical nature of the universe. Arising after 1600, this new idea of nature was developed largely by Galileo and contemporaries. Viewed as a giant machine, the universe was seen to be explainable by mechanical forces independent of man and God. By 1700, it became the dominant philosophy of nature.

Described in greater detail in Chapter 14, reductionism was introduced by Renè Descartes during the Enlightenment. Like mechanistic philosophy, reductionism was a boon to science and technology. By this method problems are approached by breaking them down into their parts. It enabled problems to be solved that otherwise were unapproachable. Believing that God had created the world for man's selfish use, people were generally unaware of how this reductionist method could savage the environment. The use of an holistic approach, concern for the whole more than the parts, is now recognized as essential to environmental well-being.

Emerging from the scientific revolution in the early seventeenth century, the Enlightenment, or the Age of Reason, attained its greatest influence in the eighteenth century. With the advent of the Industrial Revolution in the eighteenth century, the Enlightenment was accentuated by greater freedom from subservience to the church and monarchs. Striving for intellectual unity and the use of reason as opposed to revelation, it was one of the most important contributions to civilization.

Still in the eighteenth century, faith was lost in the promise of science, and reason eventually lost to theology and the greater emotional appeal of myth and dogma. Pointed out by biologist E.O. Wilson,[15] the greatest breach in human thought today is between scientific cultures and prescientific cultures. Mysticism, however, has been an abject failure in shedding light on reality. Without the ratiocination of natural science, people are trapped in a cognitive prison. Reality is generally counterintuitive and cannot be understood without science.

The Enlightenment concept of history is the idea that modern history is driven by the expansion of knowledge and the consequent power over nature.[16] By virtue of new knowledge, major improvements in life could be expected by way of moral, social, political, intellectual, and material benefits. The French philosopher Condorcet and Benjamin Franklin believed that progress must be equated with political and social liberation. Science and technology were considered as instruments for achieving these goals, which would provide an alternative to monarchical, aristocratic, and ecclesiastical institutions. Invention was not considered as belonging to the individual but to society.

Before the Enlightenment of the eighteenth century, the authority of the church and Aristotelian physics dominated thinking. During the Enlightenment the protestant belief that people should think for themselves greatly assisted the process of science and economic growth. The philosopher Bertrand Russell[17] described the Enlightenment as "essentially a revaluation of independent intellectual activity."

Theology played a major role in the development of seventeenth-century technology.[18] For the Puritan, hard work represented their salvation. For Francis Bacon and other Protestants, knowledge, industry, and trade were ways to enhance social benefits. Drawing heavily on the Bible, Bacon believed that seeking power, fame, and profit were not befitting a Christian. He thought that technology must progress solely for society's benefit.

After Bacon's time and in stark contrast to his economic philosophy, a Protestant ethic emerged that approved pursuit of self-interest. This approach was believed to best serve the public good, and economic freedom would be advanced by Adam Smith's economic theory. Contending that pursuit of economic self-interest was outside of social control, he published his idea in 1776 in his book *An Inquiry into the Nature and Causes of the Wealth of Nations*. Extolling free market capitalism, Smith believed that competition establishes an equilibrium between supply and demand. He called this process the "invisible hand."

As opposed to benevolence, Smith believed that from the self-interest of the tradesman is derived the well-being of everyone. No real conflict exists, according to this theory, between the interests of both parties. Economic life was not believed to be a zero-sum game. For capitalism to develop, the social attitude had to be established that self-interest was in concert with religious beliefs.

Jeremy Bentham (1748–1832), in his utilitarian philosophy, saw a compromise between Bacon's and Smith's economic theories. Although he was a proponent of laissez faire, he also believed that governments could interfere by intelligently promoting the cause of natural law.[19] All men under the law were to have equal rights in the quest for happiness. Because happiness is dependent on social stability, equality and security were the dominant considerations. Politically, he favored benevolent despotism.[20]

During the 1840s, Americans were beginning to disregard the Enlightenment concept of history. Capitalists believed that the great profits derived from new technologies were rightfully their own. Not surprisingly, they were firm believers in technological progress. Political liberation would be a by-product of the American Revolution and the founding of the republic. Such a view was transformed gradually into the technocratic view of progress.

The technocratic view values technological innovation as an end in itself, whereas the social and political ramifications take care of themselves. Reductionist methods of attacking problems, showing little concern for how the modification of a part affects the whole, is technocratic. Exemplified by economies of scale, standardization of process and product, and control of the workplace, Fordism in this century is classical technocracy.[21]

Since the ancient Greeks, people have recognized the give-and-take of technology. Only in about the last twenty years has society begun to weigh the relative benefits of invention. Each new technological achievement not only creates improvements but problems as well. Other new technologies follow to address the problems. An infinite regress, this paradox largely explains the tension between extreme views concerning the merits and shortcomings of technology. The problems incurred by new technologies were seen by Florman[22] as being not problems of technology but "the pressure of human desire." Too many people that want too many things.

After World War II the rise of existentialism posed a serious intellectual threat to technology. As Florman stated, "The essence of the existential view is disenchantment with conventional creeds, a resolve to dispense with comfortable delusions, and an insistence on looking inwards for new truths." "Among all existentialists . . . there is a shared scorn for the truth of science and the promises of technology." By this philosophy, complete autonomy was given to the individual. It was the despondency caused by the Cold War, the hydrogen bomb, the environmental crisis, and the elusiveness of security and comfort that, according to Florman,[23] fueled a revival of existentialism. Although existentialism may have some merit, its extreme antitechnology position seems too contrived.

Antitechnology is essentially an antimaterialism view. Not only the existentialist view, but Greek and Judeo-Christian heritages defile materialism as one of society's most serious shortcomings. If materialism is characterized as greed, then the criticism may be valid. But if it includes material things in general for improving the well-being of the masses, then the criticism is surely false. Unless people can strive to solve problems, not only by thought but by the use and invention of material things, where is the substance of our existence? Why deny a reality that we can touch and observe with feelings of certainty?

An existential appreciation of life stems from the striving, the struggle, and the occasional victory. Problem solving, invention, and discovery are signs of a life lived to its fullest. The other extreme, the technocratic view, believing that all technologies are good without concern for effects on social and political matters, leads to disasters. Examples are environmental contamination and resource depletion. Unless society can see the flaws in technocracy and antitechnology, social evolution will be stymied by these extremes of belief.

## Technology Assessment

Shortly after the National Academy of Sciences published a report in 1969 on a procedure for technology assessment, Congress established an Office of Technology Assessment.[24] For true value, assessment must be of both the short-term and the long-term. The latter requirement has not been developed with any degree of confidence. It is this difficulty of method that gives strength to both the technocrats and its detractors, and it remains a serious impasse to rational control of technologies. Despite this difficulty, diligent efforts should be made to control potentially harmful technologies. Unfortunately, the Office of Technology Assessment was abolished by technocrats of the United States Congress, which is a reflection of the lack of understanding of science and technology by the electorate in general.

The social scientist Peter Drucker[25] believed that it is not possible to predict the impact of technology, which is a response to the convergence of many factors other than technological. Examples of fallacious predictions of the consequences of new technologies are abundant.[26] Edison was ridiculed by Britain's scientists claiming that his concept of electric lighting for cities violated the possibilities of science. Edison wanted alternating current to be banned as unsafe, and for the same reason James Watt wanted high-pressure steam to be banned. Drucker's recommendation was that technology should be allowed to progress. Only after careful monitoring would it then be possible to regulate its progress fairly.

Whatever approach is followed, biodiversity, our most valuable resource, will continue to be of great value for so long as it is preserved. The number of species doomed each year is estimated conservatively to be 27,000. "Only in the last moment of human history has the delusion arisen that people can flourish apart from the rest of the living world."[27] Biodiversity possesses a vast store of knowledge, minimally revealed so far, that can greatly enhance our economic, medical, scientific, agricultural, and general well-being. Not the least of importance, ecosystems enrich the soil, create the air we breathe, and, perhaps most important, influence climate. Without an as yet undetermined critical level of biodiversity, *Homo sapiens* could not survive.

### Growth of Industrial Research

By the middle of the nineteenth century, invention was going at such a rapid pace that competition between nations became a symbol of prestige.[28] It fired the economy of factories, and productivity grew at an enormous rate. The steam engine stimulated the science of thermodynamics in the same fashion as the airplane stimulated the science of aerodynamics. Consequently, pure science became established, and applied science continued to promote productivity and a wide range of new products.

The first industrial research laboratories were established in Germany in the late nineteenth century.[29] Copied by other industries throughout the world, Bell Telephone Laboratories in New Jersey, Philips Laboratory in Eindhoven, and the ICI corporate laboratory in Runcorn are examples of the giant organizations that resulted. By the 1930s, industrial research was a major new variety of technical enterprise.

The development of large corporate laboratories enabled the pursuit of knowledge on a more idealistic and exploratory basis. At the onset of World War I, this approach was radically changed to practical directions with a great sense of urgency. War changed invention from the idealistic and recreational to the broad utilitarian needs of the marketplace. In 1913, Henry Ford established the first assembly line in his Detroit factories. This was tagged "mass production" and led to major cost reductions and affordable automobiles for the masses. Mass production became a household word between the World Wars and was believed to be a mechanism for the conquest of poverty.[30]

Except in the area of communications, pure science was used on a limited basis during World War I. Between World War I and World War II, progress in scientific theory and instrumentation led to some major inventions. X-ray diffraction for studying the structure of materials, electron microscopy for observing small particles, and the development of television and radar were some of the more significant results.[31]

By World War II, a new era of science had begun which led to the development of the atomic bomb. Amateur invention was no longer of major import, and high technology offered sophisticated inventions having great social impact. As Price[32] described, antibiotics for the control of infection and steroids for birth control have increased our life span and changed our family structure. Transistors, microelectronic chips, and computers are developments that are continuing to change society and the way we approach science and technology. Rocketry technology, developed during World War II, has led to space travel that is expanding our knowledge of the universe.

Invention is no longer the primary province of lone innovators struggling in a cluttered garage. Now entangled in the more complex aspects of science, innovation often requires substantial financing, large teams of scientists and engineers that will interact a variety of disciplines, inordinately expensive equipment, and enormous patience. The path to invention is still an enigma. It is intertwined with a modest understanding of how the brain functions and the heuristic of how to create on command.

## CONCLUSIONS

Perhaps only when the most unyielding philosophies—religious and economic—are intimately tied to society's penchant for greater material, social, and environmental well-being does technology peak. Paradoxically, progress in invention and scientific theory is a consequence of shedding the bonds of conventional thought and brewing in a milieu of unconventional, free thought. A blend of these extremes, traditional versus unconventional, is the eclectic ideal for greatest progress. Harness the tremendous power of prevailing, philosophical conviction, and mix, gingerly, with small amounts of philosophical, scientific, and technological iconoclasm. It is an ominous mix, but one from which consequences of great social merit can evolve.

Intellectual unconventionality can be a powerful method for breaking the shackles that inhibit novelty. It is a trademark of people who contribute major breakthroughs. This is not at all surprising in that invention and revolutionary theory are derived generally from previously unthought of or unaccepted ideas. Creative scientists and technologists, to varying degrees, fit this mold.

Although the ideal blend of philosophical conviction and iconoclasm has been a superb mix for technological growth, in many ways it has been a disaster for the environment and our natural resources. More than a commitment to objectivity in science, an ecological conception of knowledge could help win the battle to save the environment.[33]

We are at the mercy of entrepreneurs and politicians who, by the nature of their professions, are concerned largely with short-term gain. Voluntarily taking action to protect the environment not only may decrease profit but often puts the entrepreneur at a competitive disadvantage. Similarly, politicians who wish to stay in power must address the short-term demands of the electorate. Asking sacrifice for long-term benefit is generally lethal to a political career. Additionally, it is not the nature of people, generally, to sacrifice short-term gain for the greater uncertainty of long-term benefit.

Evolving largely to address short-term change, our brains are not structured to be as concerned with the long-term as is needed by modern society. Primitive *Homo sapiens*, in particular, would not have survived without giving primacy to the short-term. Emphasis on the short-term in companies is especially true where the effects of critical change are not seen within a budget period, or even within a career. Without significant incentives for the long-term, society will continue to be the victim of short-term greed. Establishing an attitude of long-term greed is, perhaps, a utopian goal, but one that could give a tremendous assist to the goals of a healthy environment and greater contributions by science and technology.

Throughout history technology has delineated society.[34] Cultivation of stone tools and domestication of plants and animals gave rise to the Neolithic revolution and the first permanent settlements. Increased use of coal and steam power along with many new tools for the manufacture of cotton textiles effected the industrial revolution. Technological growth in navigational equipment and seafaring promoted the commercial revolution. In a similar fashion, information processing is bringing about today's control revolution.

Perhaps what is needed most today is a new revolution in rationalism, a new Enlightenment. For this purpose, technology, and for that matter all of knowledge, would be approached holistically as permitted by the extent of reductionist knowledge. This would entail such goals as enhancement of creativity through consilience, environmentally safe practices, judicious utilization of natural resources, minimalization of waste, and population control. A significant challenge, increased technology perforce means increased social complexity.[35]

The tremendous potential of invention—material, theoretical, or philosophical—is our primary hope for the solution of many problems, for prosperity, and for an increasingly humane lifestyle. Although we will create problems in the process, building the learning curves of technology assessment and environmental impact can help minimize harmful effects. Careful monitoring of new technologies and judicious incentives and regulation can help to give the greatest weight to social and environmental well-being.

With the emergence of modern technology and science, the world had reached a critical juncture. Invention had increased to such a high rate that it was difficult to balance it with environmental well-being. Recognizing that this balance with nature was essential to the well-being of life on earth, a more profound form of science was gradually emerging. As more and more knowledge was gained, the holistic approach to science and technology led to the interaction of more and more knowledge patterns. Not only has this been a more creative and productive approach to technical problems, but it has helped to balance technological progress with the vitality of nature.

The next two chapters are designed to give the reader some insight into the technical world, and some potential mechanisms for the enigmatic problem of creativity. These chapters will set the stage for considering the new model of creativity reviewed in Part II.

*Chapter 4*

# The Nature of the Technical World

With a much more sophisticated development of science and technology during the scientific revolution in the latter part of the Renaissance, the plethora of great inventions of modern technology might have been predicted in general terms. Knowledge begets knowledge. Since archaic man, it has increased exponentially, which probably bodes unimaginably great strides for the future. Understanding the fundamental nature of the technical world is critical to an understanding of how science and technology delineate society's progress.

## SCIENCE

According to biologist Lawrence Slobodkin,[1] "science in its purest sense is focusing on the interface between the empirically known and unknown." In fact, if there were not this attempt to bridge the known with the unknown, fundamental progress in science would not occur, and, indeed, technology would be suppressed severely. Slobodkin's definition can be elaborated by adding that pure science is an attempt to gain empirical or elegant theoretical understanding, and to ask increasingly profound questions about the interface between the known and unknown. Approaching characterization from a different angle, the physicist John Ziman[2] defined the goal of science as "the search for the widest possible consensus among competent researchers." Science is the product of human brain evolution and the history of thought processes leading to objective thinking as applied to nature.[3]

To many outsiders, esoteric vocabulary and seeming tediousness make science appear routine and boring. In reality, science and technology can be inordinately titillating, particularly when great motivation promotes the creative path to discovery. Generally defying common sense, the unexpected results of dissecting the elements of the world and the surprising connections sometimes found between them can arouse the excitement of the most impassive observer. A critical driving force of science—the spirit that such excitement can generate—can consume yet vitalize the researcher. No profession can arouse the spirits more. "It is, after all, not the answers which scientists uncover, but the strange magic lying behind the questions they pose to their world . . . which is the true impulse driving conceptual transformation."[4]

Although the uninitiated often have a strong aversion to the skepticism of science, the philosopher Morris Cohen[5] distinguished scientific doubt from dogmatic skepticism. Science cultivates doubt until natural limits are defined. Such doubt is delineated by logic and is based on the assumption of truth's existence. Dogmatic skepticism denies all truth. Promoted by doubt, progress in science is facilitated by the search for better explanations.

Science is a method for extending our grasp of reality far beyond that which our senses alone permit.[6] Because we only see what our nervous systems allow us to see, science is a description of how nature interacts with the human mind. Our sensory perceptions are restricted, and we sense only a portion of reality. The limitation to understanding posed by the unaided brain, therefore, is monumental. Experiments, observations, hypotheses, conventional and unconventional thought, laws, theories, mathematics, and instruments enable scientists to study, measure, and interpret many things that cannot be seen directly. By such means we can study genes, molecules, and quarks far below our resolution ability with the unaided eye. In similar creative fashion, we can determine the distance of celestial bodies light years away. We can establish elegant theories, such as the theories of relativity and evolution, incomprehensible without the methods of science.

Arthur Miller,[7] Professor of the History and Philosophy of Science, University College London, believes that science has developed by the extension of our intuition into an understanding of nature beyond our perceptions. In so doing he follows the doctrine of scientific realism, which conforms to the notion that universals exist outside the mind. Thought experiments—as Einstein's boyhood dream of riding on a light beam, which eventually led to his special theory of relativity—form the basis of intuition and extrapolation to reality. As theories are established, a new foundation has been created for further intuition.

The quid pro quo of science and technology is reflected by the observation that science could not have developed without initial advances in technology. Pointed out by the physicist Frederick Seitz,[8] some form of mathematics was developed by all civilizations leading up to the Greeks and was used for accounting and land measurement. In addition, celestial cycles were used to guide agriculture and religious rituals. Such types of invention were essential to the development of meaningful science. In similar fashion, much of modern technology has been developed from major discoveries in science, as relativity theory led to the harnessing of atomic energy. Science and technology are interdependent and thrive on each other.

Science is as much a process as it is a collection of knowledge. It is a specific way of envisioning the universe, a guide and not a definitive formula for a better understanding of reality. Science entails the establishment of a set of rules (mathematical model) that can be used for explaining and predicting the nature of phenomena.[9] The philosopher Karl Popper viewed science not as a body of knowledge but as a system of hypotheses. These guesses cannot be fully justified, and our interpretations of all physical phenomena possess varying levels of uncertainty. Scientific method, then, becomes essential for surmising which hypothesis is in greatest agreement with reality. Because presuppositions about reality are continually progressing, science is another aspect of Darwinian evolution.

One of the most effective ways to justify a scientific theory, at least tentatively, is through the confirmation of prediction. If the theory is expressed in mathematical language, ambiguity is minimized. Perhaps the most famous example of confirmation is Dmitri Mendeleev's prediction of undiscovered elements to fill vacancies in the Periodic Table. He grouped the known elements in concert with similarities in chemical properties. In accord with obvious gaps in the table, it was possible to predict the existence of unknown elements. Confirmation of prediction, however, is not a definitive demonstration of a theory's validity. It simply means that the theory can be considered as valid until the next test of prediction. But as explained by Boden,[10] although prediction is of great importance to science, it is secondary to explanation. Successful prediction and repeatability of related experiments, however, remain as the most meaningful ways to tentatively verify explanation. Prediction, repeatability, and explanation are the fundamental goals of science.

Distinguishing science from other belief systems is facilitated by two fundamental properties.[11] First, such that they can be used by all, the rules of science are clear and detailed. Although generally requiring extensive training, the rules of science can be used effectively without special insight or inspiration. Secondly, the rules of science are public, and there are no private truths as there are in many other belief systems. Science is distinguished from pseudoscience by six features: (1) repeatability, (2) economy, or the most elegant of explanations, (3) measurement, (4) heuristics, methods that provide direction in problem solution, (5) consilience, establishing connections with other patterns of knowledge and potentially reducing all knowledge to the laws of physics, and (6) predictability.

Nature is governed by reliable laws which limit what can be known. The physicist John Barrow pointed out that there are things that cannot be known—whether the universe is finite or infinite, open or closed, finite in age or eternal.[12] The finite speed of light limits what we can observe to a small portion of the universe, and the inherent character of laws of nature or rules of reasoning impose limits as well. Organized complexity, exemplified by atomic order in crystals or life itself, could not exist without limits to nature. In imaginary worlds without limits, neither crystals nor life could exist. Science is understood largely through mathematics. Becoming less and less accessible at the frontier of physics, mathematics needed for superstring theory is understood by only a small number of people. If mathematics becomes much more complicated, no one will be able to understand it. These limits according to Barrow give sharper definition to our understanding of nature than those things that can be known.

Belief in omnipotence discourages science, sabotages belief in the consistency of the laws of nature, and pirates one's thoughts into the imaginary world of mysticism where everything is possible. Science is born only in those intelligences that can see the limits of nature. For science, therefore, the concept of impossibility along side the possible is an essential backdrop.

Defining science is considerably more difficult when the complexity of chaos theory and the unpredictability of subatomic events are considered. Chaos theory suggests that certain aspects of nature may not be predictable and are, therefore, incomprehensible. Seeming to preclude predictability, minute changes in initial conditions, the butterfly effect, may lead to substantial changes in system trajectory. Weather prediction is a prime example.

Although scientists generally presuppose order and causality in the phenomena that they study, there are seeming limits to order, which may limit the reach of science. In a different context, science may fail because the phenomena in question may not be responsive to scientific methods. Because of our preoccupation with order, we may see pattern where it does not exist.

These are some of the complexities and uncertainties in science posed by the philosopher John Dupré.[13] Evolutionary processes have not been so thorough in the development of our brains that we can learn every aspect of the universe. Designed by natural selection, our brains are better equipped for survival and breeding than for discovering profound truths. Presumably, certain aspects of nature will always elude us.[14] Quantum theory shows that everything cannot be known.[15] To know the world we must observe it, but the act of observing causes random events in the world and even changes the nature of what is being observed. Bohr's principle of complementarity—particle-wave dualism of light—implies that everything cannot be known at one time. The condition for knowing one thing can exclude knowledge of others.

To understand a phenomenon completely, according to Kurt Gödel's incompleteness theorem in mathematical logic, one must view it from the outside.[16] For example, students who flash cards in football stadiums to spell out certain cheering expressions cannot see the pattern that they are displaying. To do so they must go outside of the system.[17] On this basis, the deepest secrets of the universe may not be understood without viewing from the outside, which poses striking limits to our understanding of reality.

Gödel's theorem simply voids a complete understanding of a system in mathematical terms. Many aspects of chemistry, biology, and psychology are understood without the aid of mathematics. Certain phenomena, however, such as quantum mechanics could not be understood without the analytical power of mathematics. Although science is confronted by limits, the physicist Freeman Dyson observed that Gödel also showed that mathematics is inexhaustible.[18] Similarly, Dyson believes that science, though limited in certain directions, is inexhaustible in other directions. In this sense, both science and technology have limits, yet are inexhaustible.

Theoretical physicist Lee Smolin does not believe it necessary to view the universe from the outside for a complete understanding.[19] In his cosmological theory of natural selection, he constructs a science that views the universe as a coherent whole, whereby its internal dynamics promotes organization. This is opposed to the Newtonian idea that space and time are absolute, which necessitates viewing from the outside to gain full understanding.

If we accept the contention that full understanding can come only from the outside, as is suggested by Gödel's incompleteness theorem of mathematical logic and Newton's contention of absolute space and time, then the necessity of an intelligence outside our universe becomes a transcendent necessity responsible for everything. And it becomes an infinite regress to determine the cause of the cause of the cause. In stark contrast, general relativity disparages the idea of an absolute reality, according to which the geometry of the universe changes with time. All of the structures in the universe are dynamical, which must be understood by the relations among things. It is not clear that the universe will ever reach equilibrium. If it does not, it would be a permanent, self-organized, non-equilibrium system, potentially promoting life for the time of its existence.

Reinforcing his belief that an intelligence external to the universe is unnecessary, Smolin indicates that self-organizing, non-equilibrium systems characterize the universe on every scale. This condition of non-equilibrium on Earth arises from the continuous influx of energy from the sun. In accord with complexity science, self-organization emerges from complex systems far from equilibrium, fueled by a continuous influx of energy. In his concept, the laws of physics are created by natural forces that are time-bound; the universe is self-made, constantly evolving, and it can only be understood from an historical perspective. In this sense, the concept of the absolute is passé!

Similarly, quantum physics can only be understood as an entangled whole, and in this sense is in agreement with general relativity. Whatever we study, the Heisenberg uncertainty principle allows us to know only half of the potential knowledge needed for full understanding. The properties of an electron are a function of every particle it has interacted with from its inception. Such a view nullifies the world of classical physics, where particles are absolute, independent of their history. To derive a full description of an elementary particle or any part of the universe, it is also necessary to have a description of the whole universe. To make a quantum theory of cosmology, so as to know everything, a new mathematical formalism would have to be invented that would apply to the whole universe. Thus, Smolin's relational view of the cosmos is in accord with the idea that synthesis of disparate phenomena, to the extent possible, promotes the greatest penetration of reality.

Despite limits to science, a great amount of knowledge has been accumulated, which enables scientists to accurately predict many events and to continuously develop new technologies. It is in no way certain that our present knowledge limits will not be transcended by a persistent effort to penetrate these barriers to human understanding. Nevertheless, the popular maxim that "anything is possible," though prevailing in pseudoscience, is without foundation.

In one sense, these limitations to understanding may seem to be cause for adopting a nihilistic outlook and for raising the black flag of anarchy. Indeed, such has occurred via the anti-scientific rhetoric often referred to as the "post-modern critique" and "cultural relativism."[20] Followers of these beliefs are scornful of the search for truth and see "facts" as contaminated with theories, which are believed to be severely biased by moral and political doctrines. Although there is some truth to their arguments, cultural relativism is, on balance, nihilistic sophistry that would seem to deny the predictive benefits and abundance of technology derived from science.

From a positivistic approach, the limitations of science—alongside its inexhaustibility—are to be noted with great care by every individual bent on discovery. Uncertainty in science leaves the door wide open for change, novelty, and the most monumental of eurekas! Perseverance in science may well overcome many of the uncertainties, at least to the extent of permitting much greater predictive and technologic progress. The theoretical physicist Stephen Hawking[21] takes an optimistic view of the future of science and contends that "the remarkable progress we have made, particularly in the last hundred years, should encourage us to believe that a complete understanding may not be beyond our powers." This state of mind or way of thinking may be the most conducive to discovery.

Perhaps most important, science profoundly respects the power of the human intellect and offers greater hope than any other concept for the potential achievement of humanity. Unable to answer certain questions, human thought often turns to explanations without foundation—all too convenient denial, which dulls the tremendous potential of the human brain.[22]

## TECHNOLOGY AND DISCOVERY

The mathematician John Casti[23] referred to what is known as "the General Electric Syndrome." If GE is doing it, it must be science. As explained by Casti, if GE is doing it, it probably isn't science, but it *is* technology. Technology is a technical method of achieving a practical result. In a more realistic sense, technology is problem solving and taking shortcuts to address the profit picture expeditiously. It is often pragmatic, without a clear understanding of the underlying mechanisms.

Technology is applied science sometimes, perhaps in the modern world most of the time, but it is also strictly technological at other times—not derived from science. To be sure, technology began long before science was invented. Consider the Neolithic period when people developed stone tools, pottery, and weaving, cultivated grains, and domesticated animals. Even the inventive genius of the Chinese occurred long before modern science began in the seventeenth century, and before they had a process of thinking that could be considered scientific.

Observed by the chemist Henry Bauer,[24] science is universal and technology is particular. For example, except in singularities of black holes, laws developed in science presumably apply everywhere. Technologies generally can be approached from many different directions. Such flexibility of approach often makes industrial proprietary knowledge a source of challenge to other companies who diligently explore many different avenues to the same problem. This versatility of approach to a common problem is the reason that patents are often circumvented.

Innovation is a major function of technology, and it begins with invention and concludes with commercialization. In the strict sense of analogy, innovation is modern alchemy. Alchemy was a medieval, speculative, chemical philosophy with the aims of transmuting base metals to gold, of developing a universal cure for disease, and of prolonging life indefinitely. In the industrial minerals industry, we attempt to transmute minerals, not to gold, but, similarly, into forms of greater value. And with invention, we attempt to cure the diseases of our companies and by the same means prolong their lives indefinitely.

"Brooding meditation" characterizes the antecedent of invention much more effectively than the glib notion of "a flash of genius."[25] What seems to be a discovery arising solely from the moment has actually been preceded by innumerable failures and the diverse discoveries of innumerable people.

Each failure and each related discovery is a building block for the break-through. The notion of "a flash of genius," therefore, is myth. Invention, often, is simply an existential phenomenon pursued for the sake of solving the puzzle—intrinsic enjoyment.

Inventions are driven by need, but even more so by intrinsic motivation—sheer curiosity—often where demand for such a novelty has not yet developed. Opposed to the heroic notion of invention arising from a unitary genius, novelty is generally the product of the scientific and technologic past and present, having great vertical and horizontal extension. Many people have contributed, and the end result is a product of a cumulative process.

A prime example of the cumulative nature of invention is the steam engine.[26] James Watt has been considered the unique inventor, inspired by steam rising from a teakettle's spout. In fact, the idea arose from his doing repair on a steam engine invented by Thomas Newcomen 57 years prior. Many had already been manufactured in England. Newcomen derived his idea from the Englishman Thomas Savery who patented a steam engine in 1698. This was preceded by a steam engine designed by the Frenchman Denis Papin around 1680, in turn, preceded by the Dutch scientist Christian Huygens and others. Presumably, the earliest steam engine concept was a toy invented by Hero in ancient Greece.

The chain of events that leads to inventions does not occur linearly, and the sum of the parts does not equal the whole. A machine, such as an automobile, has the emergent property of motorized mobility, but the disassembled sum of the parts is without utility. Creativity invariably possesses this nonlinear property. One invention leads to others, ad infinitum. Again, the sum of the inventions is less than the collective interaction of the whole. The rate of evolution of inventions increases with each new invention, which generally is of increased complexity. The more we know, the more we can know.

As pointed out by James Burke,[27] an authority on the history of technology and science, the scratch plow, which he considers the most fundamental invention in the history of man, brought civilization into being. Because the plough was the instrument of surplus food production, it triggered almost every subsequent innovation. Surplus food led to urbanization, which, in turn, created greater need for new tools and other instruments of civilization. Industry thrived, and this led to an endless array of inventions that promoted further growth. This triggering mechanism, or the interaction of the past with environmental change, ideas, materials, and people over a broad geographic range, is the fundamental fuel of invention. Disequilibrium in social structure, as urbanization, generally leads to a flurry of inventions to accommodate changing needs.

Untethered invention may approximate a Koch curve, which is in concert with Vannevar Bush's "endless frontier" (Chapter 1). Such a curve is an infinitely long line surrounding a finite area.[28] It was named after the Swedish mathematician, Helge von Koch, who described it in 1904. An example can be any triangle, where an equilateral triangle is constructed on the middle one-third of each side. This fractal transformation can be carried out in one's imagination infinitely, producing an infinite length. Similarly, invention can lead to chain reactions where one major invention creates an avalanche of new ones. These new inventions may create similar avalanches, symbolized by the infinite array of triangles on the Koch curve.

Inventions can be synergistic combinations of fundamental knowledge, combinations of synergistic knowledge, or combinations of fundamental and synergistic knowledge. If there is a limit to fundamental knowledge, it is represented by the finite interior area of the Koch curve, and inventions ultimately would be limited to new combinations of synergistic knowledge and new combinations of synergistic knowledge with existing fundamental knowledge. Assuming the correctness of this analogy to fractals, invention may have infinite potential, even if fundamental knowledge is limited. But unless all possible combinations of knowledge can lead to invention, then limitations do exist.

Science probably will not penetrate all realms of nature, which further limits technology. The finite potential of the human brain, the possibility that human beings will not survive, and excessive costs for the process of achieving some inventions are potential deterrents. Additionally, perhaps sometime in the distant future, rate of increase of inventions will become asymptotic, which might discourage pursuit of this technical enterprise. Excluding these potential obstacles and to the extent that all inventions will give rise to an equal or greater number of new inventions, as has been the case so far, the potential for such novelty seems to be unending.

From a practical point of view, the analogy of invention to the Koch curve might be considered in a finite sense. If the smallest subdivisions of matter are the elementary particles, such as the electron and the quark, then the fractal transformation of the Koch curve would be constrained by at least this limitation. Although further reduction is possible within our imagination, nature does have limits, vis-à-vis the cosmic speed limit or the speed of light. In a similar vein, invention may have a reductionist limit, as in the case of an asymptotic petering out of invention. In such an event, invention may cease to be cost-effective. Nevertheless, such an ending to knowledge gain is probably so far in the future of *Homo sapiens* that today the end of new knowledge seems almost meaningless.

Discovery is new knowledge, which may or may not have been derived by creative cognition. Uncommonly, it may come about simply through the conventional, generative processes of the scientific method. Although invention generally has many alternates, discovery is definitive. The laws of thermodynamics and the discovery of atomic energy are finalities. Robert Root-Bernstein, Associate Professor of Natural Science and Physiology at

Michigan State University, distinguished invention and discovery in different terms.[29] "We invent with intention; we discover by surprise."

In the context of this book, three kinds of discovery need to be distinguished, revolutionary scientific, normal scientific, and serendipity. Revolutionary scientific discovery relates to new knowledge pirated from just across the border in unknown territory—the frontier of knowledge. As a consequence of this kind of discovery, a modified or new theory may be developed, and the related paradigm may be changed beyond recognition. Einstein's theories of relativity are cogent examples.

Technologic discovery, which is a type of normal scientific, generally occurs within the borders of a well-established paradigm. Discovery within an established paradigm can occur through careful scientific planning and thought (normal scientific) or by accident (serendipity). Accidental discoveries can occur in either revolutionary or normal scientific research. Such discoveries or anomalies are not strictly accidental and are, in a sense, anticipated by carefully planned research. In an example given in a later chapter, a man might be searching for a needle in a haystack, but serendipitously come up with a farmer's daughter. Discovery of any type is the purpose of research, accidental or otherwise. If researchers are well prepared with knowledge and curiosity, they are much more apt to recognize anomalies and to pursue them for greater understanding. If the new knowledge is straight forward, as new information showing unique performance of materials under controlled conditions, the discovery is normal scientific. If new knowledge can be used to produce a new product, a new order has been discovered that is both technologic and synergistic (total effects are greater than the sum of the effects taken independently).

The discovery of stone tools by Neolithic man was clearly not scientific, and such novelties must have resulted from serendipity—accidental observations of synergistic interactions. But in either case, technologic or accidental, a new order may be established. The new order is the discovery of knowledge where the whole is greater than the sum of the parts. It represents the emergence of a nonlinear, holistic, novel property. When Neolithic people secured together a wooden handle and a rock of appropriate shape, they reconstituted matter having greater utility than simply the sum of the disassembled components. Other examples are new machines, or, in the case of chemicals or industrial minerals, a new synergistic composition of matter. Usually not leading to discovery, the normal scientific process of targeted research is the first step in the reduction to practice of what was generally known.

In normal scientific, technologic discovery, theories generally are not changed, but a new, synergistic pattern of knowledge has been developed. It is invention, often derived by a combination of accident, conventional generative methods, and by creativity. This kind of discovery in normal science occurs at a different frontier than the discoveries of revolutionary scientists. It might be considered as the internal growth of discovery, whereas revolutionary scientific discovery is an external growth.

Biochemist and science fiction writer Isaac Asimov[30] described the relation of science and technology in the most perceptive context:

The fact is that science and technology are one! Just as there is only one species of human being on Earth, with all divisions into races, cultures, and nations, but man-made ways of obscuring that fundamental truth; so there is only one scientific endeavor on Earth—the pursuit of knowledge and understanding—and all divisions into disciplines and levels of purity are but man-made ways of obscuring *that* fundamental truth.

For science and technology to progress, creativity is essential. The next chapter is an analysis of the nature of creativity.

*Chapter 5*

# The Nature of Creativity

From the creative explosion in the Upper Paleolithic, the second period of the Stone Age 40,000 years ago, to the present, human beings have demonstrated a depth of creativity that has produced an immense array of discoveries and inventions. Science and technology have grown in knowledge, in thought processes, and in tools, enabling discovery at an ever-increasing rate. Through the pressure of changing environments and the essential development of cooperation in complex social systems, the *Homo sapiens'* brain has evolved to a state of sophistication that promises a future of remarkable discoveries and inventions.

Biologist Christopher Wills contends that we are still evolving and that the pace of our evolution is accelerating.[1] Although physically we are becoming smaller and weaker, our brain evolution is increasing. Because less intelligent people often have more children, prophets have claimed that IQ scores are going down. Wills points to a study by the New Zealand psychologist James Flynn in the early 1980s showing that rather than going down, IQ scores were generally going up throughout the industrialized nations, and in some cases very far up. Three potential reasons have been suggested to explain why recent generations have been smarter on average than their parents:

1. When people play fast-moving computer games, they improve their cognitive skills. Viewing images on television that flash in rapid succession may similarly speed up reaction time and brain function.
2. Since World War II diets have improved significantly in both balance and completeness.

3. Improved health care has brought about a significant decrease in childhood diseases. Crude genetic and environmental damage are dominant reasons for diminished intellectual capacity. Otherwise, everyone's brain is capable of high performance.

Advances are being made in the development of smart pills, which may play a role in enhancing intelligence of future generations. The new technology of reprogenetics (extraction of harmful genes and insertion of favorable genes in the human egg before insertion into the womb) bodes well for the future robustness of *Homo sapiens* and its variants, or even new species of *Homo*.[2] It is potentially a mechanism for speeding the pace of evolution. The creative world, seemingly, will continue to be penetrated in ever more decisive ways.

Creativity does not seem to be amenable to clear definition. As a rough approximation, it is the interaction of disparate knowledge patterns by the use of both conventional and unconventional generative methods in a way that gives rise to useful, challenging, and illuminating new concepts. To be creative, the product must be both novel and useful. To these requirements the psychologists Teresa Amabile and Elizabeth Tighe[3] added a third condition; the solution path, rather than algorithmic, must have been heuristic (exploring many different pathways)—an open-ended process rather than straightforward. Finally, to be creative, a product must be judged as such by the peer review process. This last requirement imposes implementation, and in most cases creativity is meaningless without empirical evidence. Exceptions are Einstein's relativity theories, which were adjudged creative before they were empirically substantiated.

As creativity is unpredictable, it is not yet amenable to scientific explanation. On the other hand, it has been suggested that unpredictable happenings may occur in the brain via subatomic events as quantum changes in energy levels of electrons. Such subatomic events, however, potentially can be predicted on the basis of probability.

In concert with the definition of creativity noted above, the historian of philosophy and science Arthur Miller[4] divided creativity in science into two parts: (1) network thinking, and (2) the nascent moment of creativity. In network thinking, selected concepts from different disciplines are interacted by metaphor to achieve a novel concept. Nonlinear, this line of thought can be nonconscious. For the interaction to be creative, an analog medium consisting of lists of information concerning the immediate problem as well as lists of information concerning other problems must be a part of the picture. Selection mechanisms to discard most of the abundant possible explanations of phenomena are indispensable, and they include mathematics, aesthetics, intuition, and conventional and unconventional thought.

Network thinking corresponds closely with a basic theme of this book: creativity is promoted by diversity of input and interaction. Creativity has arisen from the interaction of disparate knowledge patterns in a continuing dialectic throughout history and over a wide geographic area. It is constantly being nourished by new observations from diverse research, events, hypotheses, and psyches. Miller described intuition, metaphor, and mathematics as mechanisms for extending ideas beyond those phenomena that can be seen.

The neurologist and educator Howard Gardner[5] emphasized that products of creativity arise from long-term, intensively pursued, highly organized efforts that generally occur within one domain. A notable exception is Leonardo da Vinci who was creative in, at least, two domains. Gardner outlined a set of four commonalities with respect to his study of seven highly creative individuals:

1. A continuing dialectic between childhood curiosity about nature and a mature intellectual understanding of a discipline. Breakthroughs tend to be confined to the early part of their professional career, which Gardner suggested may be due to the difficulty in sustaining some noeteny [childhood character].

2. A period of withdrawal from the world; but after their fundamental insight, they return to the world.

3. Daring, bold, and persevering outlooks.

4. Possession of some degree of marginality as, for example, living within a relatively alien culture—as a Jew among gentiles.

The importance of the individual to the nature of the novelty developed is illustrated by an example provided by anthropologist Gregory Bateson.[6] Marxian philosophy contends that the great creators (e.g., Charles Darwin) were, for the most part, irrelevant to the changes they instituted. In Darwin's time, it is argued, society was ripe for a theory of evolution that would justify the decorum of the Industrial Revolution. This setting, as proposed by Karl Marx, precludes the importance of Charles Darwin.

As Bateson expostulated, if Wallace had been the prime mover, the theory of evolution would be substantially different today. Alfred Russell Wallace, an English naturalist, evolved a similar theory of evolution at about the same time as did Darwin. Based on Wallace's analogy of the steam engine with a governor and the process of natural selection, Bateson suggested that the cybernetics movement may have been advanced by as much as 100 years. In this context, it is of paramount importance which individual promotes change—a primary reason for the unpredictability of history.

Further along the lines of personal characteristics, introverted people have an elevated sensitivity to cortical arousal, which is essential to creativity. Not only easy cortical arousal but emotionally responsive dispositions are important. The neurologist Richard Restak[7] believed these characteristics to be evidence of a neurological basis to creativity.

Creativity has peaked during periods when differing points of view have been prolific. Rivalries between small states, according to an extensive study by the psychologist Dean Keith Simonton,[8] have been an important basis for creativity throughout history. This was true in ancient Greece, in Renaissance Italy, and in seventeenth- and eighteenth-century Germany. These are among many examples in which political fragmentation and cultural diversity have stimulated novelty. Competitive companies today are similar in spirit to these earlier small states. If corporations become highly successful and monolithic, however, the characteristics that initially produced success rapidly atrophy. By their very nature, large, authoritarian institutions promote conformity and are alien to the creative spirit.[9]

The relationship of the brain to the cosmos is the subject of neurocosmology, which can be the source of many metaphorical speculations about reality. Also, this unique approach provides a novel way of generating a broader range of potentially viable hypotheses. The artist and neurocosmologist Todd Siler[10] suggested that nuclear fusion and fission processes may relate to similar processes in the brain. Creativity may be a fusion process in which the thoughts of both hemispheres of the brain merge for an instant and cooperatively generate a novel idea. Biofeedback researchers call this cooperative activity "synchrony." Such moments of inspiration in brain activity have been observed in electroencephalographic recordings as high amplitude alpha waves and lower amplitude theta and beta waves. In contrast, reasoning may be a fission process representing an asymmetrical event in which one hemisphere dominates the thought mechanism.

Psychologist Donald B. Calne speculated that intense temporal lobe electrical activity (microseizure or microsynchronization) may be the physiological basis for intense aesthetic experiences.[11] Both the flow experience attendant with creativity (Chapter 1) and ecstatic religious experience seem to fit in the category of microseizures. In fact, one common form of epileptic seizure leads to altered states of consciousness, which is also related to intense electrical activity in the temporal lobes. This kind of epileptic seizure and psychoses have led to wild hallucinations, such as seeing the heavens open, speaking with God, or even becoming God. Paradoxically, then, excited states of electrical activity in the brain, particularly in the temporal lobes, may be the fundamental basis for the emotional intensity attendant with both creativity (flow) and mystical experience.

Such observations seem to place psychotic episodes and the rational experience of creativity in rather precarious juxtaposition. But aside from intense electrical activity in the brain, the two states of mind seem to be in sharp contrast. Without falling into the trap of mysticism, it is this intense, excited state of mind that greatly increases one's ability to unravel complex phenomena. The major surge of mental energy accompanying inspiration, unfortunately, cannot be measured as units of energy. Its source is equally mysterious, and its activity cannot be predicted or controlled with any certainty. What can be done is to increase the probability of inspiration, which is an overall theme of this book.

If Einstein can be considered the quintessential representative of creativity, then some of his personal characteristics should be considered as well. To say that he was independent of mind is an understatement. His intense opposition to authority led him to challenge senior figures with abandon. He took pride in not knowing the literature of his field and insisted on going back to first principles to derive a theory. As different from the conventional scientific method (using basic principles, mathematical reasoning, and visual-spatial imagination), he revolutionized the way reality is viewed. Elegant theory, in his mind, was infinitely more reliable than empiricism. Holding in great disdain scientists who would not tackle difficult challenges, he conceded that only monomaniacs make scientific discoveries. As a creator, he was essentially burned out by the age of 40, at which time his reflective wisdom constituted another form of contribution.[12] Such an approach may not be appropriate for all creators, but his independence of action and the confidence that it reflects would seem to be essential for creativity.

Elaborated by philosopher and psychologist Margaret Boden,[13] creativity is not due to chance alone, and serendipity implies some degree of judgment. Simultaneous discoveries in science are relatively common as, for example, the theory of evolution discovered at about the same time by Charles Darwin and by Alfred Wallace. Opposed to coincidence, such events are generally due to the convergence of complex social events, which can facilitate a ripeness for certain kinds of inventions. Archimedes developed expertise in observation and in manipulating the concepts of density and volume. This made him ripe for his Eureka! discovery—how to measure the volume of a crown replete with filigree. Hero of Alexandria invented a steam engine to be used as a toy in the second century A.D. Industry had to wait 2,000 years for ripeness, the appropriate convergence of technical and social conditions.[14]

Howard Gardner[15] described three elements that he considers to be fundamental to creativity: (1) human being, (2) object or project, and (3) other individuals. This is in concert with psychologist Mihály Csikszentmihályi's[16] view that creativity is understood better if examined from a systemic perspective, including the social and cultural context. He believed that "creativity is not an attribute of individuals but of social systems making judgments about individuals." Creativity does not exist solely as an individual attribute, but within a complex framework. In addition to the individual, there is the domain and the field, where the domain is the body of knowledge, laws, and theories governing a discipline, and the field is the individuals working within that domain.

Csikszentmihályi illustrated the fickleness of time and judgement by the example of Mendel. In his era his experiments with peas were considered as an impressive demonstration of hybridization but not of great theoretical significance. Only 50 years later was it recognized that what Mendel had observed provided a fit with the genetic model of evolution that was then in contention. Mendel could not be adjudged creative until more knowledge had been acquired within the domain, and only then did the field recognize the theoretical importance of his work.

Criteria for judging contributions change with time, and evaluations are different among experts. Judgement of creativity, therefore, is not objective and varies as does judgement of aesthetics and other abstract qualities. Current social beliefs and attitudes become the arbiter of creativity independent of the individual. Csikszentmihály then asked, "Where is creativity?"

The superstructure that promotes creative activity, in Gardner's view, entails the relationships that occur within three fundamental elements: (1) interaction of the adult mind with the worldview of the child, (2) the relationship of the individual to the work in which he or she is engaged and how that domain is altered as a consequence, and (3) the interaction of the individual and others in the immediate or related domains. He, along with Mihály Csikszentmihályi, viewed creativity as a dialectical or interactive process among all three elements.

Gardner diagramed these three nodes as the triangle of creativity. Common to all creative activity is the ongoing dialectic between talented individuals, disciplines, and those charged with judgement of creations. Nurturing creators and their products are the tensions or asynchronies associated with this interaction or dialectic. Such an interactionist view generally persists throughout concepts of how creativity arises. It emphasizes the holistic nature of the creative act or the synergistic interaction of diverse fragments of reality to create a unique, new order.

By way of this systems view of creativity, no result of the interaction can be creative without a contribution from all three components, and the creative product evolves over long periods of intensive effort.[17] Creative results are the product of historical and contemporary forces, a complex of contributions arising from many people.[18] The computer, for example, arose from a creative ecosystem[19] as much as it did from creative individuals.

In his study of the creative lives of Sigmund Freud, Albert Einstein, Pablo Picasso, Igor Stravinsky, T.S. Eliot, Martha Graham, and Mahatma Gandhi, Gardner found that at least ten years of uninterrupted work within a discipline were required to achieve a creative breakthrough, and that another decade was necessary to achieve the second breakthrough. In contrast, Alan Turing, one of England's great twentieth-century scientists, made intellectual contributions in five-year intervals.[20] Clearly, long periods are required to achieve major creativity. Each of the individuals studied by Gardner needed peers of similar interest who could stimulate each other. By virtue of discovering a problem area, the potential was uncovered for discovery. Each individual possessed an element of unconventionality that precluded their full acceptance by the scientific society. Opposed to becoming part of the establishment, they championed intellectual unconventionality, and they kept their work equally unconventional.

Profoundly respectful of the potential fruits of hard work, all of these creators required support from a companion who understood the nature of their goals. In the pursuit of these goals, each creator found it necessary to strike a Faustian bargain—to sacrifice a part of themselves either by becoming an ascetic, by isolating themselves from others, or by the exploitation of other people. Such opprobrium seemed to be their conception of how to cling to their special talent.

The basic idea of creativity as conceived by psychologists is divergent thinking. Intelligent people are thought of as problem solvers and, therefore, as convergent thinkers. They converge on a unitary solution. Creative thinkers have great flexibility and derive many different approaches to problem solving, some of which may be novel. Not surprisingly, this distinction is generally complicated by shades of gray. Divergent thinking, however, is equivalent to the lateral thinking of Edward de Bono described in Chapter 16. It is an extremely important factor of creativity, among many. Explained by Gardner, beyond an IQ level of 120, psychometric creativity is independent of psychometric intelligence.

Freud believed that the energy of libido can be sublimated into creative pursuits. Such sublimation is characterized by creative activity in the arts or by discovery in science and technology. Psychologist Frederic Skinner's behavioral approach ascribed creative activity to past reinforcements, such as rewards for success. More recent work disputes the viability of competition and rewards.[21] Excessive competition can discourage new students and promote fraud in the struggle for funds. Extrinsic rewards, such as compensation and promises of evaluation, discourage risk taking and promote satisfactory but not outstanding results. In contrast, intrinsic motivation, the motivation of intense personal satisfaction and enjoyment that would be carried out passionately without compensation, is considered to be paramount to creativity. The extrinsic rewards of recognition within one's professional community is the exception that reinforces intrinsic motivation.

Biologist Lawrence Slobodkin[22] alluded to child prodigies in music and chess, but to their absence in science. He suggested that prodigies occur in those disciplines in which understanding is in simplified form. The child thinks in terms of the whole world, whereas scientists have learned to simplify complexity into understandable units. For there to be a child prodigy in science, he or she would have to learn this process of simplification. Highly sophisticated simplification in science is called elegance, and to acquire this ability to simplify necessitates extensive training. Profound knowledge and empathy within a field is requisite to creativity.

Essentially all of us are psychologically creative in the sense that we create new and useful ideas that are novel to ourselves. Historically creative people are the exception, and they create new and useful ideas that are unique to civilization. Many people are historically creative, and the extent to which that is recognized is a function of the usefulness of the new ideas that they create. Certainly creativity is elusive and at times may seem to come via a lightning bolt of illumination. But in reality, it results from purposeful, long-term, painstaking effort. According to the writer Daniel Cohen,[23] creativity has been recognized for only about the last 50 years as a widespread characteristic of human beings. Most important, it is a quality that can be cultivated.

Creativity according to Csikszentmihályi[24] arises, in part, from the kind of problem on which one works, presented or discovered. A presented problem is tacitly understood from the standpoints of formulation and method of solution. The probable answer is easily extrapolated. Correctly derived targeted research is in this category, and for those companies that concentrate on such work, creativity is less likely to be cultivated. Creating intellectual tension and without a direct method of solution, understanding is limited in the discovered problem. The solution path can lead to creativity of great significance. Scientists who choose to solve discovered problems are the protagonists of Kuhnian revolutions (Chapter 14). Those who have such a discovery orientation—the intrinsic motivation—and the energy to tackle the complexity of discovered problems are the revolutionaries who do violence to the status quo. They are most responsible for progress in the understanding of reality.

Creativity is the product of uncommon logic—not magic—and according to the physicist Joseph Schwartz,[25] is the mystification of achievement. In this connection, an editor once gave an aspiring writer the formula for an ideal beginning to a successful piece of fiction. The formula contains three parts: (1) sex, (2) high society, and (3) an unconventional situation. On the basis of this formula the writer came back with an unbeatable beginning: "Damn it," said the duchess to the king, "take your hand off of my thigh." In a similar fashion, a formula for invention can be derived, also containing three parts: (1) a sexy technical problem, (2) a highly spirited group of scientists and engineers, and (3) an unconventional solution. On this basis, the female personification of basic research said to the male officers of the company, "Damn it, stop harassing me, and perhaps then we can consummate in creative bliss."

Some of the conclusions of Cohen[26] in his book on creativity are that madness is not a corollary of creativity, which may be enhanced by good physical and mental health. Intelligence and creativity are not necessarily related: each of us possesses some level of creativity; the right hemisphere of the brain may be the source of inspiration and intuition; the most creative are more venturesome and eccentric. If creativity is to flourish, social conditions elicit an attractive environment—Plato was most incisive in his statement, "What is honored in a country will be cultivated there."

The next chapter continues the discussion on the nature of creativity with respect to mechanisms and models. Along with the systems hypothesis of creativity described in this chapter, these mechanisms and models will serve as guidelines for the abstract dialectic between mind and nature. They will be transformed into a pragmatic approach to creativity and discovery in Chapter 18.

## Chapter 6

# Mechanisms and Models of Creativity

Having briefly considered the present state of intellectual development, the nature of the technical world, and the nature of creativity, it is now pertinent to consider some potential mechanisms of creativity and how they can assist the innovator. The systems theory of creativity, outlined in the previous chapter, gives insight as to the interactive and social nature of creativity, and it can be considered as an adjunct to hypotheses described in this chapter. Definitive answers for creativity do not exist, but some likely aspects are gradually emerging that can give some insight on how to achieve goals.

Provocative routes to potential understanding of why and how creativity arises are embodied in three approaches: a theory of creativity derived from Darwinian ideas, a quantum mechanical explanation, and a mechanism derived from the new science of complexity. These approaches are recounted in brief form.

## DARWINIAN CREATIVITY

Psychologist Dean Keith Simonton[1] described the Darwinian approach as "a perspective that disparages myths" attendant with some theories of creativity. Simonton outlined the Darwinian theory of creativity under the headings of (1) thoughts and processes, (2) products and ideas, (3) persons and personalities, and (4) schools and cultures.

Under thoughts and processes, variations are produced by the interaction of such things as concepts, feelings, and memories. Arising by chance, the variations are blind. A selection procedure exists that excludes variations that are nonadaptive psychologically. Those that are selected favor near-

term advantage. It is through this mechanism that the short-term orientation of people may have developed that can be so detrimental to the creative
process. Although evolutionary forces have led to this impasse, it is to be
hoped that evolutionary forces have also given us the capacity to overcome
this scourge of modern industry.

Generation of blind variations follows from interaction between thoughts
with every imaginable combination, which can give rise to unpredictable
but novel stabilities. Perhaps some of these variations arise in the nonconscious mind as well, which can be the basis of the *aha!* experience. Some
serendipitous discoveries can be explained by this process. After a choice
is made, thought is focused exclusively on this one idea.

Serendipity is a perfect example of the chance composition of thought
derived from blind variation. An example is the discovery by Archimedes,
his "Eureka!" that induced his purported nude run into the streets of Syr-
acuse. Even our most notable historical creators did not directly will their
creations. They did increase their odds of success, however, by diverse,
determined, and monumental efforts. As stated by Simonton, "True geniuses must have the patience to relinquish their fate to the vicissitudes of
chance."

To optimize chances for discovery, there must be an impressive array of
thoughts and approaches that traverse the brain. By this means, the chance
combination of ideas that are viable will be enhanced. Some degree of
pragmatism must be at play such that any process that has even remote
potential, no matter how outrageous, can be considered freely and objectively.

Those people who produce the greatest number of intellectual works
have the odds in their favor for generating the most creative products.
Although much of this work will not meet the highest standards and some
will be poorly conceived, the greatest mistake is limiting direction to a
paradigm or to a small number of works. Diversity in effort seems to be
of major importance to inspiration.

Under persons and personalities, the emergence of a creator seems to
require the confluence of certain childhood experiences that will set the
stage for innovative directions. A mentor that encourages and gives hope,
who does not discourage unconventionality, and who inspires great confidence can be the catalyst for an otherwise budding creator. Emphasized by
Howard Gardner and by Simonton, marginality is of great assistance in
providing motivation. That is, the individual may be marginal with respect
to a discipline, as a physicist working in biology, or with respect to race,
as a Jew working among gentiles.

With respect to schools and cultures, the competitive struggle between
opposing paradigms functions similarly to the variation-selection mechanism already discussed. Only those paradigms that seem most adaptive and

that provide the most useful and predictive explanations of phenomena will be retained by the community of scientists.

## QUANTUM CREATIVITY

A substantial similarity exists between the Darwinian approach to creativity and the quantum mechanical approach. The quantum explanation, however, does deviate somewhat and greatly expands the potential understanding of the creative process. Many physicists today agree with Einstein's contention that quantum mechanics is incomplete. Physicist Roger Penrose[2] concluded that there are laws even deeper than quantum mechanics essential for the operation of mind. Quantum mechanics, to date, is in concert with experiment, but additional theory is needed for a complete picture of the world.

The laws of quantum mechanics hold for molecular, atomic, and subatomic particles, and the laws of classical physics hold for large objects, such as billiard balls. Somewhere between a new law is needed to understand how the quantum world connects with the classical. Penrose believed that such a concept is essential to an understanding of the human mind. This is a highly controversial area, and the neuroscientist and Nobel Laureate Gerald Edelman,[3] for example, believed that consciousness is unrelated to quantum mechanics. He contended that it is a consequence of biology, as in the evolution of brain structure. Extraordinary processes emerge from matter, and mind is a process arising from special arrangements of matter.

Physicist and astronomer Victor Stenger[4] pointed out that the quantum approach requires that all the parts of the universe must communicate at infinite speed. This results from the quantum concept that atomic and subatomic particles are interdependent throughout the universe. Infinite speed has never been demonstrated and is in conflict with the basic concepts of physics—in particular, Einstein's speed limit, or the speed of light. We are conditioned to see the world from a Newtonian mechanical perspective making the quantum world seem nothing short of bizarre. French physicist Louis Victor De Broglie explained why quantum effects are not seen in the macroscopic world.[5] Wave properties of particles become smaller with increase in mass and are imperceptibly small within our visual world. If an object has a quantum wavelength greater than its size, it behaves in quantum fashion; but if its wavelength is smaller than its size, it behaves in classical Newtonian fashion.

Although there is doubt that a relationship exists between creativity and the quantum world, it is useful to consider the striking correspondence between the current ideas of quantum mechanics and creativity. Philosopher and physicist Danah Zohar[6] explained this idea by contrasting it with classical or Newtonian physics.

Determinant and without surprises, every event in Newtonian physics happens in a specific way. Quantum systems, on the other hand, are indeterminant, probabilistic, and full of surprises. Furthermore, Newtonian systems are defined by a single set of parameters that characterizes one reality. A world of multiple reality, the quantum world consists of superposed systems, some of which can be diametrically opposed. In this quantum view, an object has all possible histories, all equally real. Describing quantum reality, the Schrödinger equation contains multiple realities and an infinite array of possibilities in accord with Heisenberg's uncertainty principle (Chapter 16). Newtonian physics describes matter as either a wave or a particle, whereas quantum physics has matter as waves *and* particles.

Perhaps most significant is that Newtonian physics is causal, and quantum happenings are chance occurrences that can be acausal. "Nonlocal" relationships, as with two photons shot from a source, show a relationship independent of distance apart. Despite this separation, the photons always have opposite polarities and act as if they were part of a larger whole. Matter appears to be made up of particles and waves all of which are interconnected and, perhaps, cannot be fully understood as isolated entities. For such communication to occur, infinite speeds are necessitated. This is where the conflict with Einstein's speed limit, or the speed of light, arises. From nonlocal relationships is derived a quantum mechanical, holistic approach to scientific problems (Chapter 15).

By the use of what mathematicians call an "imaginary number" in Einstein's equations, special forms of matter called "tachyons" are postulated to exist.[7] Assuming their existence, tachyons can travel faster than the speed of light. With reduction in energy, they travel faster and faster, until with no energy they travel at infinite speed. Seemingly, something of the nature of tachyons would have to exist to explain superluminal speed.

Physicists Tony Rothman and George Sudarshan explain the quantum concept of nonlocal in a way that does not require superluminal communication between particles.[8] Two particles shot from an atom correlated from birth are not two distinct systems having different wave functions. There is one wave function for both particles no matter how distant their separation. Although the two particles remain correlated, no signals are exchanged between the two particles nor need be. Correctly stated, nonlocal in quantum mechanics means "extended and nondecomposable." In this context, the quantum world becomes less bizarre.

Because Newtonian particles are hard and impenetrable, they rebound when they collide, but quantum particles merge in a manner similar to that of water waves. By virtue of being indeterminate, the properties of quantum particles can go into nonlocal correlation, and the two systems then become part of a larger whole. This larger whole cannot be reduced to its parts, and, because of this new relationship, new properties have been created.

Zohar continued by explaining that there are reasons to believe that an analogy exists between quantum mechanics and the physical basis of our conscious life. One of those reasons is the similarity of the unity of the quantum world to the unity of consciousness. We are continuously bombarded by sensory data as we observe surrounding phenomena, and separate modules in the brain control these responses. That we do not sense these many observations in fragments is, indeed, mysterious. From the quantum perspective, the psychological integrity of "I" can be viewed as a holistic phenomenon. It is seemingly equivalent to the unity of multiple reality in quantum mechanics, each component superposed and blended to form a single complex unit. We hold in our brains innumerable, even contradictory, imaginations at the same time. Feelers are put out in all directions in the same fashion as quantum systems, "virtual transitions" to determine the most stable and meaningful variation.

Our capacity for creativity, Zohar contended, has quantum underpinnings. Apparently many people have been enamored with the similarity between mental and quantum processes. On the other hand, they have been foiled by the very hot or very cold temperatures seemingly required for quantum systems that have the necessary coherence—as lasers and superconductors. Such self-organizing quantum systems have been observed, however, since the 1960s in biological tissues. Zohar believed that human consciousness is a quantum mechanical, self-organizing system. The products of consciousness, such as ideas and creations, are the coherent patterns that we generate.

The example of Schrödinger's cat, invoked by Zohar, is helpful in understanding the supposed quantum-consciousness relationship. This cat, as you might imagine, has quantum characteristics. Kept in an opaque box, he is supplied with food, poison, and a radioactive device that randomly releases poison or food. Having the versatility possessed only by a quantum cat, he devours the poison and the food simultaneously, thus becoming dead and alive simultaneously. Both states are in quantum superposition. An electron is neither a wave nor a particle until it is measured, in the same fashion as the cat is neither dead nor alive until the box is opened and seen by an observer. Because the act of observing a quantum system, for unknown reasons, converts quantum reality into everyday actuality, the cat becomes either alive or dead only when the box is opened.

Erwin Schrödinger, an Austrian theoretical physicist, did not believe that quantum mechanics would apply to objects so large as a cat, and he did not intend this example to be taken literally. He devised this thought experiment to show how ridiculous it is to apply quantum theory to the macroworld.[9] The idea holds, however, if we consider the cat to be subatomic in size.

Schrödinger's cat is again a world of multiple reality with coexisting contradictory states. A similar bizarre phenomenon is believed by Zohar to exist in our consciousness. If, on the other hand, we focus on a possibility for purposes of actualization, we lose contact with all other possibilities. This has been referred to as the collapse of the Schrödinger wave function. Creative efforts, therefore, and for best results, are never structured tightly and pursued by a rigid algorithm. Our thoughts exist in quantum superposition only if our minds are unfettered, where the confined world of Schrödinger's cat presides, and we are adrift in unrestricted and contradictory possibilities. Zohar believed that creativity is inherent in our brain's structure. This gives emphasis to the contention that we are all creative and that such ability can be enhanced.

Also supporting a quantum mechanical explanation, physicist Erich Harth[10] suggested that minute changes in the subatomic world migrate upward to become action potentials of nerve cells. All of the uncertainties and unpredictabilities of subatomic behavior may influence our thoughts and actions, which have been called bottom-up control. The selection and elaboration of the chance events from the bottom-up quantum influence is the function of consciousness. Feedback loops within the brain form mental images providing the substance of imagination and creativity. These feedback loops, sensory paths that relay information back and forth between the sensory organs and the cerebral cortex, amplify and improvise giving a modified and personalized version of reality. These loops may use quantum effects and the influence of experience as the sources of unpredictability and, occasionally, creative illumination.


## COMPLEXITY

Nobel Laureate Ilya Prigogine and philosopher, chemist, historian of science Isabelle Stengers[11] believed that order can develop spontaneously out of chaos by a process of self-organization. Systems in far-from-equilibrium conditions are ultrasensitive to even minor changes in external conditions by which unexpected and strange things can happen. In nonlinear systems, which is the case for most of nature, small perturbations can lead to dramatic changes, which is often referred to as the butterfly effect. The usual example is one of hyperbole, where the flutter of a butterfly in Rio de Janeiro can cause a chain reaction resulting in a weather change in New York. Laminar flow of fluids beyond a critical flow rate may change into turbulent flow. On the macroscopic scale, turbulence appears chaotic, but it is highly ordered on the microscopic scale. As Prigogine and Stengers point out, this transition is to a state of self-organization. In the human brain, inspiration seems to be a product of self-organization arising from a chaotic blend of information.

Such occurrences relate to the new science of complexity. Closely related to chaos theory, the two sciences often are referred to collectively as chaoplexology. Order can arise spontaneously from chaotic complex systems. Although to some degree this science seems to smack of vitalism, the exponents insist that it does not and that self-organization is driven by the internal dynamics of complex systems.[12]

In Darwinian evolution, increase in complexity is not inevitable and change is effected by natural selection. Combining elements of both, the internal dynamics of complex systems and the external forces of natural selection, the new science contends that increase in complexity is an inexorable drive. In striking contrast to conventional wisdom, self-organization in complexity science becomes an agent of evolutionary change along with natural selection.

While controversy abounds in the quantum mechanical explanation of creativity, self-organization may offer a graceful way out of this dilemma.[13] In this budding science, self-organization can emerge spontaneously from chaos by local interactions. Emergence of life is a prime example. Whereas inanimate objects are relatively stable, biochemist Stuart Kauffman[14] considered life to be poised at the edge of chaos, making it sensitive to change or mutation. In a similar vein, the brain can be viewed as a neural network poised at the edge of chaos. A slight fluctuation, the butterfly effect, as may be produced by a new fragment of knowledge, may be all that is needed to move to a different metastable state. Such change can lead to the emergence of new ideas that can be tested against reality in the selection process. In such a system quantum effects are unnecessary.

## MODELS OF CREATIVITY

Figure 6.1 shows a schematic for industrial creativity, but it should be equally applicable to academe. It is a schematic that is complemented by the systems theory of creativity described in the previous chapter. Modified after a classical model for creativity, it was originally elucidated by German scientist Herman Ludwig Ferdinand von Helmholtz in 1891 at a banquet celebrating his seventieth birthday.[15] He divided the process of creation into three parts: (1) preparation, in which all important information is collected and collated, (2) incubation, the time when the nonconscious mind is helping to solve the problem, and (3) the happy idea, or the time of illumination. Jules Henri Poincaré,[16] a French mathematician, also characterized similar steps involved in creativity. In both cases, the hard work of verification follows the three steps. Since Helmholtz and Poincaré, variations of their model have been published in the literature to fit idiosyncratic needs. In a similar fashion, and for purposes of this book, two additional steps have been added to the Helmholtz model to aid in the elaboration of the processes involved in discovery and creativity. These steps are knowledge gain and stimulation.

Amabile and Tighe[17] outlined a similar model that also includes four stages: (1) problem presentation, (2) preparation, (3) idea generation, and (4) validating the generated ideas against criteria. To be characterized as

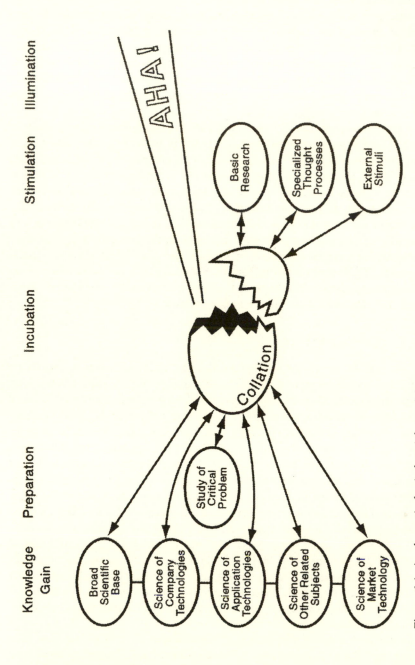

Figure 6.1. A schematic for industrial creativity.

creative, stage 1 must have been unusual and accurate, stage 2 must have involved a sufficient wealth of information and skill in the domain, stage 3 must have evolved at least one unusual and viable idea, and stage 4 must have led to the choice of an idea that optimized novelty and usefulness. Although these criteria clearly outline prerequisites that lead to creativity, which, generally, will be followed throughout this book, stage 1 does not necessarily have to be unusual, although it is common and generally advisable to facilitate creativity. Evolution, for example, was not an unusual problem even in the time of Darwin. It had been around since the ancient Greeks and, between that time and Darwin, was approached in diverse ways. Natural selection, the mechanism of evolution proposed by Darwin, was, indeed, unusual, and so it was the solution and not the problem that characterized Darwin's idea as being creative.

With the guidance of the schematic (Figure 6.1), the critical nature of each stage shown in the model will be considered, not only to achieve but to manage discovery and creativity. Although the sequence of each step is generally not critical, the usual order is as shown in the schematic. Models of creativity are approximations, and the process can branch in every conceivable direction. Knowledge gain is, however, a priority, and it would be difficult, if not impossible, to discover without appropriate background. Acquisition of both diverse and focused knowledge is an essential first step.

## CONCLUSIONS

If the Darwinian or the quantum approaches to creativity are accepted, and, therefore, the role of chance, the importance of quantity and variety of knowledge and ideas can be seen as essential. In the science of complexity, emergence of order occurs most readily in high input, increasingly complex systems. In all three of these potential mechanisms of creativity, the greater the richness of the intellect, the greater the chances are that variations in knowledge will interact with ideas to produce novelty. The conscious, perhaps even nonconscious, selection process will improve with experience. By persisting to discover and invent, and as learning accompanies each failure, chances for success will increase.

The ultimate success will depend largely on the ongoing acquisition of knowledge and the number of failures that the researchers and the sponsors are willing to tolerate. If goals are lofty, the number of failures that will precede success will be great in number. By being persistent in efforts, prolific in work, diverse in research and thought processes, and conscientiously objective in evaluations, creativity and discovery can be a reality. By evading highly structured environments until after the selection process has brought into awareness the best solution path, the probability of success can be enhanced greatly.

With the new model of creativity, possible ways of improving chances for creativity can be readily discerned. Part II is a detailed description of this model, and the first chapter in this section explains the nature and criticality of knowledge to discovery and creativity.

*Part II*

# A New Model for Creativity

*Chapter 7*

# Knowledge Gain: The Nature of Knowledge and the Origin of Science

The history of science and technology has shown that there are many pitfalls in pathways to discovery. Religious influences can be both helpful and detrimental to progress in knowledge. Mystical thought, inflexible tradition, and suppression of the dialectic are among the many nemeses of invention. Originally highly creative, the Chinese persisted in their pagan beliefs and were ultraconservative in their intellectual and political world. Neither did they develop science nor continue with their supremacy in creativity after the mid-fourteenth century.

In Renaissance Europe and during the Enlightenment, empiricism, reductionism, and mechanistic philosophy were new, successful ways of approaching the technical world. They were a key to the industrial revolution and a boon to science and technology. Modern science has advanced to such a high level of knowledge that it is at a crossroads, where the holistic approach to discovery, in lieu of reductionism, is a key to maintaining a healthy environment and a robust technical world.

Some technical areas have become so sophisticated that enormously difficult, esoteric advances in mathematics are required. Large teams of technical people interact to achieve discoveries of great complexity. The potential for discoveries and new viable theories in science and the potential for new processes and invention in technology seem to be inexhaustible. Even if they are not, the potential for new knowledge seems to be so great that science and technology are probably still in their infancy. Knowledge requirements, in both extent and depth, for discovery have increased immensely. Thus, the first step in creativity is embraced by knowledge gain— an invigorating but endless process.

"The first time a school boy realizes that a little learning is a dangerous thing is when he brings home a poor report card," so Mark Twain quipped.[1] A broad range of knowledge and extensive knowledge interaction are the basic nutrients that fuel discovery and creativity. The researcher who confines his research to his immediate concern severely undermines his chances for creative achievement. Thomas Huxley incisively expressed an analogous thought: "If a little knowledge is dangerous, where is the man who knows so much as to be out of danger?"[2]

By virtue of gaining abundant knowledge about a subject, interest in that subject is stimulated. Put another way, the more ways that a problem is addressed, the more self-interest that is generated. Acquisition of such invaluable knowledge is critical to the maximum development of the intellect, but equally important, it helps generate the motivation that fuels perseverance. It is virtually impossible to know a subject well unless it has been approached from many different directions, and without perseverance, the stubbornness of discovery would be overcome rarely.

## THE NATURE OF KNOWLEDGE

Psychobiologist Henry Plotkin[3] viewed knowledge as an extension of instinct and instinct itself as a form of knowledge. He considered evolutionary epistemology, learning and intelligence as Darwinian evolutionary processes, to be a new science of knowledge, no longer the exclusive realm of philosophy. He defines knowledge as "The relationship between the organization of any part of a living creature's body and particular aspects of order in the world outside of that creature." The fleshy, water-conserving stem of the cactus, built into gene memory, is a form of knowledge just as is our brain understanding that the sun will rise each morning. Knowledge pervades even in life forms that do not have brains. Negotiating obstacles and learning by experience, a paramecium does not possess neurons. It is surmised that the cytoskeleton may control its behavior.[4] Adaptations are forms of knowledge and knowledge is adaptation. Thus, it follows that evolution is the process by which knowledge is obtained. Without knowledge there would be no life.

Without evolution there would be neither knowledge nor life. As Darwin's theory of evolution is selectionist, the traits that characterize the fitness of an organism develop by chance, before becoming required. Adaptive traits are initially produced independent of adaptive usefulness, and it is in this context that Darwinian evolution is considered as blind. Traits are then selected from many variants for near-term advantage and then transmitted to the offspring.

Because it is useful, knowledge has evolved and was selected in this blind sense. Making flight easier, the adaptation of hollow lightweight bones in birds have survival value. The erroneous assumption is often made, therefore, that adaptations have purpose rather than occurring by chance.

This false notion has been around at least since Aristotle, who formalized it 2,000 years ago.[5] It is one of many examples where common sense can lead one astray.

Creative ideas, according to William James, arise through random variations unique to an individual's thought process, independent of external influences. External events may then become prominent in affecting the selection process. In a similar sense, science can be characterized as evolutionary. The cycles of conjecture and refutation evolve by selection into increasingly plausible explanations. The connections between different patterns of the world are gradually being understood by science. Perhaps one day there will evolve a grand unified theory. In both examples, creativity and science, Darwinian evolution is operative.

Plotkin[6] divided knowledge processes into three categories: primary, secondary, and tertiary heuristic. The primary heuristic refers to the processes by which variants are generated, selected, and propagated. It is the gene pool that propagates our knowledge of instincts. In that it promotes characteristics for the future that have worked in the past, the process is inductive. Instincts of the primary heuristic are the precursors of rationality and intelligence. The secondary heuristic comprises mechanisms within the immune system and brain, which have developed to supplement the primary heuristic. Constraining what the secondary heuristic can do, the primary heuristic feeds to it prior knowledge. That is why our intelligence is perceived to have *a priori* knowledge.

Plotkin considered intelligence the collective term for the secondary heuristic operating in the brain. It has evolved to address the limitations of the primary heuristic. Such limitations are posed by high frequency changes, which take place faster than the primary heuristic can adjust through adaptation. The tertiary heuristic includes the processes of culture, the sharing of knowledge, which Plotkin saw as the most complex thing on earth. Just as with change in species, change in intelligence and culture is the result of evolution. Conventionally understood, knowledge is a product of intelligence and culture. To this understanding of knowledge must be added instinct.

Psychologist Merlin Donald[7] described the modern brain as "a mosaic structure of cognitive vestiges from earlier stages of human emergence." Our brains represent the cumulative contributions of all of our hominid ancestors and even of certain apes. The idiosyncratic nature of cultures has a major effect on how we use our brains and how our intelligence is developed. Hence, cultures play a major role in our intellectual evolution and readily influence restructuring of the mind. Adaptations represent shades of truth, which become more inaccurate going from primary to tertiary. Because the tertiary heuristic, culture, is less amenable to control, it is generally less true than the primary and secondary heuristic.

Konrad Lorenz showed that no learner can acquire knowledge about every aspect of the world. The learner is not a generalist. He contended that learners possess innate teaching mechanisms, embodied by the primary heuristic, that constrain the extent of learning. Plotkin[8] believed this to be the most important concept of evolutionary epistemology. The most important spinoff that arises from this concept is that the English philosopher John Locke's idea of the original state of the mind as a *tabula rasa* is fallacious. Intelligence is limited by the primary heuristic, and the slate is already scribed when intelligence becomes operative. Without this being true, intelligence would not exist. Because learning is so rapid, it could never start from scratch, and it starts from a position where it is known that which must be learned. The importance of this observation will become more apparent under the discussion of rationalism (Chapter 13).

## THE ORIGIN OF SCIENCE

According to physicist Freeman Dyson, science developed from the fusion of philosophical thinking that began in ancient Greece and the tradition of skilled crafts that developed even earlier.[9] Concepts were derived from philosophy, and tools were derived from skilled crafts. Scientific revolutions can arise either from new tools for observing nature or from new concepts for understanding nature. Dyson contends that most of the recent scientific revolutions have been tool-driven. Frequently borrowing from each other, philosophy and skilled crafts became inextricably linked only in the twentieth century. Such intimate linkage is a fundamental basis of discovery.

Physicist Alan Cromer[10] described two views of how knowledge has been acquired. In the modern view, science develops in every civilization. In contrast, the traditional view is that science is the unique product of ancient Greece. As Cromer explained, the shortcoming of the modern view is that human beings evolved about 200,000 years ago. Yet, significant scientific knowledge has only developed in the last few hundred years. He concluded that this long period of ignorance shows that some barrier exists to objective human thought.

The Middle Ages represented an authoritarian, devoid of objectivity, religious hiatus of about 1,700 years between the objectivity of the ancient Greeks and the Enlightenment, sometimes called the Age of Reason. Knowledge grows on knowledge and increases exponentially (Chapters 3 and 21), which seems to be a partial answer to Cromer's barrier to objective human thought. With this realization, it is natural that the overwhelming gain in scientific knowledge would be accrued in recent years. On the other hand, the religious, anti-intellectualism of the Middle Ages is a perfect example of a major barrier to objectivity.

For science to develop, certain precursors are a necessary part of a culture. Cromer listed seven factors in Greek history that promoted objective thinking:

1.  the assembly where the art of debate had to be well developed for one to succeed;
2.  a maritime economy that precluded parochialism;
3.  a widespread, Greek-speaking world for the interaction of scholars and travelers;
4.  an independent merchant class that could afford to hire its own teachers;
5.  the *Iliad* and the *Odyssey* representing liberal, rational thinking;
6.  a religion not dominated by priests; and
7.  the persistence of these factors for hundreds of years.

Cromer believed that free debate was the most important vehicle that set Greece above other nations. People of Greece studied the techniques of debate extensively and the most adept received high honors. The process of debate involves competition, argument, and persuasion of peers, all aspects of objectivity prerequisite to science.

To the extent that free debate occurs in organizations, opportunities can arise for the interaction of a broad range of information. Such interaction greatly enhances the possibilities for the chance but synergistic combination of knowledge patterns that will lead to novelty. All those who participate in such debate will continuously accrue insight into the workings of the organization and how to expedite improvements and innovations. Organizations that promote open debate will reap the benefit of a powerful tool of science, the dialectic.

A maritime economy requires interaction with many different people and situations in the various ports of call. Permitting easy communication for travelers and wandering scholars, most of the ancient Greek world was Greek-speaking. Frequently leading to altogether new and viable concepts, the innovative interacted new ideas from different and distant lands with their own. Similarly, organizations that have worldwide contacts get from these distant locations new approaches and concepts that can affect great change for those who open their minds to the possibilities of diversity. The "shuttle effect" is a common source of new ideas by which scientists from different backgrounds and cultures interact to generate novelty.[11]

The wealthy independent merchant class of ancient Greece hired teachers for their children, which enabled the establishment of the teaching profession. Free from religious and civil constraints, schools arose that provided an open intellectual climate. In modern industry, excessive concentration on short-term objectives and secrecy imposed by proprietary constraints, commonly preclude intellectual openness. These strictures are important reasons for stagnation in industrial research. The problem of intellectual openness can be addressed by stressing the necessity of continuous learning of diverse knowledge patterns and intensive knowledge interaction between individuals in the group. If carried to the outside, such knowledge interaction can be even more enlightening.

In the *Iliad* and the *Odyssey*, Homer alluded to gods of finite character, and this limitation imposed on the supernatural had a sobering effect. In this way, humans could seek help from the supernatural, but have a ready explanation for failed requests. The Greek gods were subject to natural law that gave credence to realism and noncontradiction, both of which led smoothly into the objectivity that science attempts to impose. Without the authoritarianism of priests, mythical concepts were less apt to become established and to interfere with the objective needs of science.

Within the stricture of a company technology group, high priests of theory commonly develop. Such theories become the material of company paradigms that dictate the direction of research and the nature of interpretation of research projects. Although a necessary condition for progress in research and technology, the paradigm limits versatility of research direction and interpretation. Particularly if the paradigm is deeply channeled and misconceived, such a stricture can be a major disadvantage to any research effort. Events of this nature are not uncommon. Scientists and technologists can be helped greatly if they make a conscious effort to broaden perspective and to generate alternate more useful hypotheses that will inhibit the devastating effects of mind-sets.

The persistence of all seven of these conditions in ancient Greece, that stimulated intellectualism for a thousand years, enabled the development of science. It was a discipline uniquely originating in Greek culture and one that need not and, perhaps, would not have developed in any culture since. With careful thought, similar conditions can be cultivated in companies to promote the spirit of science and technology and the indelible motivation to discover. A case can be made, therefore, that laxity in intellectual spirit is a prime cause for paucity of innovation and low productivity.

Science is heretical in that it demands that phenomena be seen objectively through experiment and observation rather than as is wished or intuited. It is through carefully designed education that this higher plane of thought is achieved. The *Iliad* emphasizes the tradition of debate in ancient Greece that required independent thought and objectivity as opposed to the precepts of myth. The discipline of debate represents an important early phase in the development of objectivity and, therefore, scientific thought. Although most scholars of the scientific revolution believe that a major change in thinking took place between Aristotle and Galileo, Cromer suggested that the greatest change came with the Greek's discovery of objectivity.

In science, objectivity is respect for consensus in the scientific community. This definition may appear to be contradictory to the cause of creativity and can be if the excepted paradigm (set of beliefs and skills held by a community of scientists that shape research direction) is considered immutable. Because the empirical method of science—and for sundry other reasons—never results in certainty, the final arbiter of objectivity is the weighted opinion of the scientific community. In contrast, paradigm shifts, as quantum mechanics instead of Newtonian, are potential refutations of community opinion, but they are not considered objective until the community passes favorable judgment.

The biologist Lewis Wolpert[12] elaborated key reasoning processes for people to learn before a clear sense of science can be realized. These include the variables involved in causal events, the necessity of changing one variable at a time in experimentation, the concepts of probability and correlation, and the general idea of abstract models to facilitate explanation of phenomena. Stemming from their lack of necessity in daily existence, these basic concepts of science are rarely learned by the laity.

Christianity replaced 500 years of Greek dominance, and the myth of egocentrism replaced objectivity. To illustrate the devastating effect of the loss of objectivity, Alan Cromer[13] invoked the psychologist Jean Piaget who showed that for most of history, human beings, believing that they are somehow connected to the powers that govern the world, have had difficulty in separating internal thought from the external world of objects and events. They have clung to the idea of personal knowledge and a direct link to nature. Cromer contended that until this connection is severed, which is contrary to human nature, science cannot develop. He believed that this stubborn connection is the fundamental barrier to objective human thought. Any dogmatic belief subdues intellectual adventure. Successful scientists dispose of their egocentrism in favor of a superior sense of potential truth. This is public objective knowledge arising from a consensus in the scientific community.

Cromer's central thesis was that science is the unique product of ancient Greece and that all civilizations learned their science from the Greeks. China produced many technologic developments but did not develop science. It was not until the scientific revolution in sixteenth- and seventeenth-century Europe that the limits of Greek science were exceeded, and this came about partly because of the development of a large scientific community. Science began to evolve again, primarily because faith was replaced by reason and observation. Superior knowledge develops only from the interplay of free and informed minds.

In contrast to Cromer, the late biologist and astronomer Carl Sagan[14] saw a profound predisposition toward science in first graders and even among the !Kung San hunter-gatherers of the Kalahari Desert in the development of their skills in tracking and hunting. Many of Cromer's criteria for objective thinking can be found in hunter-gatherer peoples. Sagan even saw this penchant in chimpanzees when they were tracking on patrol of their territorial borders. Because it is the fundamental basis of our survival, a predisposition for science throughout the history of *Homo sapiens*, Sagan contended, has been inherent. He believed that "When, through indifference, inattention, incompetence, or fear of skepticism, we discourage children from science, we are disenfranchising them, taking from them the tools needed to manage their future."

The next chapter continues the discussion of knowledge gain. Having now a better feeling for the nature of knowledge and how science originated, it may be beneficial to gain some insight into problems in understanding science, how knowledge is evolutionary, and the importance of a broad range of knowledge to achieve discovery.

*Chapter 8*

# Knowledge Gain: Problems, Dynamics, and Essential Knowledge Patterns

It is striking how many people express doubt about things for which there is evidence, yet believe tacitly about things for which there is no evidence. It is even more striking that the ancient Greeks, over 2,000 years ago, were the first civilization to adopt objectivity and to make great strides in the development of science. The great contributions of this beautifully thoughtful civilization were lost to the emotional crassness of the European Middle Ages, preserved by Islam, and, happily, returned by the Crusades. Hence, it is appropriate that obstacles to understanding science and the essential knowledge patterns for successful technical people are explored in this chapter.

## PROBLEMS IN UNDERSTANDING SCIENCE

Logical thinking processes, according to physicist Alan Cromer, do not come naturally and are learned only through formal training.[1] With their passion for debate and their development of mathematics, these special cultural conditions of the ancient Greek civilization provided a fertile field for the cultivation of logical thinking. Unable to distinguish astrology from astronomy, as many as one-third of Americans believe in astrology. Half or more believe in extrasensory perception (ESP), about 17% have consulted psychics, and between one-third and one-half believe in unidentified flying objects (UFOs). The extent to which many people are superstitious and seem to be selectively oblivious to critical thinking, makes one wonder about the quality of education in America.

In contrast to Cromer, Sagan[2] believed obstacles to scientific thinking are political and hierarchical. In cultures with conservative stability where fundamental change seems to be unnecessary, new ideas are not encouraged or may even be prohibited. Thinking is generally as conservative as the attendant culture. Where environmental, biological, or political change occurs, the old ways may be ineffective in dealing with new problems. Both Cromer's and Sagan's explanations of cultural impediments to science seem to have validity. Thinking with both the creative and logical processes of science seems to require appropriate conditioning and encouragement. Such thought processes are essential in all areas of endeavor for the most productive and useful existence.

Without appropriate education, science will not prevail. In this regard, Sagan[3] emphasized that our cultural milieu, educational systems, and communications media do a poor job, if at all, of distinguishing science from pseudoscience. Mystical, unfounded beliefs as astrology, the lost continent of Atlantis, channeling, the shroud of Turin, UFOs, the paranormal, among a long list, occur even amidst the otherwise well educated. The media shirks their responsibility in not making known the refutation of these unfounded notions.

Harms that may arise from such superstitions have been summarized by the National Science Board,[4] the policy-making arm of the National Science Foundation:

1. a decline in scientific literacy and critical thinking;
2. the inability of citizens to make well-informed decisions;
3. monetary losses (psychic hotlines, for example, offer little value for the money spent);
4. a diversion of resources that might have been spent on more productive and worthwhile activities (for example, solving society's serious problems);
5. the encouragement of a something-for-nothing mentality and the belief that there are easy answers to serious problems (for example, that positive thinking can replace hard work); and
6. false hopes and unrealistic expectations.

Healthy skepticism and critical thinking can lead to a more reliable and effective society, and unfailing belief without evidence is a dangerous, devolutionary path. Without clear evidence of the truth or falsity of phenomena, reservation of judgment is the most meaningful state of mind. Being open-minded to ideas that have some semblance of credence is essential for the covering of all bases, but skepticism is essential to eliminate preposterous notions for which there is no evidence. To the extent that tough, logical thinking is pushed aside, people make themselves targets for deceptions of every stripe. Never having totally departed, the Dark Ages could easily undergo a major resurgence without a general social empathy for the creativity and rigorous logic that are inherent in reliable knowledge.

Astronomer John D. Barrow[5] points out that in the history of conscious life, irrationality is in much greater evidence than is rationality. Mystical, symbolic, and religious thinking have dominated all cultures, past and present, to an extent that this propensity suggests there may be an adaptive advantage to such beliefs. Through emotional intensity and blind acceptance of sacred beliefs, greater benefit for survival may be afforded. Although the source of many false ideas, sharing of mystical beliefs can promote social cohesion and a united front against external dangers. Often requiring irrational boldness to address fragmented understanding and difficult problems, the esteem arising from heroic deeds and the acceptance of a supernatural power that will come to our aid in this and a later life often can arouse the necessary courage to tackle the most intransigent problems. Suspension of reason to maintain tribal cohesion during times of great social stress seems to be an adaptive advantage that generally overwhelms the idyllic goal of rationality.

Rationality is essential for understanding nature; irrationality seems to be beneficial sometimes to deal with some of life's worst problems, as horrendous firepower during war, death of loved ones, and dangers encountered in exploring the earth and the solar system. Barrow suggested that, perhaps, rationality breeds too much caution to address such problems in the most effective way. In this sense, rational societies may not have discovered the New World, produced heroic soldiers, nor walked on the moon.

On the other hand, rational societies conceivably might be so technologically advanced that they would defeat any enemy on the battlefield without much danger to themselves. They might explore the solar system with such technological superiority that danger would be minimized. Furthermore, and perhaps most important, if all societies were rational, war might become, at best, obsolete, and, at worst, a rare phenomenon.

Emotions and biases are often the basis of decision making, which can be manipulated by charismatic leaders. When united with an emotionally charged purpose, large groups of individuals can be transformed into a highly disciplined automation. Indeed, this can be done exclusive of reason and even without invoking mysticism. Sustained by cultural imperatives and ultimately for the sake of communism, Chinese soldiers in the Korean War obeyed orders and sacrificed their lives in mass infantry attacks. In World War II, religiously motivated kamikazes made suicide attacks on American warships. Hitler captured his followers in a mass hysteria and by cleverly designed eristic convinced many of the German people of the correctness of heinous acts against Jews, homosexuals, and others. These examples reflect the most profound reasons why critical thinking is essential to effective democracy and to the long-term well-being of civilization.

Mystical systems are not a mechanism for knowledge gain but are crutches that may help psychologically in time of great need. On the negative side, by sometimes excluding creativity and critical thinking from the thought process and by promoting irrational beliefs that were instituted by ignorant, agrarian, and nomadic societies that lived many hundreds of years ago, mystical beliefs can impede the evolution of society's intellect and long-term well-being. The rationalism of critical thinking and scientific method is the only way to acquire reliable and, hence, the most enduring knowledge patterns.

A totally rational society would subdue the diversity needed to optimize creativity. But if we assume the existence of a society in which the great majority are rational and thoroughly conditioned with critical thinking, progress in understanding ourselves and the rest of nature, conceivably, would accelerate at a dizzying pace.

Described by Howard Margolis,[6] senior lecturer in the Graduate School of Public Policy Studies at the University of Chicago, our brains store knowledge by the agency of many patterns, and cognition consists of relating the closest fitting pattern with the observation. Learning is dependent on this repertoire of patterns that also acts as a constraint. Discovery pivots on the use of existing brain patterns in new ways but, nevertheless, in a way that seems to be familiar. With continued use and incremental adjustments, the new pattern becomes fully established in one's repertoire. We learn with comparative ease those things that fit our existing network, but we learn with difficulty those patterns that deviate from our repertoire. A new pattern becomes progressively easier to recognize each subsequent time it is seen in that system. Similarly, as we increase the number of patterns in our repertoire, the incorporation of other new patterns becomes easier as well.

Entrenched ideas that can come from working in a domain for many years or otherwise becoming too attached to a paradigm, become progressively more difficult to shed. This can be true even in the light of overwhelming contrary evidence. Margolis gave many examples, such as Priestly, who would not give up the idea of phlogiston; Mach, who denied both relativity and the reality of atoms; and Lord Kelvin, who in the latter part of his life was unable to accept any of the new important ideas, such as evolution, X rays, and transmutation of the elements.

It follows that discovery that displaces an established habit or pattern is most often made by those who are not deeply entrenched in a paradigm. Without notable involvement, however, the discoverer could not have the knowledge to solve the critical problems in that field. Thus, partial outsiders are the frequent source of discovery. A classic example is the discovery of DNA by Watson and Crick who used techniques alien to traditional biologists—X-ray crystallography and structural models.

Edward de Bono,[7] an expert in systems behavior, emphasized the dangers of too much knowledge to creative thinking. Abundant knowledge can promote mind-sets and preclude serendipity. This danger indeed does exist, particularly if one has worked many years within one paradigm. Escape from the paradigmatic trap can never be easy, but three approaches can be helpful. The first is diversity of research that helps to maintain a broader perspective of reality. By this mechanism, one acquires a broad range of knowledge that precludes minute detail and requires the insight to recognize and remember the most critical parameters.

The second approach is to remind oneself constantly of the dynamic and uncertain nature of knowledge. To the extent that such conditioning is effective, scientists are more likely to maintain rational flexibility in their approach to problems and in their interpretation of data. The third approach is to constantly seek, through mind experiments, alternate hypotheses that may provide a more workable explanation.

Psychologist Teresa Amabile[8] believed that it is not possible to have too much knowledge to be creative. If knowledge is stored according to rigid algorithms, creativity is not favored. If it is stored in broad categories for easy access of association, abundant and diverse knowledge can only aid creativity. To contend without ramification that excessive knowledge hinders creativity contradicts a fundamental basis for novelty. To be incarcerated in a paradigm, a theory, or a hypothesis is the nemesis of the scientist who wishes to be creative, but without abundant knowledge creativity will not happen. Highly creative people have solved this paradox.

Science fiction writer and biochemist Isaac Asimov[9] pointed out that scientific creators have always thoroughly understood the science that they have displaced with more viable explanations. Copernicus fully understood Ptolemaic astronomy, Galileo mastered Aristotelian physics, Vesalius was fully versed in Galenic medicine, and Einstein completely comprehended Newtonian physics.

Major shifts in thought patterns, as Kuhnian paradigm shifts (Chapter 14), apparently require determined efforts by people who are desperately searching for a path out of the quagmire of conventional approaches. Even if a viable, new approach is found, the old guard will be difficult if possible to convince. Margolis, therefore, alluded to Planck's dictum: "For radical discoveries the new view triumphs less by converting the old guard than by outliving it." The philosopher and psychologist William James was, indeed, cynical about the fate of a new idea: "First it's absurd, then maybe, and last, we have known it all along."[10]

A fundamental task of the scientist is to observe and record experience with objective accuracy, but this is far more difficult than is generally understood or is readily admitted. Psychologist Abraham Maslow[11] cautioned that by cultivating "the humility of the empirical attitude," the channels of the mind are opened to new concepts. Humility, however, is only for the uncertainty of empirical conclusions. The best scientists have great confidence and perseverance and feel anything but humility in their efforts to make discoveries.

Because people often fear and resist the understanding of themselves, knowledge concerning other things is generally better developed. Maslow emphasized, therefore, that the better we know ourselves, the better knowers we are about other things. Defenses such as hallucinations, illusions, delusions, repressions, and denials are the enemies of clear understanding. Psychological health can be improved by self-knowledge through introspection and brutal honesty. Reliable knowledge demands this intense honesty with ourselves—that we transcend our egos no matter how great the obstacle. The verification and the peer review process in the scientific community help to neutralize our mistakes in knowledge created by our individual pathologies. It is partly by introspective efforts but largely through testing reality in the scientific community that we can hope for any significant objectivity in scientific concepts.

Maslow[12] differentiated the classification of things from the contemplative enjoyment of the way things are. The latter method is Taoistic knowing, and the former corresponds to the method of science. Both kinds of knowing are important and their integration is a special kind of holistic knowing. Taoistic knowing is most often associated with artistic appreciation. Biologist E.O. Wilson explained the distinction in similar fashion: "science explains feeling, while art transmits it."[13] Understanding the nomenclature of music is scientific, but passively listening and appreciating its aesthetic qualities is Taoistic. To gain full understanding of a culture, one must live with its people and experience the breadth of their being. In this process one achieves Taoistic knowing, and then many questions can be understood introspectively.

Penetration of their companies' and their customers' cultures gives technologists a critical background for new product development. This penetration is from the standpoints of operational, functional, psychological, and aesthetic needs. Living with customers to the extent feasible is the only way of closely approaching full knowledge or clear definition of their new product needs.

Taoistic knowing is not the sole prerogative of people who appreciate art, and it may be related to the hierarchical scheme of information occurring in the human brain. When an object or a system is studied, knowledge is gained that is stored according to this hierarchical scheme. Most of these modules operate outside of consciousness. With certain cues our attention may be directed to this otherwise hidden knowledge, or it may come to us via hunches or intuition.

Split-brain research has reinforced this view and has shed light, although controversial,[14, 15] on a unified consciousness. Serving to monitor and synthesize messages coming from different parts of the brain, a module known as the interpreter (homunculus) is thought by some to occur in the left hemisphere of the brain.[16] On the other hand, many scientists do not believe that a central controller exists.

According to computer scientist Christopher Langton,[17] many emergent properties, as in immune systems, economies, countries, corporations, and living cells, would not be possible with a central controller. Without central supervision, the system is more robust, adaptive, flexible, and innovative, than, for example, centrally controlled systems that we build. An analogy can be made with corporations or companies where all divisions are under rigorous central control and are treated with inflexible polices. Rigorous control is anathema to creativity, whereas flexibility allows for the diversity and openness essential to creation. Certain types of people exert rigorous, rigid control over their personal lives and their work, as if they had a central controller. Accuracy and precision of their work is usually flawless, but their creative production is, nevertheless, negligible. Both types are critical to the technical world.

Zoologist Matt Ridley, with the example of stress, describes in the most analytical fashion the non-centrality of physiological functions of the human body.[18] In dealing with stress imposed by the outside world, the brain alerts its hypothalamus, which signals the pituitary gland to release a hormone that, in turn, signals the adrenal gland to secrete the hormone, cortisol. Stress is equated with cortisol. All of the actions leading up to and including the secretion of cortisol are involuntary and nonconscious. No one thing is in charge, and all of the bodily actions described evolved as a result of chance—natural selection. Neither our brain, our genes, nor any other part of our body is in charge. "You are not a brain running a body by switching on hormones. Nor are you a body running a genome by switching on hormone receptors. Nor are you a genome running a brain by switching on genes that switch on hormones. You are all of these at once." Our bodies are intricately interconnected systems without a central controller.

For the brain to achieve creativity, therefore, it seems to require independent action on the part of various brain modules, ductless glands, and perhaps other bodily functions—yet intricately interconnected. Similarly, discoveries arise with those who have intricately interconnected, unique, combinations of knowledge consisting of a complex body of evidence, theories, and models. This core need of creativity can be addressed by continually researching all of the knowledge patterns related to one's field of study. Even doing research in areas of science related but largely outside the scope of one's field can be enormously helpful. Continually attempting to interact different patterns of knowledge often will result in a new, viable idea.

Faraday was most adept at connecting seemingly unrelated patterns of knowledge.[19] He showed the connection between electricity and magnetism and their relation to light and how electricity is involved in the construction of matter. The highly creative child psychologist Jean Piaget[20] carried out a widely different network of projects including epistemology, logic, history of science, psychology, sociology, and biology.

Even seemingly unrelated areas as poetry, prose, music, and art can be helpful avocations to improve abilities to think metaphorically, to draw analogies, to visualize, and to recognize patterns. By this approach one cannot learn as much detail about each discipline as does the specialist, and knowledge choice is that which best reflects the larger perspective. Such broad learning gives a better opportunity for knowledge interaction and the quantum leap to discovery.

## THE DYNAMICS OF KNOWLEDGE

In industry, research generally addresses strategic company goals, which Michael Wolff[21] tagged "directed basic research." "Non-directed basic research," is considered as fundamental work that does not lead directly to a commercial application. Both types of basic research are invaluable, and it has been shown that at least half of all inventions stem from nondirected basic research.[22]

Some people in industry make the argument that all basic research, if really needed, is best consigned to outside laboratories. This would allow companies to pursue immediate and more practical problems. Often this action may be the only practical approach. On the other hand, basic research generally has greater intrinsic value when done in-house. People who do research gain a depth of understanding, an empathy, and an insight, much of which is Taoistic. Such knowledge is impossible to transfer fully to others. It is this subtle but critical depth of understanding which can lead to outstanding new product development teams.

Although simply a part of scientific method, attempts to explain data collected from experiments are stimulating and compelling, continuously presenting new challenges. This reflects the overwhelming power of the combined effects of experiential and reflective thinking. Under these conditions the mind is continually driven by a barrage of new information that requires explanation. There is no better way to arouse diversity of thinking, to explain anomaly, and to gain a better understanding of phenomena. Directed or strategic basic research is critical to new product development. Nondirected basic research in most companies is probably best reserved for academe.

Projects carried out in industry generally are of a restrictive nature, designed to emphasize practicality and targeted direction to nontechnical management. Often the needed underlying science is absent, and for that reason these projects are generally failures. Even more damaging, highly limited breadth of study inhibits creativity. Multiplicity of research projects is important to the creative process. To justify diversity in projects, it is critical that each area of study, no matter how indirect, be shown to management to be related to strategic company goals.

Efficient procurement of knowledge is facilitated by a continuous awareness of its dynamic nature, and by being constantly alert to the possible derivation of original and more viable answers. As described in greater detail in Chapter 8, knowledge is not absolute and is subject to change. This stems, in part, from the inadequacies of deductive and, especially, inductive reasoning. Additionally, knowledge is provisional because of the finite nature of the phenomena we investigate. This latter point assumes the holistic concept that all phenomena are interrelated and interdependent.

Knowledge can also be dynamic because of evolution. Described by physicist Joseph Schwartz,[23] the structure of the protein molecule is determined by the sequence of its amino acids. A typical protein of 100 amino acids has $20^{100}$ possibilities of arrangement. Permitting any combination of the 20 naturally occurring amino acids, the laws of physics have to some degree been excluded from the evolution of life. Evolution has been confined to a much smaller group of proteins. Historicity, therefore, is pivotal to living matter. Schwartz emphasizes that molecular biology has shown that because of its historical nature, life cannot be understood in the same terms as physics.

In the physical world, evolution also plays a role. The second law of thermodynamics, entropy, for example, is evolutionary, specifically devolutionary in the sense that all matter moves toward disorder. In this sense, however, biological evolution again deviates from physics, often moving toward greater order. The relentless movement toward disorder is interspersed with bursts of biological evolution slowing the short-term pace of entropy. Complexity theory shows that in far-from-equilibrium systems spontaneous organization can slow further the pace toward randomness.[24] Such organization can lead to planets and galaxies as well as cells and organisms. In the long-term, however, it seems that entropy will dominate.[25]

Asimov explained this seeming inconsistency.[26] The second law of thermodynamics applies only to closed systems, where energy is neither gained nor lost via the outside. The disordering influence of the second law applies only if the universe is a closed system, which is believed by Asimov to be the case. Subsystems can increase in order, as the evolution of life, as long as another part of the system (e.g., the sun) decreases in order at a much faster rate. It is not a zero sum game, and the overall movement toward disorder will always be positive.

There is some debate as to whether the evolution of life necessarily moves to greater complexity. Both interpretations have been offered for Darwinian evolution. In the new science of complexity, evolution necessarily moves toward greater complexity. These aspects of knowledge uncertainty are notable admonishments about the dangers of mind-sets and intellectual elit-

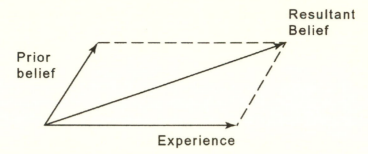

**Figure 8.1**. Parallelogram of forces showing how prior belief modifies the interpretation of experience. As prior belief and experience vary, so does the resultant belief.

ism. Furthermore, overt awareness of the dynamics of knowledge can keep the mind open for the recognition of flaws in understanding and receptivity to the necessity of change.

Another critical aspect of knowledge is the sociological view described by David Bloor.[27] Knowledge is not a reflection of reality that can be seen in the same light by any individual. It is a product of the interaction of our experience and cultural influences with the new experience. Such an effect can be viewed diagrammatically by the parallelogram of forces (see Figure 8.1). Each individual and each culture provides a different response to new experience that accounts for the highly varied opinions offered by society.

Evolutionary psychologists and behavioral geneticists have shown that genes play a significant role alongside environmental influences.[28] Each person has a unique genetic makeup and a unique environment—even some of this environment is determined by the genes. Genes affect a propensity for behavior, which may be modified by the environment. Our genetic constitution and what we have seen preconditions our interpretation of the present; such bias often preclude our seeing things in broader perspective. As observed by Bloor, our perceptual and thinking facilities are in conflict, and our perceptions are the dominant force.

How highly intelligent people could receive the same information and derive different and often contradictory conclusions, at first, seemed puzzling. The conflict between conservative and liberal points of view is a perfect case in point. These sociological and evolutionary perspectives of knowledge explain much of the inconsistency and seeming inanity of some public opinion. On the positive side, the wealth of ideas provided by this system is a critical parameter of creativity. Just as there are many different and potentially valid approaches to phenomena that are essential to understanding, there are many idiosyncratic ideas that when interacted can lead to the eclectic.

With the seeming impossibility of acquiring perfect knowledge in frontier areas of science, consensus in the scientific community (Chapter 12) looms particularly important. With time and continued confirmation, knowledge increases in reliability and may eventually gain the status of textbook science, which is not likely to be refuted. Physicist Alan Cromer[29] pointed out that some things can be said with absolute certainty. Because of maximum cohesive force caused by the electrons, no substance is solid above 5,000°C. Melting points of solids preclude maximum operating temperature of turbines and the maximum thrust of rocket engines. But the tenuous nature of frontier science gives emphasis to the need for the extensive use of the dialectic. From these sources the eclectic may be found and the interaction of different approaches may lead to a synergism of major import. This process can further the cause of knowledge reliability.

Psychologist Robert Sternberg[30] pointed out that considerable evidence exists that intelligence is not a fixed entity—that it can be increased through guided instruction. People who adjust to new environments are using, conceivably, a process for enhancing intelligence. In the last 2.5 million years there have been many abrupt changes in climate caused by the retreat and advance of continental glaciers, where survival demanded major adjustment. It was during this time that the Great Encephalization occurred, when our brains enlarged to their present size.[31] In concert with Darwinian evolution, brain enlargement was a chance development that addressed a critical need. Drastic change in environment as a major cause of intelligence growth seems to be highly reasonable speculation (Chapter 2).

Elaborated by Richard Restak[32] and originally observed by Darwin, domesticated rabbits have smaller brains than wild rabbits. The many challenges of nature require a greater range of brain use by wild rabbits, whereas reduced need has led to the partial atrophy of the brains of domesticated rabbits. Rats bred to be maze-smart have more developed brains in the sense of a higher content of the neurotransmitter, acetylcholine. Furthermore, the cerebral cortices of animals subjected to differing levels of stimulation show measurable structural differences.

Neuroscientist Fred Gage of La Jolla's Salk Institute carried out experiments in the 1990s with mice raised in either stimulating environments or deprived environments.[33] He showed that very young mice exposed to a stimulating environment gain neurons as they grow up. Stimulated mice were shown to be more clever than others and were better at dealing with the unexpected.

Nobel Laureate and neuroscientist Gerald M. Edelman[34] saw the brain as the most complex object in the known universe. Seemingly, the brain is continually being modified, and the more the environment demands our adjustment to new challenges, the more complex the brain can become. Containing between $10^{12}$ and $10^{14}$ nerve cells, the neuronal cables establishing links between these cells are several kilometers in length within one cubic millimeter of cerebral cortex.[35] The combinatorial explosion of potential connections would stagger even the largest of existing computers. Equally exciting is the potential for new ideas that could stem from these nerve cell connections. The notion that mental exercise can modify the brain is recent and should have great significance in the cultivation of one's ability to conceive problem solutions and creative illuminations.

In a similar sense, it seems that research, particularly where it involves a broad range of projects, provides a significant stimulus for the continued growth of intelligence. Although studies in ethology have shown that intelligence is about 70% to 75% genetic,[36] the remaining 25% to 30%, which is environmental, potentially can still have a notable influence. Biologist Christopher Wills[37] pointed to studies showing that the intrauterine milieu plays a significant role in affecting intelligence and can cut the heritability estimate in half, giving much greater weight to the influence of the environment.

Zoologist Matt Ridley indicates that events within the womb have three times as much effect on intelligence as our home environment did after birth.[38] The remainder includes school, peer groups, and other outside influences. Gene influence increases with age—heritability of childhood IQ is about 45%, but late in adolescence is about 75%. As you mature, you leave behind many environmental influences and gradually establish your innate intelligence. It is this emergence of innate intelligence which enables you to pick the most suitable environment. Ridley points out that two vital things are proven by this self-orienting choice of environment: "that genetic influences are not frozen at conception, and that environmental influences are not inexorably cumulative."

While environmental conditions other than the extreme generally have little effect on intelligence, it seems reasonable that an intensely intellectual zeitgeist involving diverse research constitutes an extreme. Knowledge gain from diverse research must be coupled with a persistent effort to interrelate not only the obvious but the yin and the yang. Such a procedure usually requires a continuous adjustment to new concepts and disturbingly different relationships that can knead and reshape the intellect.

Many neurobiologists theorize that learning leads to new synaptic connections.[39] Synapses are gaps between nerve cells, and communication across gaps occurs via chemicals known as neurotransmitters. The neuronal and chemical change in brain structure is called plasticity. Varying among animals, plasticity is highly limited in insects and strongly developed in human beings.[40] Among humans, it is strongest with children but still functional in adults. Thus, every experience affects brain modification, and learning may be a mechanism of enhancing not only our capacity for knowledge but our ability to think progressively more profoundly. As we improve the quality, the content, and the range of our knowledge, we increase the chances for new connections leading to new concepts. It is a potential mechanism for overcoming some of the negative aspects of inherited intelligence. Seemingly, our ability to comprehend and to conceive unique approaches to problems should only grow by virtue of a more complex synaptic network.

Changes that take place in the brain as we learn are reflected by positron emission tomography, PET, where radioactive isotopes are injected into a vein.[41] When the blood carrying the isotopes enters the brain, it accumulates in the areas of greatest activity. From this activity, a color-coded map is produced. Different thought processes or states of mind produce different color-coded images. It has been observed that trained musicians use their left hemisphere for processing music, whereas people listening to music purely for enjoyment show dominant right hemisphere processing. Such brain mapping may further our understanding of how we solve problems.

The potential benefits that may be derived from brain plasticity deserve additional speculation. If people can change their brains for the better by exposing themselves to appropriate environments, then the path that the determined creator must follow is clearly marked. By exploiting the brain's plasticity, preferably beginning in childhood, through exposure to diverse intellectual interests and by working equally hard at understanding the interrelationships between phenomena, people might even become geniuses. At worst, they will be profoundly more knowledgeable, and their thought processes will have been provoked and incensed to a higher level of understanding.

As large quantities of knowledge alone are insufficient for achieving discovery, kneading and reshaping of the intellect are critical to the growth of new concepts. Change of basic assumptions and thought processes is sometimes necessary for the appreciation of anomaly—to see with the most penetrating illumination. If researchers are too enamored with the conventional beliefs of their mentors, colleagues, or of the existing paradigm, their chances for discovery can be greatly diminished. For the most profound understanding of nature, new knowledge can be scanned with a kaleidoscopic outlook until a particular fit coincides with the most acceptable hypothesis of reality.

Biologist Lawrence Slobodkin[42] observed that rebellions in German concentration camps during World War II were limited to the best-fed prisoners. Slave rebellions in America were often led by the most privileged, just as the French, British, Russian, and American revolutions were initiated by the prosperous. As Slobodkin analogized, "If it requires the physically well nourished to rebel, then major doctrinal revolutions are most likely to occur among the intellectually well nourished." There is no better recommendation for the acquisition of the broadest range of knowledge.

## ESSENTIAL KNOWLEDGE PATTERNS FOR TECHNOLOGISTS

To be in the best position to accomplish their innovative tasks, technologists have in-depth understanding of the knowledge patterns shown in

**KNOWLEDGE
GAIN**

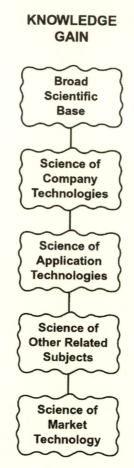

**Figure 8.2.** Minimum knowledge essential to technological discovery.

Figure 8.2. They continuously do research on these patterns, which provides new knowledge to mine for potential profit.

A critical example of the science of company technologies relates to the fundamental properties of materials, which are understood, in-depth, for efficient new product development. This subject, generally, is complex and inadequately understood. Basic research is carried out continuously on relevant materials to enable companies to differentiate their products from the competition. Because this kind of work often does not lead directly to a practical application and because of pressures for technical service, basic research—long-term knowledge gain projects—in many companies is cavalierly pushed aside. Although it can be essential for long-term company vitality, it is treated often as a luxury to be had only under the most perfect of conditions. In those companies where short-term problems are not being addressed effectively, it is often even more difficult to gain management approval for long-term knowledge gain projects. As long-term knowledge gain is commonly essential for the most efficient resolution of short-term problems, this conflict can become a serious catch-22.

The science of application technologies relates to mechanisms of inter-action (e.g., how the clay mineral kaolin interacts in paper coating, paint films, plastics, etc.). Many companies take the shortcut or pragmatic route to new product development, which is concern only for superficial problem solution. This approach commonly excludes an understanding of mecha-nisms of interaction and can take on an air of witchcraft. Such a short-term approach can lead to developmental failure and inadequate knowledge for technical service of products. The better the mechanisms of interaction are understood, the easier it is to improve product quality, or to develop distinctly new products.

Many related subjects can be helpful in creating new approaches (e.g., new kinds of instrumentation), unique approaches used in other disciplines for problem solving, understanding how to interact the use of left-handed and right-handed thinking, studying metaphorical relationships with dif-fering aspects of nature, intuition, mathematical formalisms, ad infinitum. Attempting to recognize connections between various aspects of nature can lead to a wealth of creative approaches and discoveries.

The science of market technology is a subtle but critical extension of the science of materials applications. Customers have unique problems that cannot be understood adequately by laboratory work alone and often can-not be anticipated without inside information. This is where Taoistic knowledge becomes indispensable to developmental work. Without a pro-found understanding of customer needs, it is impossible to carry out an efficient new product development program.

The nature of the needed market knowledge is generally outside the scope of typical market research, which is not meant as a pejorative comment on the excellent work of most marketing departments. Perhaps best described as the final extension of applied science that must be understood, this effort can be carried out most profitably by the technologists directly involved in the development program. To facilitate on-site experience, these same tech-nologists, ideally, have close customer contacts. By this mechanism, the technologists can begin to sense or intuit the most important aspects of a customer's system. During this time, the technologists may develop an em-pathy for the most critical needs of a potential new product. The specific nature of market technology needed by technologists is outlined below. To distinguish it from conventional market research, this approach has been designated a technological market survey.

1. Determine customer's use or potential use of your product.
2. Determine nature and function of all related customer system components. As much as proprietary constraints allow, combine this data with costs.

3. Research literature.

4. Collate and interpret data.

5. Project new product needs and how your knowledge might be focused to address these needs.


These surveys can be of a general nature covering many different areas of application from which several new product needs may be derived. On the other hand, they may be specifically directed toward a partially formulated new product concept. By virtue of a survey, a new product concept can be characterized with great accuracy. This can decrease the amount of time wasted in attempting to develop a product that is significantly short of customer needs, that may not have sufficient breadth of applicability, or that may not be cost-effective. Investigations of intelligence testing have shown that a common reason for failure is poor definition or understanding of the problem.[43] Preparation of customer surveys is time consuming, but it can more than compensate for time wasted stemming from poor problem definition, and it can greatly enhance chances of successful new product development.

All of the knowledge patterns under knowledge gain interwoven with an understanding of product economics are the minimum knowledge areas that each member of a new product development team, ideally, possesses. Although some degree of specialization is unavoidable, each member, for greatest benefit, acquires an in-depth understanding of each pattern. Psychologist and philosopher Margaret Boden[44] indicated that the distinguishing characteristics of a highly creative person do not relate to special powers, but to greater knowledge, practiced expertise, and high motivation. Thus, the practical in-depth understanding of a broad range of knowledge is essential to creativity. For creativity in academe, knowledge patterns include as many as possible, but especially a broad scientific base and that derived from interdisciplinary research.

To address the minimum knowledge needed for creativity and discovery, all of the knowledge patterns in the schematic under knowledge gain are researched continuously. The purpose of the research is to gain a greater fundamental understanding of base materials, of the mechanisms by which base materials interact in applications, and of modifications of base materials required to make them behave in applications in custom-tailored fashion. But the question invariably arises, how can technologists or scientists find the time to do all of this research? Because pressing current problems take precedence, the usual answer is that the time *cannot* be found. This nearly ubiquitous trap bears abundant responsibility for low levels of industrial competitiveness and relates to why otherwise capable scientists are not more productive. The answer to this problem of doing adequate research is not simple. It entails a greater administrative understanding of the needs of research, and a greater understanding by technologists of the broad commitment necessary to be successful inventors.

Each person has limits beyond which expansion of projects is counter-productive. An obsessive desire for knowledge and a clear commitment and desire to do all of the projects undertaken is the most positive pathway to success. Additionally, the projects undertaken are viewed in the sense of pleasure—never as necessary chores or done with a concentration on monetary reward. Creative science and technology without full commitment are not apt to happen. If this simple observation were to be fully recognized and somehow expedited, productivity would skyrocket.

If one generates a new viable concept, the extent to which it can be transformed to a successful innovation is dependent, partly, on the quantity and quality of relevant knowledge. Research and development laboratories, for goal achievement, have the perseverance and the passion to accumulate knowledge continuously, such that they will be right when the competition is either wrong or innocent. Mark Twain expressed a similar thought with notable sagacity when he said, "Let us be thankful for the fools. But for them the rest of us could not succeed."[45]

The most important motivation of many technical people is the subtle yet profound stimulation that stems from knowledge dynamics. In extensive research on creativity, psychiatrist Albert Rothenberg[46] found that motivation is the only characteristic common to all creative people. Scientists or technologists who have found their ability to discover new knowledge or to be creative have about them an aura of excitement, intensity, confidence, and permanence. Such enthusiasm is infectious and can become epidemic. Even those who are not inveterate inventors are apt to be caught up in these positive emotional forces. Scientists and technologists with this syndrome are rarely, if ever, unhappy with their work—unless their curiosity is being seriously thwarted. Scientists and technologists who have the propensity are allowed to do research, to hypothesize, and to invent, or their organization will lose the most important resource of creativity and successful companies—motivated people!

The essence of the knowledge gain step, then, is that one's conceptual base is expanded continually, not only within one's discipline but in related fields as well. This can be accomplished by the pursuit of diverse research projects and by the interaction of different knowledge patterns as much as possible. Expansion of knowledge base in as many areas as possible, even seemingly unrelated to one's profession, can lead to unsuspected connections and promote creative cognition. Thus, the first step in the creative process, knowledge gain, is ongoing while discovery is the goal. It anticipates the solution to many problems and is invaluable for the next step in creativity, preparation. Socrates believed that the greatest cause of evil is ignorance. Knowledge was the touchstone of ancient Greek thought,[47] as it is for all creators.

Preparation, the next chapter, is a focus on approaches to the solution of specific problems. Ways of problem study that have been found to be most effective are elaborated.

*Chapter 9*

# Preparation

With the buildup of a broad range of knowledge, both technical and general, researchers are prepared to tackle difficult technical problems in their discipline and even in related disciplines. Preparation (Figure 6.1) was Herman von Helmholtz's first step in his outline of the creative process (Chapter 6). Although similar, knowledge gain is classified as general and preparation as specific. If studied from every conceivable direction with intense concentration, visualizing, agonizing, and reformulating repeatedly, an enigmatic problem has the greatest chances of being resolved. In industry it is critical to management and helpful to the motivation of technologists to understand how problem solution will advance business goals.

## CRITICAL ASPECTS OF PROBLEM STUDY

If one has the privilege of choosing an area of study with discovery as the goal, the choice of the problem is critical. Most scientists seem to work on routine problems that have a popular appeal. Emphasized by geophysicist Jack Oliver,[1] it is difficult to assert leadership in an established field by working on fad problems. Problem studies that are most apt to lead to discovery are those that have been overlooked or ignored, especially anomalies. Frequently, important problems are removed from consideration because of their complexity or because they are not popular. It is in these areas that one has the greatest chance to excel and to make major breakthroughs in understanding.

For initial approaches to problems, a preferential way is to proceed by way of an algorithm of one's own composition. Somebody once said, the trouble with life is that you're halfway through before you realize that it's one of those do-it-yourself-deals. To do good research or to solve problems, people must dig deep for their best and most novel ingenuity. After a lecture given by the linguist Noam Chomsky, a student praised him and expressed explicit trust in whatever the noted linguist had to say. Professor Chomsky responded by imploring the student not to trust anyone, and, in essence, said that his primary aim was to arouse the intellect of others such that they think for themselves.

Algorithms can provide a mechanism to facilitate coverage of all bases, mind-stretching, and initial approaches to problems. They do not, however, guarantee discovery and are not considered to be absolute. In one's early research career, programs may not be well-conceived. Furthermore, if one is tied too closely to the logical empiricism of the scientific method, creativity is often stymied. Algorithms can be formal or informal. A mathematical formula, as Newton's for gravitational attraction, is formal and applicable to only a highly specialized problem. The scientific method is informal and a tremendously powerful algorithm applicable to the whole of science. If followed with rigidity, however, scientific method becomes formal and generally unproductive of creativity.

Using a principle similar to the scientific method, algorithms can be formulated for an initial approach to problem solving. Steps can be incorporated to stimulate novel ideas, which may include continuous expansion of conceptual base and extensive knowledge interaction, the utilization of an holistic approach where possible, and the practice of both conventional and unconventional thought processes.

Expansion of the conceptual base comes through a broad range of literature and laboratory research and through an exchange of ideas with peers. It is not the acquisition of knowledge per se that leads to new ideas, but the interaction of different knowledge patterns in unique ways. Just as biologist and geologist Stephen Jay Gould[2] believed that organisms arise from the interaction of genes to give rise to nonlinear, emergent characteristics, so the interaction of knowledge patterns can lead to nonlinear, novel concepts. This interaction is analogous to the moiré phenomenon, where the combination of different sounds of two or more rhythmic patterns in appropriate ways can produce a third coherent pattern or sound. For example, two very high frequency patterns can be combined in a way that produces a low frequency sound audible to the human ear. This emergence of a new low frequency sound typifies the nonlinearity of nature and the necessity of unique interaction to effect synergism, or creativity.

Anthropologist Gregory Bateson[3] suggests that this phenomenon may be more common in nature than is generally realized. Indeed, it does seem to be related directly to a human creative principle. Not just any combination of knowledge patterns will do, and those that can be interacted viably must be chosen with considerable knowledge and insight, or by serendipity. The more disparate the knowledge patterns that can be interacted favorably, the more creative a resulting new concept is apt to be.

To optimize chances for the most fruitful knowledge interaction, the broadest range of mental gymnastics are essential. Such interaction can be promoted by extensive dialogue in-house and among worldwide technical contacts, by ideation and problem-solving sessions, and by the use of unconventional thought processes (Chapters 15 and 16). Frustration of many technologists being pressed for world-class ideas, stems from an inadequacy of conceptual base and a system that fails to promote extensive knowledge interaction.

Ideation and problem-solving sessions can take many different forms such as brainstorming, synectics, think-tank systems[4] and skunk works.[5, 6] These are informal algorithmic approaches, any one of which can be a powerful tool if used with appropriate leadership and follow-through. Elaborated by Souder,[7] incisive and probing leadership is characterized by openness, suspension of too critical judgment, and concerted efforts to make new ideas fit into problem-solving mode. New ideas are generally the progeny of elevated egos, and if idea generation is to be promoted, they are treated with tender loving care. A general understanding of company functions and strategic needs is essential if the most pertinent ideas are to be generated. Giving weight to the benefits of broad company exposure, those who have had the broadest range of experience are generally the most practical and versatile of idea generators.

Perhaps most useful for hypothesizing, Edward de Bono[8] advocated an aleatory approach to the achievement of novel ideas. He called this process provocation. Richard Restak[9] pointed out that the English novelist, Anthony Burgess, used a similar system that he called aleatory composition. He would direct his plot by creative connections that he would sometimes find with random words selected from a reference book. With the two hundred billion interconnected neural cells in the brain, Restak expostulated, there are abundant possibilities for long-range connection and for creative interaction with a random word. Searching for chance connections with seemingly unrelated words or ideas sometimes can provoke new approaches to problems or bring to light unexpected relationships.

With analysis of data, only the patterns already existing in our minds are recognized. New ideas, therefore, come with considerable difficulty. Lateral thinking (Chapter 16) can address this problem and can be promoted by following certain techniques developed by Edward de Bono in his book *Serious Creativity*.[10] He derived each of these techniques in detail, and they can be quite helpful in extricating one's thought process from traditional channels.

A company that is strongly supportive of technology necessarily promotes strong motivation for idea generation. Conversely, waxing and waning of technology support is devastating to the creative spirit. The

foundations for innovative ideas build on a complex of knowledge interaction over many years—a process that generally is not brought to fruition
quickly after a long hiatus of dispassionate attention. Unless a company is
willing to support long-term knowledge gain projects without serious dis-
continuity, their innovative return on research investment undoubtedly will
be disappointing. Intermittent research expenditures designated for innovation can become a serious waste of capital.

Holistic approaches to projects are one way of imparting a broad range
of knowledge interaction into the scientific method. Although described in
detail in Chapter 15, holistic thinking involves the interaction of many
different knowledge patterns associated with a phenomenon. In the ultimate sense, this would include the universe, but in practice, only a holistic
flavor can be realized. For example, one might interact all of the different
surface chemical and surface physics properties, structural and composi-
tional properties, particle geometry, optical properties, properties related
to interaction with areas of application, rheological properties, and so
forth, for the clay mineral, kaolin. This would be as opposed to studying
an isolated property of kaolin, for example, base-exchange capacity. The
latter approach is reductionist and less conducive to creativity.

Discovered knowledge, re kaolin, which may lead to new products, for
best results are interacted not only with all of the properties described
above, but with plant logistics, crude availability, customer needs, and cost-
effectiveness. Commonly, such new knowledge is not clearly transferred, or
it may be transferred but not clearly understood. If the new knowledge is
understood, self-interests in other areas may preclude adequate attention.
In the most productive system, the technologist discovering the new knowledge has the onus of approximating its potential impact on profit. There
are three reasons for taking this unconventional position, and the first, just
alluded to, is to ensure follow-through in studying and making known the
approximate profit potential.

The second reason relates to the common criticism that research-oriented
technologists are not practical. By virtue of studying the broad impact of
new knowledge, technologists can begin to understand the limits of an
invention. By this means, they can gain insight on how to approach problems with a more knowledgeable frame of reference. Most of this knowledge interaction relates to practicality, and therefore, to the technologist's
understanding of the pragmatic needs of invention. At this stage only a
rough approximation of costs and logistics is generated. To the extent that
impasses are spotted, efforts can be made to address such issues before the
project is terminated by other but less informed and committed authority.

Problem-solving efforts can be hampered by a premature concentration
on costs and logistics by people that feel they have nothing to lose by not
solving new product impasses. Focusing on economics, for example, with
an eye toward acceptance or rejection, at an early stage of new product

development produces a tunnel vision that is devastating to creativity. To do so is another instance of the collapse of the Schrödinger wave function and the end of idea generation. Only after a problem has been solved technically in most of its ramifications is there a concentrated study of economics. Even then, if the new product appears not to be cost-effective, Herculean efforts can be made by everyone involved to reduce costs. This includes such people as the discoverer, process engineers, and operations personnel—even the company president. Such efforts are often successful, and not taking this difficult step is a common reason for new product failure.

The third reason for the technologist to approximate profit potential is, perhaps, the most important and relates to a fundamental need for tapping creative potential. That need is knowledge interaction with the widest range of knowledge patterns. Again, the holistic approach enhances chances for creativity.

## ALGORITHMS FOR THE INITIAL STAGES OF PROBLEM STUDY

Continuous expansion of conceptual base and a holistic system of knowledge interaction are fundamental points of departure for deriving an algorithm, and the specific objectives to be addressed are as follows:

1. Problem definition and opportunities.
2. Characterization of key in-house knowledge re the problem.
3. Delineation and prioritization of research needed to enhance problem-solving ability.
4. Derivation of direct approaches to problem solving.
5. Promotion of maximum interaction of groups' collective knowledge, creativity, and wisdom.

From these objectives the algorithm shown in Figure 9.1 was formulated to be used in the initiation of problem solution. Intuition, curiosity, metaphorical recognition of other approaches, and so on, may assume control of research direction at any stage. John Bransford and Barry Stein[11] described a similar problem-solving technique, the IDEAL approach. In this system I = identify problems and opportunities; D = define goals; E = explore possible strategies; A = anticipate outcomes and act; L = look back and learn. Loosely applied in terms of order and need, this strategy can lead to creativity.

The first part of the algorithm (Figure 9.1) provides a mechanism to characterize the problem clearly, which is critical to efficient solution. Definition and redefinition should be undertaken within the company, and if

---

**Individual Effort**

- Give a clear and concise definition of the problem.
- Consider the opportunities offered by problem solution and list all potential goals.
- State concisely, preferably in one or two sentences, key knowledge regarding the problem. Carefully analyze this supposed knowledge for unjustified assumptions.
- List the basic knowledge that you believe should be understood to facilitate problem solution. Highlight critical research areas.
- List prioritized critical research.
- Postulate how base materials can be modified to address problem.
- List extrapolated tentative solutions.
- Expedite mechanistic method of new product derivation (see Figure 9.3).

**Group Effort**

- After individual presentation of algorithms, group development of eclectic approaches.
- Periodic review of research for group edification, re-evaluation, and appropriate directional change.

**Individual and Group Effort**

- As new knowledge is discovered, conceptualize the use of this knowledge in as many different ways as possible. Consider a variety of ways for representation, visually, mathematically, verbally, or graphically. Evaluate impact on whole of knowledge and, if applicable, on effectiveness in potential areas of application.

---

**Figure 9.1.** An algorithmic initiation to problem solution.

solution means a new product, it is helpful to solicit the aid of potential customers. It is much too easy to develop a new product for which customers have no interest. All parties who might potentially be involved in the development, manufacture, testing, sale, and use of a new product, potentially, can enhance product vitality with their input.

With problem solution more than one opportunity for application may exist. Each goal may redefine the approach and allow for a variety of novel ways of achieving a successful conclusion. Identifying all problems and opportunities is a major step in the creative process.

Characterization of key knowledge is an additional way of gaining a better idea about the nature of the problem. Particularly at this point but throughout the algorithmic process, identifying unjustified assumptions can assist problem solution or the opportunity for creativity. Characterization of what is known about a problem can be carried out by a process that de Bono called fractionation. By this mechanism, the problem is broken into its component parts, which can be dealt with separately at first and finally as a whole. An example of fractionation is shown in Figure 9.2 under basic knowledge.

By defining what is known about a technology, which requires focusing also on what is not known, a first approximation of the solution path has been outlined. This leads to the next step, prioritization of critical research. By outlining the physical and chemical properties of base materials, for example, the weakest links of understanding can be highlighted and prioritized. Similarly, outlining of mechanisms of product interaction with applications can enable recognition of critical areas in which research can be conducted to strengthen problem-solving ability. This mechanistic approach can be used to derive new product concepts as well (see Figure 9.3). Commonly, published research has been carried out in all pertinent areas. Such research often is not complete and may answer only some of the questions, or the answers may be inappropriate to the idiosyncrasies of a problem. Under these conditions, consideration can be given to extending research from the literature to the laboratory.

An example of the algorithmic approach is shown in Figure 9.2. The algorithm can be developed in considerably more detail than shown, but the primary purpose here is to illustrate rather than to be thorough. If more than one individual prepares similar algorithms, the mutual interaction of all of them can lead to eclecticism.

An example of mechanistic new product derivation via rheology is shown in Figure 9.3. From this mechanistic approach, it can be derived that the most desirable kaolin rheology would be produced by a clay having a broad particle size distribution, containing particles having the lowest possible aspect ratio, and a low colloid content. Other than adsorbed monovalent cations, kaolin surfaces should be clean. The most stable dispersion can be obtained by the use of a dispersing agent that will give uniform and optimum zeta potential. Mineralogical purity is important to preclude interference by viscosity-increasing minerals. Second order derivations that have been underlined indicate areas where research is needed to clarify how these kaolin characteristics can be optimized.

The research questions that are posed include:

1. What is the precise nature of the size distribution that will give best packing, and what is the optimum particle size range?

2. How can the most viscosity-damaging colloids be removed efficiently?

3. What is the nature of the natural surface contaminants and how can they be removed most efficiently without irreparable damage to the kaolin crystal?

4. How can the viscosity-increasing mineralogical components be removed or inactivated most efficiently?

How one poses questions is critical, and if narrowly stated can limit dangerously the nature of the needed research. For example, if one were to ask

Potential Goals:

1. Improve kaolin brightness by the reduction of lattice iron to the ferrous state.
2. Improve dispersion, suspension stability, and rheological properties by removing iron and other impurities from the kaolin surface.
3. Improve kaolin brightness by the maximum extraction of iron.

Key knowledge: Conventional wisdom that iron can be removed most efficiently by sodium dithionite reduction of ferric iron to the ferrous form in acidic kaolin-water suspensions followed by filtration and rinsing. A small additional amount of iron can be extracted via magnetic separation from well-dispersed kaolin-water suspension.

Basic Knowledge: Occurrence of iron in kaolin.

1. ionic iron held in base-exchange sites on kaolin surfaces—can be extracted by exchange resins or by the mass action of other multivalent cations
2. oxides and oxyhydroxides as incrustations on kaolin surfaces—can be extracted by the standard bleaching process described under key knowledge
3. <u>ferrous and ferric substituted for aluminum in octahedral positions of the crystal structure</u>—extraction method not known without dissolution of structure
4. lattice substituents and surface incrustation on TiO2 minerals occurring in kaolin—can be extracted by magnetic separation, flotation, or selective flocculation
5. discrete iron minerals—can be extracted by magnetic separation
6. <u>organic complexes of iron as incrustations on kaolin surfaces</u>—partially extracted by oxidation and bleaching
7. <u>iron orthophosphate complexes as incrustations on kaolin surfaces and as discrete particles</u>—best extraction procedure to be determined.

Prioritized critical research:

1. organic complexes of iron—study nature of occurrence, how influential, and how to extract
2. iron substituted for aluminum in octahedral positions—determine nature and extent, and how to reduce, extract, or otherwise minimize influence
3. iron orthophosphate complexes—study occurrence, influence, and methods of extraction

Solution postulations: Ferric iron as a sustituent for aluminum in the octahedral layer of kaolin may be reduced to the ferrous form by the expansion of the structure with certain organic compounds followed by bleaching. Stabilization of iron in this reduced state may be achieved by the introduction of certain monovalent ions into the structure to neutralize the resultant electrical imbalance. Brightness may be improved by the reduction process.

Organic complexes of iron may be removed by the combined action of high shear, high temperature, and oxidation in alkaline solution followed by bleaching a low pH and rinsing. Other surface contaminants may also be removed by this process.

Figure 9.2. Problem: For brightness enhancement, how can iron be removed most efficiently and economically from kaolin without damage to the kaolin crystal or, alternatively, how can the effect of iron be minimized without extraction? Underlining highlights topics for potential research.

| First Order Requirements | Second Order Requirements |
|---|---|
| (f)* dense packing | (f) <u>broad particle size distribution</u> |
| (f) lowest particle volume concentration | (f) lowest aspect ratio particles |
| | (f) <u>minimum colloid content</u> |
| (f) optimized surface chemistry (high uniform zeta potential) | (f) <u>cleanness of surfaces</u> |
| (f) mineralogical purity | (f) nature and level of dispersant |
| | (f) <u>minimum smectite, halloysite, noncrystalline colloids, etc.</u> |

**Figure 9.3.** Mechanistic derivation of best kaolin rheology. *Note:* *(f) = function.

only how viscosity-increasing mineralogical components could be removed efficiently and neglect to ask how, alternatively, they could be inactivated, a potentially creative solution might be neglected.

If the answers to these research questions are not known or cannot be found in the literature, a clear need exists for conducting relevant research. If the essential basic research appears to require inordinate time, then the practicality of the related targeted research should be reevaluated. As described in Chapter 8, conducting targeted research without basic understanding of the relevant science is a common source of wasted capital. When these research questions are answered, however, the conceptual framework of a new product has been derived. The needed investigation, then, becomes largely algorithmic.

This system of mechanistic derivations can be carried to the finest detail desirable—third, fourth, or higher orders of derivation. To the extent that any mechanism is inadequately understood, a critical research area has been delineated. The highlighted problems in the algorithm and the mechanistic derivation become the directed basic research, the keys to strategic problems. If related targeted problems are to be resolved, such research is expedited. This strategy is applicable as a starting point for any research problem whether it is applied or basic.

Problems often are resolved in a moderately satisfactory way and then stopped. Persistence toward optimum solution is a characteristic of highly creative people. Routine answers to problems can be easy, a syndrome of risk-avoidance cultures, but the novel and most useful answers take thoroughness and perseverance. If the original goal is not achieved, the result should not be called failure, which in science and technology occurs only if insufficient effort is put forth toward problem solution. If the original question is not answered, despite a noble effort, a considerable amount has been learned. Such knowledge is not only a necessary foundation for the solution to certain other problems but may eventually lead to the resolution of the original problem.

Finding the weakest links of understanding by outlining physical and chemical properties and by the mechanistic approach to new products is similar to an approach developed by William Shockley at Bell Labs. His approach led to the development of the transistor.[12] He delineated his process with an acronym, ACCOR. A is for finding key attributes and the Cs are for comparison operations. O and R are for orderly relations that are the results of the process. Shockley pointed out, you don't even begin to understand something until you have examined it from many different perspectives.

Until work is carried out on the highlighted problems, it will not be possible to develop the most informed approaches to problem solution. Nevertheless, the high probability is that the technologists assigned to the problem already have considerable expertise. Early extrapolation of how to solve the problem, even before conducting necessary research, can be a mind-stretching exercise. This approach can lead to unexpected viable ideas in group sessions by knowledge interaction. In limited cases, problems are more amenable to early solution by means of trial and error, which can lead to a pragmatic solution prior to the understanding of mechanisms. An example of trial and error success was the cloning of Dolly, which was achieved prior to the understanding of the appropriate science.[13] Certainly, the inventor Thomas Edison was a champion of trial and error, and his many successes attest to the sometimes validity of this method. Generally, the greater the amount of background information the greater the success of trial and error. This approach, however, often is an endless task, and limited budgets generally demand the greatest efficiency that can be achieved. Perhaps the experience of most researchers, the testing of hypothetical projections based on a substantial background of knowledge, learning from each failure, and doing basic research to understand related science in depth, generally, are the most meaningful and efficient springboards for action.

The last part of the algorithm is to evaluate the potential impact of the new knowledge on profit. As indicated above, this can include such things as the availability of appropriate crude, relation to plant logistics, relation to areas of application and customer needs, and cost-effectiveness. This holistic approach often stimulates new more viable paths to problem solving. The algorithms that have been discussed are designed essentially for technology groups; but for greatest effectiveness, knowledge interaction can be extended to the entire company and to external contacts.

To the extent that this algorithmic approach is deemed desirable, its redesign may be needed to fit the idiosyncrasies of a technology group. These approaches to problem solution are not absolute but simply are guidelines to help technologists focus more clearly on the nature of the problem and on efficient problem solution. For best research, technologists always have the freedom to follow their intuition and their curiosity and to conduct their work with a minimum of interference.

The basic question for the initial approach to a scientific project or a technology problem is what is the most efficient strategy or the optimum path to arrive at a fundamental understanding? Limitation of funding for the project demands that efficiency be a prime consideration. The use of some semblance of scientific method in problem solving is essential. For greatest effectiveness, however, the method can be modified to incorporate continuous expansion of conceptual base and extensive knowledge interaction.

Expansion of conceptual base, besides the pursuit of diverse research projects, can be expedited by an holistic approach where possible. Knowledge interaction, which depends on both internal and external dialogue, can advance this process as well. Both conventional and unconventional thinking (Chapters 13–16) can be intimately interwoven into all aspects of problem approach. Idiosyncratic algorithms and mechanistic derivation of new product concepts can be an important part of characterizing efficient strategy. These approaches can give new life to stalled or stagnant projects as well.

The third stage in the discovery process, covered in the next chapter, is incubation, which is, perhaps, a nonconscious process of organizing data into a novel concept. Methods of promoting incubation are considered as well.

*Chapter 10*

# Incubation

---

Two stages of creativity, knowledge gain and preparation (covered in the previous two chapters), help prepare the creator for the *aha!*, an experience of profound discernment. With the understanding that knowledge is elusive and uncertain, the creator is constantly searching for a better rapport with nature, which in science can range from constructive changes in presuppositions to major modifications of paradigms. In technology it can range from new more effective processes to the development of major new products. The stubbornness of nature to reveal her secrets is often circumvented by the third stage of creativity, incubation.

Frequently, preparation does not lead directly to problem solution; but the next stage of creativity, incubation, can be the circuitous route to novelty. The most problematic aspect of creativity, incubation is a process that may take place in the nonconscious mind, which may take over when conscious thought is no longer effective. An elusive concept, the existence of the cognitive nonconscious is still to be substantiated.

The mystique of creativity, seemingly, is related to this presumed nonconscious process. Creativity has taken many forms throughout history:[1] Plato believed that creativity was divine in origin; Nietzsche believed that it was related to irrationality; Shakespeare alluded to its association with madness when one of his characters said, "The lunatic, the lover, and the poet are of imagination all compact." Others have believed that creativity arises in the unconscious mind and, therefore, cannot be understood. At this stage of knowledge development, one might have been tempted to agree with Mark Twain in his reference to another matter, "The researches of many commentators have already thrown much darkness on this subject, and it is probable that, if they continue, we shall soon know nothing at all about it." Fortunately, most of the modern conceptions of creativity have abandoned the mystique scenario.


## NONCONSCIOUS THINKING

Referring to experiments by D.N. Perkins, philosopher and psychologist Margaret Boden[2] concluded that abundant evidence exists in support of alternative explanations for nonconscious thinking. Time away from a difficult problem does not necessarily mean a total break from that thought pattern. Conscious thought about the problem may return at opportune moments, small increments of the solution may accumulate, or the solution may have been close at the time of the interruption. With a return to the problem, the solution may emerge readily, which, opposed to incubation, is a process of memory. During a respite from a problem, a clue may be picked up, which may lead to solution. In this case, the process of enlightenment has been serendipity.

Sleep provides a rest from conscious thinking about the problem that can lead to relaxation of logical restraints. Here the phantasmagoria of dreams may stimulate formulation of an unconventional approach to problem solution. In this case, however, the clue to problem solution has arisen from a nonconscious state, giving credence to the importance of nonconscious thinking. In addition to sleep, relaxed states of mind produced by reverie or meditation may expose viable passages from a deeply channeled mindset. Such states of mind are transitional between conscious and nonconscious.

Experiments by psychologist Robert Weisburg[3] and others showed that the ability to solve problems, such as the nine-dot problem (Chapter 16), comes from expertise. Solution does not arise from a sudden insight, but from a gradual process. Weisburg concluded that intuition and logical judgments evolve through similar processes of extensive knowledge acquisition. In this sense, the idea of intuitive leaps in understanding is passé. He explained inspirations or spontaneous thoughts as arising from a sequence of associations promoted by an external event. The speed of the associative chain and the excitement of the new thought precludes reconstruction of the event. Concentration is on the result, which is perceived as the only important aspect of the inspiration.

Although these alternate explanations are often valid, the concept of nonconscious thinking seems to retain enough validity that it cannot be excluded totally from consideration. The actions of experienced drivers or athletes in the expedition of often repeated movements, or even the process of breathing, are strong indications that nonconscious thinking is a function firmly integrated into our central nervous system. Art and science may have their greatest similarity in the nonconscious, parallel processing of information. That information in long-term memory can be processed in parallel is lent support by psychological studies.[4]

Numerous experiments have shown that several tenths of a second elapse between the performance of a physical action and that person's awareness of his intention to perform such action.[5] Such evidence strongly suggests nonconscious initiation of physical actions.

Perhaps the most striking example of nonconscious thinking was revealed from research done by psychologists Nicholas Humphrey and Larry Weiskrantz.[6] Blind monkeys, whose visual cortex had been destroyed, were taught to reach out and grasp small moving objects. These researchers wrote a paper on how completely blind monkeys could learn to use nonconscious, visual information. Weiskrantz did additional work with blind people. He found that they could guess where light was located and the shape of objects, and be right almost every time. Without any apparent visual sensations, they seemed to have had a nonconscious awareness of these phenomena. Perhaps they did see but were not fully conscious of this ability. Weiskrantz called this blindsight.

## DREAMING AND NONCONSCIOUS THINKING

Dreaming often seems to be a nonconscious, aleatory method of problem solving. Witness the many claims by creators of discovery via reverie and dreaming:[7] Archimedes' discovery of how to measure volume of an irregular body while relaxing in a bath; Freidrich Kekule's dream of whirling atoms in snakelike configuration that led to his derivation of the ring structure of benzene; and Elias Howe's dream of spears that led to his discovery of putting the eye of a sewing machine needle at the bottom rather than at the top. These are a few of many examples of relaxed states of mind leading to inspiration.

Writer Daniel Cohen[8] alluded to the frequent resort to and favorable results of sleeping on a problem. Ruminating about a problem before going to sleep seems only to make solution intransigent. After a night's sleep, however, the problem may be clarified or, at least, cast in a more favorable light. The seeming explanation of this improved perspective is that the mind has continued to function during sleep. Though in a more relaxed state, the mind during sleep makes random, less constrained efforts at problem solution. The uninhibited imagery of dreaming provides a mechanism for deriving unconventional approaches. As Cohen reasoned, deviation from stereotypical ways of thinking is necessary for creativity.

Increasingly, psychotherapists are advocating creative or lucid dreaming for problem solving. This is a kind of purposeful dreaming in which the dreamer has some control over what prevails. Although not rigorously verified as a viable procedure, supposedly dreams can be controlled and manipulated in creative ways.

From detailed studies of animals and humans, biologists suggest that information learned during waking hours is sorted and consolidated by the brain while asleep.[9] Sharpening of cognitive skills by repetition is believed to occur during REM (rapid eye movement) sleeping or dream time. Dreaming can be seen as a form of insanity, which has been defined as the inability to choose among false alternatives. It consists of visions unconnected to reality, which are arbitrary but potentially infinite in variety. In an attempt to do the best it can with this random input, the nonconscious brain creates fantasy. Upon awakening, the conscious brain attempts to give the fantasy a rational explanation.

To the extent that dreaming leads to novel ideas, it seems reasonable to conclude that the process is a form of aleatory discovery (Chapter 6). Transformed into rational explanations by the conscious brain, random images from dreaming may become associated with critical problems of concern during waking hours. This association could lead to entirely new ways of approaching problems that would not be discovered without prompting by dreaming. In the world of creativity, the importance of diversity is unparalleled—even insanity can be useful!

As Cohen explained, Freud contended without scientific grounds that dreams are reflections of our unconscious minds. Scientists who study dreams today believe that the mind is never dormant or unconscious and that mental activity occurs even in the deepest sleep. The dream state of sleep is attendant with mental activity closely approaching that of the awakened state. The unrestricted imagery of dreaming and the frequent unconventional thoughts of daydreaming and reverie are not likely to be a part of fully conscious thought. They are playgrounds for the interaction of different phenomena, and this free flow of the imagination often leads to creative concepts.

## THE NONCONSCIOUS AND UNCONSCIOUS MINDS

Described by the psychiatrist Albert Rothenberg,[10] creativity is influenced, seemingly, by both the unconscious and the nonconscious minds. Both the unconscious and the nonconscious continually interact with our biases and our memories, which are influential in all aspects of our thoughts. The concept of the unconscious mind was formalized by Sigmund Freud. Specifically, Freudian unconscious refers to elements of the psyche developed from experience that are suppressed because of unacceptability. Although removed from awareness, these conflicts exert involuntary effects and influence themes of endeavor. Thus, the influence of the unconscious may be only indirectly related to creativity in the sense of bias.

Rothenberg pointed out that the nonconscious mind is considered by some scientists to be the fundamental basis of creative thought. A subtle distinction exists between unconscious and nonconscious thought. When

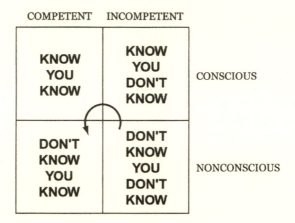

Figure 10.1. Problem solving via the conscious and the nonconscious.

creative scientists use the thought processes attendant with their creative thinking, their focus is on the result as opposed to the thought mechanisms. They are, therefore, overtly unaware of the specific nature of the thought systems that they employ. These are not suppressed thoughts because of unacceptability as in unconscious, but merely unobtrusive, behind-the-scenes mechanisms of achieving desired concepts. Thus, many esoteric thought processes used to attain creative cognition, much like breathing, may be nonconscious in character.

The brain stores knowledge at multiple levels, not all of which are accessible to consciousness. This hierarchical scheme, according to psychologist Richard Restak,[11] can explain intuition, hunches, and so forth. Furthermore, it explains our nonconscious minds. Each of us, by this account, is far more knowledgeable than our consciousness allows us to display at any given time. New knowledge input can interact potentially with a vast storehouse of knowledge in our brains. Processed in parallel nonconsciously, it occasionally leads to connections of great novelty.

The relationship of conscious and nonconscious thinking is illustrated, in part, by a diagram (see Figure 10.1), which engineering design specialist James Adams[12] obtained from Chuck House, formerly the corporate chief engineer at Hewlett-Packard and now the principal of INNOVASCAPES. The diagram has been changed to read "nonconscious" instead of "unconscious." In early life, people are unaware that they do not know how to tie their shoes, which is shown in the lower right portion of the diagram. This is the first stage of incompetency and is nonconscious. Next, they learn that they do not know how to tie them, which is the last part of the incompetent stage (conscious). After they learn how to tie their shoes, they have reached the conscious-competent stage of knowing that they know.

At the last stage of competency, tying their shoes has become a habit, and they can carry out the act without consciously thinking about it (nonconscious).

A basic problem of being creative is the ability to move from habitual action and thought to the recognition of incompetence. It is a problem of moving at will back and forth when new competencies are being learned. Learning to use the conscious mind to overcome mind-sets and habits, contrary to human nature, is a pathway to intellectual growth. Growth in science or achieving invention requires a continuous change of established patterns of knowledge.

## THE IMPORTANCE OF FLEXIBILITY

Another aspect of incubation is related to the conterintuitive nature of science, which has been described by psychologist Howard Margolis.[13] This is illustrated by the concepts of evolution and natural selection. The idea of evolution had been around for more than 2,000 years before Darwin. In the sixth century B.C., Anaximander contended that man was derived from the fish of the sea.[14]

Between Anaximander's time and Darwin's, various notions of evolution appeared. Even Darwin's grandfather, Erasmus, had published a theory of evolution in 1794. Indeed, at the time of Darwin, evolution was popular among nonestablishment scientists but was a disreputable notion among experts. On the other hand, the concept of evolution is intuitively easy. Throughout life, major transformations are observed in living things—babies into adults, seeds into mature plants, larvae into butterflies and moths, and so on. Because it was believed that the earth was only a few thousand years old, evolution was not given much credence prior to the discovery of the fossil record. The recognition that fossils represented former life existing millions of years ago saved the day for the long-term concept of evolution.

It was the theory of natural selection that caused the great dissension, and this idea did not become firmly established among biologists until the middle of the twentieth century. Natural selection is the Darwinian mechanism to account for evolution. Darwinists contend that there is no design behind evolution. The development of complicated organs, such as the brain, is the consequence of the accumulation of chance modifications by which the most functional survives longer. Such a concept is profoundly counterintuitive, as is much of science. The nonconscious mind may play a significant role in the gradual acceptance of the radically new concept, as in natural selection.

Recognition of new concepts that do not fit an existing pattern in the brain is extremely difficult for anyone. This is particularly true where conditioning to believe otherwise has been instilled since early childhood. Even if one is willing and flexible, if the pattern of knowledge is alien, understanding the idea is difficult. Perhaps the ultimate example to date of difficult ideas is the strange and mysterious world of quantum mechanics.

First described by science historian Thomas Kuhn, James Gleick[15] gave an account of an experiment by two psychologists in the 1940s. A deck of playing cards containing a few distortions, such as a red spade or a black diamond, was shown briefly one at a time to the subjects. Dealt at high speed the subjects saw nothing that seemed unusual to them. At slower speed they saw a problem but could not identify its nature. At even slower speed, some subjects correctly identified the discrepancies. On the other hand, a few of the subjects became confused and disoriented, uncertain of what they were seeing and displaying genuine discomfort.

As Gleick explained, observation by scientists of incongruities in nature can cause equal anguish. If the scientist changes his way of seeing things and accepts the new variance, he enhances his chances for discovery. It is this process of changing perception that can be enormously difficult. Perhaps it is the sole prerogative of the nonconscious mind that enables us to change our patterns of understanding and to finally comprehend and accept radical discovery.

Confidence and courage, much like the recognition and acceptance of incongruities, are also important to the progress of incubation. Their importance can be illustrated by the ignominious history of the circle. Although well known that Pavlov conditioned dogs to salivate at the ringing of a bell, it is not well known that he conditioned dogs similarly by the projecting of symbols on a screen.[16] When he projected circles, food was presented and the dogs became conditioned as they did with a bell. He then projected ellipses that were only slightly distinguishable from circles. These were shown to indicate that food would not be presented. The effort to distinguish between circles and ellipses only slightly deviating from circularity caused the dogs to lose their equanimity, to become neurotic. This bizarre response to departure from circularity has infected civilization as well.

Many cultures symbolize heaven, eternity, or the universe with the circle. Circles to the people of ancient Greece and through the Middle Ages were profoundly sacred. Most primitive societies and the ancient Greeks believed that time was circular.[17] (Exceptions were the Hebrews and the Zoroastrian Persians.) Promoted by the tides, solstices, seasons, and cyclic movements of celestial bodies, ancient Greeks and people of the Middle Ages saw an analogy between these phenomena and time. They believed that all events will repeat themselves, even that people will live again and have the same experiences. Arousing great fear, irreversible flow of time implied constant change and the end of the world.

Indeed, Newtonian physics necessitates the notion that the world be cyclical. Explained by physicist Lee Smolin,[18] if we assume that there are a finite, potential number of configurations of the universe, then the eternal universe as conceived by Newton will eventually return to former conditions. Although life as we know it is extraordinarily improbable, the determinism of Newtonian physics requires that events of the universe must be returned, no matter how long the interval, to an ordered state that permits life. Through chance alone, any possible event, according to Newtonian mechanics, must be repeated an infinite number of times.

Linear, irreversible time was established by the Judeo-Christian tradition, without which the concepts of progress and hope could not have become firmly established. It was the Christian belief in unrepeatable events, as the birth and death of Christ and the Crucifixion, which undermined the traditional notion of circular time. Belief in linear time has been an intellectual linchpin of modern science.

Until Kepler, the proposals for the orbits of the planets were invariably circular. When Kepler proposed ellipses, it is not surprising that those who were concerned with astronomy, particularly the clergy, responded like Pavlov's dogs and they too lost their equanimity. This loss of circularity implied the loss of godly perfection. Kepler was greatly upset by the proposal himself, believing that he had committed a criminal act. Despite his profoundly negative feelings about the propriety of his beliefs, he had the courage to assert this unholy proposal. Surely his feelings were deeply ambivalent believing, however, that he was more right than wrong. He had to have been a courageous man secure in his scientific competence. Clearly, successful and creative scientists and technologists, intent on making their mark, have confidence and courage. No matter how much they depart from conventional wisdom, if the seeds of discovery are allowed to incubate, they may grow into mature and useful ideas.

## THE IMPORTANCE OF DIVERSION

Because problem solving and creative illumination are expedited by mental relaxation, it is critical that various forms of diversion are a part of the striving for answers to research problems. Despite their great benefit to new ideas, playful activities are usually not part of the routine if one is constantly in a state of suspended animation, impatiently, anxiously, and unabatedly tensing for the breakthrough solution. Such persistent tension precludes the flexibility and the free rein of diverse thought processes needed to shape new concepts.

Arthur Koestler[19] alluded to tricks used to coax nonconscious processes into action. They include the smelling of rotten apples, the drinking of large quantities of black coffee, or the soaking of feet in water. Conscious thought processes peak with some people when they are in a highly relaxed but wide awake state of mind. Caffeine can assist this process. This state of mind is often accompanied by flurries of inspiration seemingly evolving from the nonconscious mind. The trick one uses generally should be idiosyncratic—whatever puts one into a state of reverie or state of free-flowing thought.

During the preparation stage when knowledge is being accumulated, determined technologists or scientists sense that the process for their gaining a better understanding of a particular area of nature will eventually come to fruition. But they do not know precisely the solution path. It is somewhat analogous to the woman who said that she did not believe in intuition but had the feeling that she would someday.

Viewed in this light, it may seem that incubation is not amenable to management influence. On the other hand, it has been shown that incubation is assisted when people have multiple tasks. Furthermore, most scientists make major discoveries only after their related projects have been abandoned.[20] It is critical, however, that potential creators' schedules not be so cluttered as to preclude a focus on original work. It is useful, as well, to have the time to follow intuitive thoughts, or to explore the anomalies of research.

These observations emphasize the stubbornness of incubation and the propitious effect of carrying out multiple tasks. An additional benefit may come from temporarily stopping a project after intense effort but persistent problem refractoriness. Seemingly, the nonconscious mind is continually rearranging knowledge until, by chance, a synergistic fit illuminates confusing and chaotic information. It is like being lost and going to bed amidst a dark and blinding storm and then awakening to a bright, clear day with a pristine mountain view.

The next chapter describes major activities that can promote discovery: research, the shuttle effect, and thought processes behind discovery.

*Chapter 11*

# Stimulation:
# Research and External Stimuli

If knowledge has reached a critical level in both extent and depth, and clever methods of preparation are utilized, then the researchers have been well served and their efforts have culminated in discovery. If not, incubation may be the option of last resort. For the most intransigent of technical problems, incubation is often a necessity and a viable stage of discovery as well. Three forms of stimuli—basic research, external stimuli, and specialized thought processes—are adjuncts to incubation and are potentially operative throughout the discovery process.

If these stimuli are thoroughly exploited, success is often the result. Research enables the acquisition of new knowledge which, when interacted with one's existing body of knowledge, can lead to creativity. External stimuli include all technical interaction outside one's organization. Thought processes behind discovery, conventional and unconventional, are categories of specialized thought processes, but because of their importance and the extent of these subjects, they are described in detail in subsequent chapters.

## RESEARCH

Although there is abundant information to support the contention that technological growth greatly affects productivity growth, the influence of basic research generally has been neglected. Behind this discrepancy lies the long delay between the acquisition of fundamental knowledge and commercialization. Computer science, genetic engineering, space travel, and the structure and surface chemistry of materials are examples, among many, of technological complexity in which basic understanding is prerequisite to invention. It is simply deductive logic that basic knowledge is beneficial to the invention process. In complex and avant-garde subjects, abundant research is needed to establish the knowledge necessary to achieve invention. In many companies, strategic research potentially can lead to new life.

It is generally understood that basic research is indispensable to the generation of new knowledge, but it is not generally understood that basic research can be a powerful stimulant for the generation of new thought patterns. The excitement that can be instilled by new knowledge, which may be uniquely that of the researcher, can be understood only through experience. It can arouse new high levels of resolve, and it can titillate the thought process to be more penetrating. According to psychologist Rollo May,[1] the greater the resolve and intensity of effort, the greater the chances of activating the creativity center of the brain.

Research can be divided into four categories: empirical, literature, dialectical, and hypothetical. All four types are essential parts of successful research programs.

### Empirical Research

Empirical research is the primary mechanism of generating new historical knowledge and is what is generally meant by the word "research" in science. It is the knowledge that is generated by experiment and observation. Studying the responses to a broad range of variables is the best way to gain a better understanding of a phenomenon, and the results provide new evidence to support or disprove related hypotheses. Although a phenomenon can never be fully explained by experiment and observation, inductive logic is an essential step, leading the way to successful prediction and technology—the irrefutable answers to the nihilists of intellectual pursuits.

### Literature Research

By becoming deeply involved in a research project, the scientist facilitates knowledge increase. Reading relevant literature, then, becomes much more meaningful, and the process of interrelating knowledge patterns becomes an excitement rather than an idle exercise. Intense involvement in research is, perhaps, the most important stimulant for knowledge acquisition. Beyond the goal of new knowledge and problem solution, the process of research can generate an intellectual ferment that can greatly increase a researcher's potential for discovery. This is a matter of tremendous importance to the cause of invention—knowledge is critical, but without spirit its value is greatly diminished.

Literature research is the primary mechanism of learning what other scientists and technologists have learned and published about nature. Gaining such knowledge about a research project before the fact may severely bias perception and give a narrow focus to research direction. Einstein generally did not make a thorough literature search until after completion of a project. On the positive side, literature research may preclude unnecessary efforts, and the knowledge gained may speed the successful completion of a project. Such prior knowledge can be a useful foundation on which to build enhanced understanding. The relative influence of prior research on new researchers may be related largely to the idiosyncrasies of the individual. If the researchers are sufficiently probing and independent of mind, they can safely explore the literature first. At the same time, the researchers can attempt to generate a unique and more viable approach.

Another aspect of literature research is independent of specific research projects. Searching the literature for new knowledge concerning general problems or potential new directions of development can be a source of information that can be used to stimulate new concepts. Reading the literature about how a material can be altered in new ways to give unique properties is an opportunity for, at least, mind experiments on how this knowledge could be used profitably. This can be done even more profitably in group sessions in which a diversity of ideas may stimulate thought for a broad range of potential commercial applications. If technologists are always aggressive in acquiring new knowledge and in probing its utility, they have the greatest chance of discovery.

### Dialectical Research

Dialectical research, exchange about research problems with a broad range of technical people, can provide a wealth of new ideas and approaches to problems. This approach can stimulate alternate and frequently more viable hypotheses than those that are generated by a small, isolated group of associates. The ultimate goal in using the dialectic is to find the eclectic components of a large group of ideas, then, by appropriate interaction, produce a new idea of greater merit than any simple combination of those ideas. Because of budget restrictions on travel and proprietary constraints in industry, this type of research often is neglected. The outstanding benefits of the dialectic are usually only apparent to those who participate, but it is a powerful mechanism for inspiring novelty.

Attendance at technical meetings and the associated dialectic can be one of the most effective ways of generating new ideas. Many people who attend such conferences do not take full advantage of this outstanding benefit. They may simply listen to the technical papers without much exertion of their own thought processes. Consequently, they generally come away from the meeting with little if any new information that stimulates their progress in scientific or technological thinking. Their primary acquisition from such meetings and the evening entertainment, often, may be a notable hangover.

One way for people to relay knowledge from technical meetings back to their organization is to simply review those papers which seem to have the most merit. This can be a rather idle, ho-hum exercise and of only minimum value to the technologists. There are more stimulating and beneficial ways of reviewing such professional meetings.

Listening to technical papers can be a superbly soporific experience. The constant drone of a monotone presentation, along with dimmed lights for slide presentation, is a nearly perfect remedy for insomnia. But there is a potential way to change this experience into an inspiring challenge. Simply listen to the papers and search each one for new knowledge, or at least knowledge that is new to you. In some cases, it may be knowledge that you have known but that has been pushed into the background, and it essentially becomes new knowledge for you.

After this initial exercise of isolating new knowledge, try to extrapolate how to change this new information into application. How can it be used to improve products or develop new ones? Does it generate new ideas for research? Does it have an impact on your existing knowledge such that at least one of your hypotheses may be nullified? Does it remind you of an aspect of your research that has been neglected that could be of great value to your goals? Extend the dialectic to associates at the meeting. From this information an essay could be written on new knowledge and its potential utility. The new dialectic could be continued back in your own laboratory. Writing such an essay is one of the best ways to mine the thought process for the most insightful and creative paths to discovery.

This approach can change a dull technical meeting into a stimulating playground of ideas—even if the papers are not particularly good. The new ideas that are generated need not be totally valid, but the great benefit can be the discovery of an approach to problems that has never been tried before—a common formula for discovery. This method of approaching technical meetings can establish a compelling, internal dialectic for mind experiments, which can excite and expand creative potential.

### Hypothetical Research

Hypothetical research, abduction, is the process of establishing hypotheses to explain phenomena. It is a critical step in the scientific method and is essential not only to give direction to research but for new data that do not fit the existing paradigm. Charles Darwin had a golden rule in his research: he would immediately record any observation that was inconsistent with theory.[2] Such observations can easily be forgotten, but their exploitation can often lead to a new, more viable explanation of phenomena. The mental exercise of balancing knowledge with potential mechanisms of phenomena provides the hypotheses that guide experimental work. Explore every hypothesis that seems to have potential, lest the research focus be so narrow as to stifle creative solutions.

Always a danger, researchers may acquire so much knowledge and skill that by sheer weight of information and experience they stubbornly follow a solitary path. Following only one path is often a dead end. Without extensive knowledge one is not likely to discover, but with too much knowledge one is apt to be narrowly channeled. It is helpful to be fully aware of this dilemma and to make every effort not to be caught in the trap. This can be done by always making an Herculean effort to ponder and evaluate all potentially viable hypotheses. Mental gymnastics of this nature cultivate a nimbleness of mind that can formulate hypotheses leading to major discovery. Elaborated in Chapter 15, Einstein's theories of relativity were hypotheses so elegant that empirical justification was not considered essential.

### Research Anomalies

Anomalies, or unexpected results, are the sources of serendipity in research. What at first appears to be adversity, may turn out to be a major opportunity. Research perforce is initiated by a preconceived focus. Unless the original focus can be kept clearly in sight and success seems probable, the vectors of subsequent research can be controlled, favorably, by the anomalies that arise during the investigation.

Anomalies represent the problems that are most apt to lead to major discovery. Such luxury of pursuit, unfortunately, is usually more the privilege of academics than of technologists. Observant investigators may find that their research direction, as guided by anomaly, diverges beyond a practical limit. Such a result generally shows that a great amount of preliminary work is requisite to solution of any related targeted problem.

Thomas West[3] gave an example of a researcher who was dutifully looking for a way to destroy DNA but after many efforts could only come up with more DNA than she had started with. Her research ended without apparent success. Years later, in a different laboratory, a scientist received the Nobel Prize for his method of creating DNA. A lost opportunity in research and technology generally becomes the province of someone else.

Although science is driven largely by anomalies, technology generally is driven by the marketplace. Understandably, technologists tend to become fixed on what their employer is demanding, while being reluctantly aloof to what the serendipity of research is pleading with them to discover. It is a notable dilemma—the employer pays their salary but anomaly is commonly the direction of proprietary new products. As Upton Sinclair said, "It is difficult to get a man to understand something when his salary depends on his not understanding it."[4]

To the extent that one pursues anomalies, new product development can become technology driven. By this approach, the successful explanation of an anomaly can be an understanding not possessed by the competition, and, therefore, the most likely source of a proprietary new product. It is commonly easier to explain an anomaly inductively than to resolve the original objective, and it may represent the best that a technologist can achieve under the circumstances. To arrive at the original objective may require a highly circuitous path, and the resolution of anomalies may be essential way stations. Although immediate necessity and inadequate time frequently preclude exploration of anomalous results, their potential importance cannot be overemphasized.

Market pull generally is used by both industry and government to guide research. This targeted research is understandable and a desirable goal, but it represents a failure to recognize a universal character of science and technology—unpredictability. Physicist and author John Ziman[5] gave notable examples: Nixon's war on cancer, nuclear fusion, machine translation of natural language, and a vaccine against malaria. Each of these projects have met unforseen obstacles that technology has not been able to conquer.

The common futility of targeted research in industry arises from a lack of the fundamental knowledge needed for problem resolution. Such blind approaches to new products are legion and a serious waste of capital. It is one of the many paradoxes of industrial research that precludes innovation. These obstacles, or any related weak link in understanding, must be resolved before the targeted project can have genuine potential.

Recognition by management of the circuitous, indeterminate path that research and technology commonly take to achieve objectives would be a monumental step toward enhancing the cause of discovery. Such increased understanding by management could lead to the greater viability of research teams. It could greatly reduce the unnecessary frustration caused by unrealistic goals and time frames, and establish a less strained relationship between technology and management. Flexibility of objectives is an important character of a company that wishes to be innovative. This does not mean that the original objective cannot or should not be pursued; it simply indicates the possible necessity of intermediate way stations. Pursuit of anomalies along this circuitous path often could lead to new products of considerable commercial value that otherwise may be lost in a hopeless backlog of shelved research. Without such recognition by management, the consequence may be failure to develop anything of commercial value.

The importance of basic research is reinforced by Edward Scolnick,[6] who showed the critical relationship between academic research and industry in the discovery of streptomycin, cholesterol-lowering medicine, neoprene, and others. Not only is it beneficial for industrial research groups to have access to new discoveries worldwide, it is beneficial if they have their own leading edge research in relevant evolving fields. The fast-moving global economy necessitates rapid integration of new knowledge into research and development and then commercialization in the shortest reasonable time. These actions are essential to maintain the sharpest competitive edge.

According to Ziman,[7] in some organizations more emphasis is now being placed on long-term strategic research. This entails a more general strategy for making connections between different patterns of knowledge, which may lead to novelty of great value. Basic and applied research are commonly being pursued simultaneously and under a common heading. The distinction between the two is becoming increasingly fuzzy. One approach merges imperceptibly into the other. In this symbiotic relationship, science grows to enhance technology and vice versa.

### Humor in Research

While doing research, humor can stimulate new and viable approaches. Indeed, humor is creativity in its own right. Aristotle said that humor is "the pleasurable distortion of what is expected."[8] The same can be said about an *aha!*, which can bring on a sense of amusement, even a chuckle. E.B. White said that "humor is a final emotion, like breaking into tears,"[9] and so is an *aha!* Humor can be generated under most conditions, but a uniquely important set of conditions in the laboratory includes the contrasts of relaxation and stress, confidence and uncertainty, and the conventional-unconventional continuum of thought processes. Further benefits are derived from eternal hope, indefatigable drive, and the realization that very little knowledge, if any, is unalterable.

Journalist Arthur Koestler[10] saw a pattern of creativity in the trivalency of humor, discovery, and art. Creative acts, therefore, range from the absurd through the abstract, to the tragic or lyric. With a story by Chamfort, he illustrates the comic effect caused by the interaction of different contexts:

The story is about a Marquis at the court of Louis XIV who entered his wife's boudoir and found her consorting with a bishop. The Marquis then walked calmly to a window and went through the motions of blessing the people in the street.

"What are you doing?" cried the wife.

"Monseigneur is performing my functions," said the Marquis, "so I am performing his."

This unexpected but logical response by the Marquis, which creates a clash of meaning, suddenly dissipates the tension and results in amusement. Interaction of differing ideas, as conceived by Koestler, can culminate in laughter, an intellectual synthesis, or an aesthetic idea. In a similar sense, laughter is common in laboratories where discoveries are made because, like the Marquis' anecdote, there is a union of seemingly incompatible ideas. As Koestler observed, "Comic discovery is paradox stated—scientific discovery is paradox resolved." Because the mechanisms of achieving humor are in many ways similar to those of achieving discovery, humor can be an indirect facilitator of discovery. Observed by professor of natural science and physiology Robert Root-Bernstein,[11] "One mental quality that facilitates discovery, then, is a willingness to goof around, to play games, and to cultivate a degree of chaos aimed at revealing the unusual or the unexpected."

### Codification and Backwater Research

In some fields of science, as chemistry and physics, there are well-established approaches to problems and a nearly fixed set of questions to be asked. Such fields are called highly "codified" by sociologists.[12] Although the research direction is clear, it may change rapidly causing much work to become obsolete. A field of low codification is earth science, which permits "conceptual pluralism." Fields of low codification promote a wider range of thought processes and perceptions, in which research results are less apt to be made obsolete. Whether one is working in a field of high or low codification, conceptual pluralism is important to creativity. Although such an open approach may be risky in highly codified fields, creativity of great merit is perforce coexistent with risk.

Some scientists change their direction to be at the cutting edge of science, whereas others continue in the former areas of research. Those that do not pursue the major advances are often said to be engaging in backwater research. These scientists can still make breakthroughs independent of the current fad. While the avant-garde scientists are at the frontier of new knowledge and theory, the backwater scientists doing applied research are the primary source of technological invention. Their discoveries may not give rise directly to new theories, but they do give rise to new holistic understanding within an existing paradigm. Both kinds of research are essential and form a vital continuum.

Science and technology are continually reinvigorating each other, forming a symbiotic relationship of great moment to society. If this continuum is interrupted, both science and technology suffer the consequences. Perhaps the most serious consequence, however, is the decrease in industrial productivity that follows from reduction in invention.

### EXTERNAL STIMULI

Dialogue about technical problems is important within an organization. It is equally important in external settings. These may include laboratories of colleagues and customers, in academic environments, at conferences, and in worldwide travel where problems by virtue of cultural and environmental differences may be approached by novel methods. Horace Freeland Judson,[13] a professor of science history at Johns Hopkins University, characterized the favorable results of this kind of interaction as "the shuttle effect." The interaction of a new technical person with a research group having different perspectives often leads to discovery.

Described by Judson, when James Watson went to work at the Cavendish Laboratory of Cambridge University, he brought a uniquely detailed knowledge of genetics. Francis Crick, already at the laboratory, was using X-ray diffraction and generating mathematical tools for characterizing large helical molecules. The interaction between these patterns of knowledge led James Watson and Francis Crick to the discovery of the double helix, the molecular structure of DNA.

Another way of promoting the shuttle effect is through the presentation and publication of research papers. Not only does such activity require the researcher to collate and interpret his data with great precision so as not to be embarrassed in front of his peers, the presentation gives him the opportunity for extensive dialogue outside the relative safety and probable bias of his employer's laboratory. The consequences of giving a paper of high quality research can be fruitful to both the individual and the organization that he represents. This is true from the standpoints of enhanced image, propitious knowledge interaction, and the establishment of entrees with worldwide technical contacts.

Although a necessary veil of secrecy exists in industry for some of its knowledge, varying degrees of paranoia preclude an exchange of harmless knowledge that could, nevertheless, promote discovery. Any level of secrecy, necessary or otherwise, that inhibits the dialectic impedes the advance of knowledge. Free exchange of ideas, to the extent feasible, can raise a sluggish, unimaginative company from the sinkhole of commodity business.

Closely allied to the shuttle effect is the "demonstration effect." This is a term used by economists for stimulation to achievement by the awareness that other people have done extraordinary things. The creative turbulence in ancient Greece in the fifth century B.C. and in ancient and medieval China illustrate the point.[14] A freeing of consciousness may account for these surges of creativity. In both countries at these times, achievements stimulated achievements, and problems were solved in many different ways without knowledge of related breakthroughs.

Whatever sparked these contagions of greatness, it is the magic bullet which researchers are constantly seeking. Perhaps one great achievement in an environment empathetic to the problems and benefits of elegant science and major invention is enough to kindle a revolution—a surge of discovery and invention that will emulate or exceed the best of the past.

The next chapter is an introduction to thought processes and their classification. Critical thinking, perhaps the most neglected subject in our educational system, is critiqued in the first part of the chapter.

# Chapter 12

# Stimulation:
# Thought Processes behind Discovery

Research and the shuttle effect are types of stimulation that are critical to discovery-oriented institutions, but acuity in the use of thought processes is the underlying genius of those who discover. Critical thinking, using a wide array of conventional and unconventional methods, opens the pathway to reliable knowledge. Thought processes used to achieve creativity, balanced by logic, are critical to the survival of *Homo sapiens*.

Once there were two gentlemen, in particular, working in the same company, who developed an intense antagonism toward each other. One was a salesman for speciality products who occasionally would work in the laboratory on new ideas. He was a man of moderate height and considerable width. The other gentleman was a scientist who occasionally helped the specialty salesman in new product development. The primary problem centered around the arrogant, demanding nature of the salesman and the slow, deliberate, loquacious style of the scientist.

Being a man of gentle nature and substantial equanimity, the scientist rarely became riled. Once, however, he exploded with uncharacteristic anger and referred to the salesman as "a pompous pachyderm educated way beyond his intelligence." The latter part of the scientist's statement seems to contain considerable truth. Education beyond one's intelligence is a trait that may be generally true, at least, in the early part of one's career.

During formal training and into early careers, technical people are deluged with information but have sparse time to think about significance and interrelationships of knowledge patterns. They begin to think more profoundly with interpretation of their theses and as their research programs in the work environment become more involved and perplexing. Such specialized development of intelligence takes time and concentrated effort to reach a level commensurate with the high volume of force-fed knowledge.

To use information or education effectively, people are greatly benefited by an extensive, diverse repertoire of both conventional and unconventional thought processes. Logical, abstract thinking does not develop naturally. Physicist Alan Cromer[1] believed that abstract thinking is important to teach in all science courses. Early in one's career much knowledge can be amassed, but abundant training and experience is required to cultivate extensive, in-depth thought processes. Those who are most ingenious in developing unique methods of thinking, observing, and analyzing are the most creative, and, therefore, their intelligence and their education come closer to being equivalent.

## CRITICAL THINKING

Fundamentalists attempt to impose social rigidity and faith in irrationality. Critical thinking, judicious evaluation, is used, if at all, for selective purposes. Spartan-like, such an environment has no room for diversity of opinion; the only haven is to project and abide by the irrationality of dogma. Within their sphere of philosophical influence, fundamentalists promote entropy as well. Such an environment is a closed system, where energy neither enters nor exits—their fate being inert uniformity.

Diametrically opposed, Athenian pluralism provides the diversity of opinion, critical thinking, lifestyle, and philosophy needed for creativity and growth to a higher level of understanding and humanity. In an open system continuously stimulated by new ideas, Athenians are highly inventive. Speed of growth, however, is tempered to accommodate a healthy environment and the ability of society to absorb change in an acceptable fashion. Such achievement may be the noblest of contributions that embraces the highest moral authority.

The freedom to doubt, characteristic of Athenians, is one of the hardest won and most precious spin-offs of the Enlightenment. Its significance is easily lost in the emotionalism of such myths as astrology, psychic phenomena, paranormal beliefs, and dogma. All of these enemies of reliable knowledge are reinforced by media exploitation and by the generally quiet consent of the populace. Progress equates with doubt.

With the use of the scientific method for problem study and with consensus in the science community, an approximate understanding of truth is realized, but absolute truth is elusive. Yet, if the question is asked, "Does God exist?" the answer is usually absolute. From lack of evidence, the answer often centers around the knowledge terminator, "faith." By this means reason is expunged, and the limits of imagination are constrained by fiat.

Imminently understandable is the need of many people to believe in first cause—God. But how people define God plays an important role in the proliferation of other mysticisms. Some scientists who are theists characterize God as being the "laws of nature, or the ultimate mathematician" whereas Judeo-Christians may see God as an anthropomorphic, vengeful or forgiving, omnipotent-omniscient entity. The latter concept is most apt to lead to other unfounded beliefs. If belief in mysticism would stop at belief in God, however, religion would have much greater credibility. This was the original deist's concept, believing in God but prone to rationalism rather than revelation, and later denying the interference of the Creator in the laws of nature. But one mysticism usually begets many other irrationalities. For a rational world, all metaphysical questions deserve the same scrutiny and skepticism as is used to establish reliable knowledge in science. The late theoretical physicist and Nobel Laureate Richard P. Feynman phrased the importance of doubt succinctly, "We absolutely must leave room for doubt, or there is no progress and there is no learning."[2]

Thinking by some people can be so convoluted that it is impossible to understand their arguments. Despite their tangled efforts at logic, if they speak with seeming charismatic eloquence, they may acquire many followers. Many, if not most people, have received little if any training in critical thinking, and they can easily become victims of smooth-tongued charlatans. With subtle genetic influences, cultural conditioning, and variable emotional states of mind, it is not always easy to be logically correct or to be sufficiently analytical to recognize clever fraud or self-deluded purveyors of mysticism. Practicing various methods of valid thinking can help one to better recognize falsity. Such methods of thinking are described in Chapters 13–16.

Strict adherence to the principles of the scientific method may stifle imagination and inhibit invention. Creativity generally stems from intuition, inspiration, and other unconventional methods—not from induction and deduction. Although great progress has been made in science and technology via the conventional, logical thought processes used in the scientific method, unconventional thought is generally the critical path to creativity. The concept is then formalized and verified by the use of logic.

Science projects generally are carried out linearly and logically. The process of discovery, however, is probably as indeterminate as is the nature of individuals. By indirection, erroneous hypotheses have led some to major discovery. Archimedes' accidental discovery of how to measure an irregular volume, Sir Alexander Fleming's discovery of penicillin stemming from the supposed unintentional dropping of a tear from his eye into a culture, Thomas Edison's inventions using wrong theories of electricity, and the many cases of the phantasmagoria of dreaming leading to invention are a few among many examples. No matter how incorrect thinking may be, if it leads to new approaches, serendipitous discovery is often the result. The path to creativity, in part, can be tortuous, nonlinear, and surprisingly chaotic. Every such successful path, however, is finally constrained by inductive and deductive logic.

Root-Bernstein[3] points out, in stark contrast, that every supposed chance discovery that has been reevaluated with new historical evidence—for example, Fleming dropped a tear into his petri dish with purpose in mind—indicates that at least some serendipitous discoveries have been derived from a carefully planned inquiry. Generally not dumb luck, discovery, Root-Bernstein contended, is usually the result of a rational, masterful approach. Significant strides in all areas of endeavor come about primarily via creativity.[4]

Rigidly using the laws of inference, logical thinking is extrapolation and interpolation of existing knowledge. New knowledge via logical thinking is simply an extension of what is already known and, therefore, is rarely novel. Using this rationale, the psychologist Robert Weisberg concluded that it may not be possible to be creative by logic alone.[5]

Intuitive thinking may produce insights that could not be derived by logical thinking. Because intuitive thinking is not bound by the rules of logic, it functions with extreme flexibility. It transgresses sacred boundaries, and it can bring together viable relationships. Those with only ordinary interests and logical thinking generally do not conceive novel ideas. Intuitive thinking is enhanced by experience and knowledge of great breadth. Often leading to unexpected but viable connections with a broad range of knowledge patterns, intuitive thinking is probably essential to creativity. It is often the first stage of critical thinking, where logic is the final arbiter.

## SOME BACKGROUND FOR THE CLASSIFICATION OF THOUGHT PROCESSES

The classification of conventional and unconventional thinking in this book is arbitrary and the reader may find significant discrepancies. Elegance, simplicity, predictive validity, and appropriateness of great ideas can lead to acceptance in the scientific community without empirical evidence. Sometimes such an idea is accepted even with opposing evidence, and, thus, takes on the air of unconventionality. Although elegant theory is the ultimate form of abductive logic, it is unconventional in the sense of rarity and novelty.

Similarly, analogical thinking can lead to creativity. It is considered conventional, however, because it is a universal form of reasoning that often does not lead to novelty. These points are mentioned to emphasize how thought processes can take on a fuzzy character between the conventional and the unconventional. The importance of unconventionality is reinforced by George Bernard Shaw's poignant statement about the inseparability of progress and unreasonableness: "The reasonable man adapts himself to the world; the unreasonable one persists in adapting the world to himself. Therefore, all progress depends on the unreasonable man."[6]

Unconventional thinking includes, among much else, thought processes that persistently probe the validity of all facts, including dogma. With the human tendency to believe certain "facts" with ferocious tenacity, often becoming more pronounced with age and experience, unconventional thought can be crucial to discovery. The fuzzy logician Bart Kosko[7] noted that science does not respond well to a truly new idea, and that it is prone to small steps of progress. He pointed out that the behavior of the science profession with new ideas is no better than was the Roman Catholic Church in its denouncement of Galileo's claim that the earth revolves around the sun.

Our ability to think stems from a unique evolutionary history. Emphasized by Henry Plotkin,[8] our method of thinking is adaptive rather than logical. Logic and mathematics for most people are difficult. He describes abundant evidence showing that we are not consistently logical. For example, most of us have a strong bias to confirm rather than to refute hypotheses. Because of this bias, otherwise obvious conclusions can be missed. What cognitive psychologists call the "availability" heuristic is equally behind failure in problem solution. By way of the manner in which our memories are organized, we sometimes make incorrect judgments. This derives from a heuristic, a simplifying rule of thumb, which may lead us astray. An heuristic is a tradeoff, a sacrifice of accuracy in the interest of saving time.

Another defect in our reasoning is the conjunction error about probability. If the chance of getting wet walking home is one in ten, expressed as 1/10, and the chance of having a headache on the way home is 1/50, the chance of both happening on the way home is 1/500. Oddly, when posed the problem, most people believe the conjunction, or both events occurring together, to be most likely.

This way, the process of thinking scientifically is different from common sense or everyday thinking. Biologist Lewis Wolpert believed that science involves a special mode of thought and is different from common sense for two reasons:[9] (1) The universe is not constructed on a commonsense basis, and scientific ideas are generally counterintuitive; and (2) Doing science requires a keen awareness of the inadequacy of common sense or natural thinking.

Wolpert gave the example of motion to illustrate the counterintuitive nature of science. A bomb dropped from an airplane will hit the ground almost directly beneath the plane's position at the moment of the bomb's impact. Not realizing that the bomb continues to move forward along with the airplane when released and that its forward motion is not affected by the downwards fall, the correct answer commonly is not anticipated by students. In another example, if a bullet is dropped from one's hand at the same moment that a bullet is fired horizontally, which will hit the ground first? Because the bullet's rate of fall is independent of the horizontal motion, both will hit the ground at the same time. A rare exception to the counterintuitive nature of science is Ohm's law which follows common sense: the greater the resistance to an electric circuit, the greater the voltage required to drive a current through the circuit.

Because of Aristotle's commonsense view of the world, many of his conclusions were mistaken. Among many examples, he deduced that a five-pound weight would fall five times faster than a one-pound weight—a mistaken view that went uncorrected for nearly 2,000 years until Galileo showed that both weights would fall at the same rate. This is not a reflection against Aristotle's brilliance but emphasizes that common sense can lead one astray. Exclusive of experiment and mathematics, Aristotle was guided by the limitations of his premises and the sociological influences of his time.

The bizarre, seemingly absurd nature of the quantum world is an extreme example of departure from common sense (Chapter 4). Despite this departure, quantum mechanics is in full agreement with experiment, which, along with other methods of science, is the final arbiter in understanding the universe.

Explained by philosopher Morris Cohen,[10] increased means of travel and communication during the Industrial Revolution played a significant role in undermining custom. When the people took charge and changed the traditional form of government in the French Revolution, questioning authority was made easier. Believing that civilized society must cherish obedience and deference, the traditionalists were frightened by unconventionality. The individualistic nature of reason is a threat to authority, but empiricism attacks reason because it is not the result of experience. Not authority, not experience alone, nor reason alone can form a rational basis for science. The interaction of induction, deduction, abduction, and ancillary, conventional thought processes is the fundamental basis of science, where authority, prejudice, and mysticism are excluded for reliable knowledge.

Elaborated by Cohen, psychological certainties (e.g., feelings) such as "our country will go to ruin if the newfangled heresies are not repressed," commonly are felt with such emotion that they preclude pursuit of truth. Lacking knowledge of opposing ideas, people may become unyielding in their opinions. Complex ideas of politics and religion often are held as absolutely certain, contrasted with great doubt concerning less convoluted and intensely studied aspects of science. Such fallacy of judgment occasionally carries over into science and undermines further the idealistic goal of objectivity.

While sharpening our ability to observe and to be receptive to change in doing science, Lawrence Slobodkin[11] emphasized that we hold our egos in abeyance. In this process the universe dictates its own brand of logic. Good science or technology requires that we discard our preconceived notions and our psychological certainties, and that common sense or natural thinking be assigned a secondary position; experiment, intersubjective observation, and logical, self-consistent theory must rule supreme. How scientists attempt to achieve this evasive goal is the subject of the section on conventional thought processes (Chapters 13 and 14).

## CLASSIFICATION OF THOUGHT PROCESSES

Three general categories of thinking include (1) common sense, everyday or natural, (2) conventional or scientific, and (3) unconventional. Common sense is based on everyday experience and like science is founded largely on inductive-deductive reasoning. Unlike science, common sense does not have the benefit of controlled experiment and consensus within the scientific community for eliminating many invalid premises. An extreme example of natural thinking is the gambler's fallacy, or the belief that an event is foreordained because it is past due.

Conventional thinking as classified in this book is scientific, which can include several different thought processes, but deductive, inductive, and abductive reasoning are fundamental. Deductive logic is essential to scientific thinking, but inductive reasoning via experiment and observation, also fundamental, is the primary method of the scientific process. Abductive thinking is the establishment of hypotheses and is equally important to the latter two methods. Unconventional thinking includes esoteric methods that commonly lead to creativity. Thinking without the restraints of logic, as in daydreams, is a prime method. The study of a phenomenon begins with conventional thinking from which a substantial knowledge platform can be constructed. This platform is a necessary point of departure for the unconventional track to creativity.

## THE SCIENTIFIC METHOD

Because conventional thinking is scientific thinking, it may be helpful to review briefly the scientific method shown in Figure 12.1. A thumbnail sketch of the scientific method is that from observations hypotheses are constructed. Experiments are conducted to verify which hypothesis best fits the facts. As new facts are garnered, modified or new hypotheses are developed. New laws of nature may be characterized by accepted hypotheses. When consensus is achieved in the scientific community, the accepted hypothesis becomes theory. As relevant new knowledge is gained, the theory may be modified but rarely is dismissed totally.

The scientific method is an ideal, which is rarely, if ever, followed to the letter. Although noble efforts are made to be objective, such an absolute method of thinking is never fully achieved, and so-called "facts" of science

Observations

Hypotheses

Experiments

Laws

Theories

**Figure 12.1.** The scientific method.

at the frontier of new knowledge are always tentative and uncertain. Even some of textbook science is less certain than traditionally portrayed. Henry Bauer[12] describes scientific research as a melange of approaches in striving to gain new knowledge: "by cutting corners; by doing 'quick-and-dirty' hunches, or by 'just playing around,' as well as by trying carefully thought-out things."

It is fortunate, indeed, that the scientific method is not a universally accepted and rigidly followed prescription for discovery in science and technology. Such blind obedience would help to assure the persistence of the status quo, thereby decreasing the credibility of the technical world. Deviation from the conventional notion of the scientific method is characteristic of the approach taken by scientists in general. Bauer makes the cogent point that "Science may be better served when some scientists generate novel ideas while others carp at everything new than if all scientists could somehow become disinterestedly skeptical."

Numerous examples exist where theory is sustained in the face of negative empirical evidence. Seeming new knowledge may be developed from detailed experimental work, from the elegance of theory, or from serendipity. Incorrect theories may lead to discoveries of major import. The paths to successful science and technology are divergent, sometimes chaotic, possessing all degrees of systematization. Despite the inconsistency of approach for discovery, the scientific method, via induction and deduction, is utilized to confirm and refine a new idea. The successes in both science and technology, generally arising from creativity, suggest that divergent approaches may be the best of all worlds.

Science usually begins with preconceived notions based on experience and deductive reasoning. These ideas contain some *a priori* notions, which are tested by experiment and observation. New hypotheses, or tentative assumptions, may be generated, which become the models for further experiment and observation. These steps may be repeated many times until a hypothesis is generated that best fits the facts. Innumerable failures, which are requisite to the advance of science, are inherent in the process. No other profession exists in which failure is so acceptable.

Never shown to be absolutely true, a hypothesis is accepted and incorporated into theory only after extensive verification, peer review, and the development of consensus in the scientific community. People involved in pseudoscience, in particular creationism, dispose of evolutionary theory as *only* a theory. This convenient and fallacious argument arises from the creationist's misunderstanding of the meaning of theory in science. Creationists allude to the popular usage of "theory" to mean conjecture or ideas whose outcome has not been determined. In science, theory has been so thoroughly challenged and tested by the science community that its degree of truth is very high indeed.

Although theories possess a high degree of validity, they are rarely considered to be perfect and are continuously being modified to fit new strands of evidence. Even in these cases, however, the fundamental bases of theories are rarely altered; only details may be changed. As astutely pointed out by Isaac Asimov,[13] "The details of evolutionary theory are in dispute precisely because scientists are *not* devotees of blind faith and dogmatism." Theory in science is not conjecture, and is generally as close to truth as can be established within the existing framework of evidence.

Models are the frameworks or the metaphors used to derive the basic goals of science—explanation and prediction. Casti[14] described scientific models as "an abstraction of some slice of reality." Examples of cosmological models are Big Bang and New Inflationary Universe. With the advent of greater evidence, these models may be replaced by theories. Only those aspects of reality that are essential to explanation and prediction are retained in models. Inasmuch as the math world uniquely enables a systematic, reliable method for generating new truths, mathematical models are used most extensively. Nevertheless, models are always approximations, and even if they provide accurate predictions, they are never fully verified.

Different brains filter different categories of information to fix in their memory structures, each building in its own idiosyncratic way.[15] Over time, these memory structures change. Observations are influenced by the nature of the knowledge already possessed, and as new knowledge is uncovered, perceptions change. Observations, therefore, are always open to skepticism, and "truth" requires the building of a consensus in the scientific community.

Try as we might, we do not always use objective standards to judge our observations. Our mental structure has evolved to use relativistic processes, as exemplified by a classic experiment:[16] three bowls are filled with hot, cold, and tepid water, respectively. One hand is placed in the hot and the other in the cold. In a few minutes, both hands are placed in the tepid. One hand will feel cold, the one that was in the hot water, and the other hand will feel warm, the one that was in the cold water.

Environmental influences also shade our judgment as illustrated by the Muller-Lyer illusion (see Figure 12.2). Although both horizontal lines are the same length, the line with the outward pointing arrows appears to be

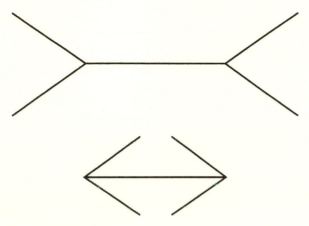

**Figure 12.2.** The Muller-Lyer illusion.

shorter. People who have grown up in round huts are less susceptible to this illusion than those who have grown up amid structures with straight lines and right angles.[17] While our brains do not routinely deceive us, illusions occur with sufficient frequency that we must be aware of this saboteur of correct observation. Illusion can be the evil twin of incisive observation or of creative imagination.

Susceptibility to illusions and persistence in irrational behavior despite its recognition is, at first thought, perplexing. As psychologist Howard Margolis[18] explained, such human fallibility seems more reasonable when it is recognized that the structure of our brains is the consequence of evolution. Each blind variation in brain structure that arises favors near-term advantage. Opposed to reconstruction, evolution adds to and modifies existing structures. Just as the primitive limbic system was once the primary brain in distant ancestors, it still exists in the modern brain and is functional along with our much more sophisticated cerebral cortex.

*Homo sapiens* have in common with many animals this primitive limbic system, an ancient part of our brain which has remained unchanged over hundreds of thousands of years.[19] This system controls emotion such as fear, lust, anger, and jealousy. With extreme duress, the irrationality of the limbic system can overwhelm the rationality of the cerebral cortex and can remain in control for days. It seems to be responsible for violent acts that the rational mind is not apt to promote. Regaining rational control is not a simple matter of turning off a switch. Fueled by these primitive emotions that have ensured survival of our species, powerful emotional currents in any individual can overpower the ability to reason. Although the human brain is seemingly the most complex thing on earth and is the basis of quintessential rationality, such as relativity and quantum mechanics, the cerebral cortex sometimes takes a backseat to man's primitive animal nature. The drive for survival and breeding is far more tangible than the optimistic goal of perfect rationality.

As pointed out by biologist Edward Wilson,[20]

The Human Brain bears the stamp of 400 million years of trial and error, traceable by fossils and molecular homology in nearly unbroken sequence from fish to amphibian to reptile to primitive mammal to our immediate primate forerunners. In the final step the brain was catapulted to a radically new level, equipped for language and culture.

Margolis believed that human cognitive capabilities evolved consistent with this principle of continuity of structure. The inadequacies of our perceptions, then, are the consequence of the defects in the evolutionary system, which can be corrected only by chance in an ongoing evolutionary process. Thought processes evolve in the context of our environment, our culture, and our genes, and small variations, such as round or square structures that dominate, can affect our brain's development.

The defects in our brains and our inability to broaden knowledge scope beyond undefinable limits, precludes the viability of doing science and technology in isolation. Although the best science is done by those who have great confidence and optimism, humility and the combined action of many brains is also essential to void errors in judgement and to expand thought and ideas into extraordinary realms of conceptualization. It is not the individual scientist, therefore, but the social contract in the scientific community that gives rise to a notable degree of objectivity as well as breadth and depth in concepts.

Despite the emphasis on individuals for their discoveries, the confirmed hypothesis is a product of the work of many scientists, past and present. Laws may be developed from such accepted hypotheses, as Ohm's law, which then may be incorporated into a larger concept of nature known as theories, such as the special theory of relativity. Laws explain sets of observations, and theories explain sets of laws.

Hypotheses are tentatively held concepts, a shaky foundation that is constantly reinforced or rebuilt until a theory can be established. According to Alan Cromer[21] "a theory is a set of logically consistent abstract principles that explain a body of concrete facts. It is the logical connections among the principles and the facts that characterize a theory as truth." They are concepts that are elegant oversimplifications, yet they are useful for explanation and prediction. Despite their seeming validity, new events or observations may undermine certain aspects of a theory. The major question is always to what extent do our theories approximate reality? Seeking answers to this question is the propellant of revolutionary science.

Aristotle saw the basic substances of the world occurring in a natural order of concentric circles, and Newton saw the universe consisting of massive objects moving through an infinity.[22] Despite the contrast of these theories to current views, they have been invaluable in promoting a better understanding of reality. They have been the foundations for strategies of research. As opposed to the strict empiricist's belief that theory-free perception enables the objective acquisition of facts, the new philosophy of science contends that the knowledge, beliefs, and theories that we already possess influence what we perceive.[23]

To illustrate this point, Harold Brown gave the examples of Kepler and Tycho Brahe. As seen by Kepler, the sun was static and the earth revolved around it; in contrast, Brahe saw the earth as a static body around which the sun revolves. Each claim was made from a presupposition that colored their interpretation. As new data is accumulated, presuppositions may change, and the view of a problem often changes beyond recognition. The moment of discovery is described by gestalt psychologists as the incorporation of a datum that fits into a maze of information suddenly shaping it into a symmetrical pattern.[24]

Our interpretation of what we see is shaded by our theories. What we perceive is influenced by two parameters: our theories and the influence of the external world on our senses. We can see things in many different ways but still within certain limits. In Kuhn's normal science, scientists begin their research program with a generally accepted scientific theory. Contradictions to this theory become research problems rather than a rejection of the theory. If the problems attendant with the theory become intransigent, then new theories are envisioned that may become the basis of revolutionary science.

As pointed out by Stephen Hawking,[25] in theoretical physics logical self-consistency has always been more important than experimental results; theory, as opposed to empiricism, therefore, dominates the scientific process in that field. To a lesser extent, this is true in the other sciences, at least in the sense of logical self-consistency. Data-rich fields, as chemistry, because of easy refutation, often follow the sequence, data, theory. Data-poor fields, as cosmology, are prone to theory speculation and generally display greater confidence in elegant theory than in data.[26] People develop such possessiveness in their theories that generally they are reluctant to give them up. Some theories may become so cumbersome with adjustments that someone less enamored with the old theory will suggest a new one.

To demonstrate the relationship of theory to science, Hawking[27] gave the example of the Michelson-Morley experiment which in 1887 indicated that the speed of light is constant regardless of the motion of the observer or the light source. For eighteen years physicists attempted to accommodate this correct but seemingly ridiculous notion, which became a major obstacle to the progress of physics.

In 1905 Einstein concluded that time is a component of four-dimensional space which he called space-time. He showed that the rate of a clock's ticking is related to the clock's velocity. As a consequence, Einstein showed that time and space are related. This was in stark contrast to Newtonian mechanics, which assumes universal time, that a clock always ticks at the same rate regardless of its velocity. An observer traveling near the speed of light and attempting to catch up with a light beam would never do so, and the beam would still be traveling at 186,000 miles per second faster than the observer no matter how closely he or she approached the speed of light. Time slows down for observers as they approach the speed of light. There is no way for an observer to advance on a point in a light beam even by a small distance.

What Einstein pointed out was that the same speed of light could be measured by observers if the idea of universal time was forsaken. Each observer would carry his or her own clock to measure individual time, which would be different if they were traveling at significantly different speeds relative to each other. Similarly, they would not agree on the distance that light traveled at a given time interval. Because the speed of light is distance traveled divided by the time interval, there must be a proportional agreement between distance and time if the different observers are to agree on the speed of light. In fact, that is the case. The faster we travel the slower our clocks run, and the shorter are our rulers. Such thinking depended on the understanding that time is not universal. What we regard as real is dependent on our theories.

Einstein's special theory of relativity shows that it is possible for time to pass at different rates. Time does not exist on its own independent of space; it is unidirectional going only from the past to the future. It is possible, however, for time to move at an angle to the future, which is why time can pass at different rates. Einstein developed this idea to accommodate a good fit between the laws that govern electric and magnetic fields and the laws that govern the motion of bodies. Experimental results were of secondary importance. Thus, reality is a variable concept dictated largely by our different theories, but which is consistent with mathematical models. As emphasized by Hawking, a theory is good if it is elegant, predictive, and accords well with observation, and reality cannot be characterized beyond this general approach. Paradoxically, theory is used to guide research, but only if observers could somehow understand reality independent of theory could there be certainty.

The widespread myth exists that scientific method is totally objective. Many believe that the method entails the suspension of preconceptions, approaching problems with our minds essentially a *tabula rasa*, and dutifully allowing the observed data to dictate objective understanding. It is surprising that such a general notion of science still permeates popular opinion. Even the Sophists of ancient Greece argued that reality is unique to each individual,[28] that understanding is subjective, and that objectivity is never fully achieved. Without the presuppositions of accepted theory, however, scientists could not ascribe meaning to their observations, know which observations are relevant, nor understand the direction in which they should proceed. Presuppositions are essential guiding principles in any research program. Inherent in this approach are the risks of cul-de-sacs and of collecting inappropriate data. On the other hand, presuppositions prescribe certain expectations, and the scientist then has the advantage of recognizing serendipity and anomaly.

Access to the cryptogram of nature for the scientist is limited to this process of theory-directed research. The process of science, then, is the interaction of theory with reality. Knowledge that becomes ours via this process is approximated by the degree of accord of this interaction. The final arbiter, however, is the social contract within the scientific community, by which a consensus arbitrates that which is considered truth. It is our last resort to objectivity. The credibility of science, then, finally depends on the nature and structure of human relationships.[29]

## THE HYBRID NATURE OF THOUGHT PROCESSES

Generally classified under conventional thinking are those processes characteristically used in scientific method. Unconventional processes in this context are considered to be those not essential to scientific method but which may lead to novelty, and which require conventional thinking for verification. Generally, all of the thought processes discussed under the conventional heading have some degree of hybrid character with unconventional thinking.

Although unconventionality greatly increases the odds of creativity, some novel ideas have come from conventional thought. Analogical thinking was used by Darwin, as the use of gradualism garnered from geological thinking, in deriving his theory of evolution (Chapter 14). Similarly, Edison used the concept of the cylinder as analogy in many of his inventions.[30] Einstein used abductive logic to arrive at elegant theory. Of course, it is an oversimplification to assume that these were the only thought processes used. Unconventional thought was undoubtedly incorporated more than historical studies of these events can recognize. It does seem, however, that the use of conventional thinking can lead to creativity with the appropriate confluence of passionate effort, a broad range of knowledge patterns, and receptive social conditions.

Major creative discoveries, it seems, can come about by thought processes limited to deductive-inductive-abductive reasoning. This occurs when hypothesizing becomes sufficiently profound to be transformed into elegant theory. Even deductive reasoning from previous knowledge has led to discoveries of major import. Conical refraction, electric waves, and the planet Neptune were discovered by deduction.[31]

An elegant example of deductive reasoning that led to discovery was described by Bronowski.[32] The example begins with Olbers' paradox. German physician and astronomer Heinrich Wilhelm Matthäus Olbers

(1758–1840) reasoned that the stars are pumping energy into space and that the universe is sufficiently old that equilibrium has occurred. Therefore, all objects in the universe are radiating the same amount of energy that they are receiving. He concluded that the night sky should be as bright as daylight. The only explanation of this paradox was the improbable idea that the universe was still very young and equilibrium had not yet been achieved.

German scientist Hermann Bondi solved this problem. He suggested three experiments that could determine which of three possible states apply to the universe. These states are contracting, stationary in size, or expanding. If the universe is contracting, night would be brighter than day as more energy would be coming from the background than the sun is supplying. If stationary, then night and day would be equal. But if the universe is expanding, then night would be dark—because the energy is going into a volume of space greater than that from which it was originating. The experiments that Bondi suggested were derived by deductive reasoning, but induction was required to arrive at the correct conclusion. His reasoning hinged on uncommon rationality. Although such things as intuition and metaphor may have aided his thought process, his deductive logic was impeccable and does not seem to have necessitated such unconventionality.

Explained by Bronowski, this information was at hand more than 100 years ago, but recognition was to await analysis of the Doppler effect. Nevertheless, Bondi's elegant deductive reasoning led to a major, though unrecognized discovery. It seems to be a superb example of the use of conventional reasoning to perfection to achieve an unconventional result.

In this sense, it might be fair to conclude that all thought processes potentially can grade from the absolutely conventional to the absolutely unconventional (e.g., hypothetical or abductive reasoning to elegant theory). The latter case may arise from knowledge breadth and depth, passion, and motivation giving rise to extraordinary effort unique to the most creative. In contrast, philosopher John Dupré[33] believed that every discovery contains "an 'irrational element,' or a 'creative intuition.' " Although this discrepancy of the nature of discovery is not amenable to clear resolution, it would be most difficult to argue convincingly against the necessity of some degree of unconventionality in creative discovery.

Described in the next two chapters, the scientific method is embraced by conventional thinking.

# Chapter 13

# Stimulation:
# Conventional Thinking I

After the philosophy and science of ancient Greece and the inventiveness of early China and the European Middle Ages, the Renaissance was the revival of scholarship, literature, and the arts. In the latter part of the Renaissance (the Enlightenment), the scientific revolution and the recognition that reason was a tool of immense power permitted civilization to advance at a dizzying pace. Of great consequence was the Industrial Revolution, made possible by diverse inventions and especially by the harnessing of steam power.

The scientific method, powered by the new concepts of empiricism, mechanism, and reductionism, enabled invention to evolve at the highest rate ever. During the Enlightenment, sometimes called the Age of Reason, mysticism and authority were replaced by the rationalism of the scientific method. Powered by the new concepts of mechanism and reductionism, the scientific method, reinforced with a new appreciation of empiricism, enabled invention to evolve at the highest rate ever. The thought patterns of the scientific method are conventional. Unconventional thinking, such as intuition and metaphorical thinking, are common sources of invention as well. Every unconventional thought, however, must be reduced to conventional thinking to justify its validity. It follows that the thought patterns we cultivate play a determining role in exploiting our intelligence.

The fundamental ways of approaching knowledge are through deductive, inductive, and abductive reasoning. Although they are basic, additional approaches to knowledge that have a major influence on thinking are included under the heading of conventional thought processes. These methods are generally attendant with the scientific process (see Figure 13.1).

The man who opened this Pandora's box of reasoning was a pre-Socratic

---

- Socratic method—dialectic or the art of separating an argument into its parts.
- Rationalism—deductive logic via *a priori* knowledge and syllogisms. Includes mathematical reasoning.
- Empiricism—inductive logic via experiment and observation.
- Abduction—tentative adoption of an hypothesis to save an appearance.
- Paradigmatic thinking—normal, thinking within a prevailing paradigm; revolutionary, thinking in a new and novel paradigm.
- Analogy—use of similar approaches for problem solving.
- Reductionism—study of a part as opposed to the whole.

---

**Figure 13.1.** Some conventional thought processes.

Greek, Thales of Miletus, who is considered to be the father of natural philosophy.[1] Denying the involvement of the gods, he is the first significant rationalist. He made the seminal pronouncement in about 600 B.C. that "the mysteries of the universe are governed by laws that can be discovered in thought." This idea marked the beginning of the transition from mythology to philosophy and science. In the context of the time, it was a heretical, courageous, and gigantic leap from a morass of mysticism.

Mathematician and philosopher Alfred Whitehead said, "It is the first step in sociological wisdom to recognize that the major advances in civilization are processes which all but wreck the societies in which they occur."[2] Thales' pronouncement, indeed, must have been a society wrecker. There followed in ancient Greece an explosion of intellectual activity that, according to the mathematician and philosopher Bertrand Russell,[3] was the most spectacular event of history. In an equally spectacular sense, an intellectual revolution of such magnitude has happened only this one time in the history of civilization.

Both philosophy and science evolved in this intellectual milieu that was ancient Greece. Besides notable contributions such as Euclid's geometry and Archimedes' mechanics, much of the Greek science was mistaken. To be wrong in science, however, is not a disgrace—it is a necessary component of the long, circuitous, and asymptotic path to truth. The biologist Lewis Wolpert[4] saw the idea that man is innately curious to be at least a partial myth. He reasoned that there is no other way to explain the lack of curiosity displayed by all societies, save the ancient Greeks. The evolution of science need not have occurred but by this chance development.

## SOCRATIC METHOD

First used by Zeno and later adopted by Socrates and Plato, dialectic argument, the art of separating a subject into its parts by question and answer, is critical to the process of science. The development of scientific societies and journals during the scientific revolution in seventeenth-century Europe facilitated the dialectic and the consequent development of modern science.[5]

As different from dialectic, eristic was practiced by the Sophists of ancient Greece and today is the art of crafty attorneys or politicians; it is a matter of twisting arguments to produce incorrect but desired conclusions. Defense attorneys may rationalize and make the worst actions of their clients appear acceptable or untrue. Some politicians regularly try to make inappropriate actions appear respectable or untrue. As Russell explained, those who practice eristic are out to win, and those who practice dialectic are out to discover the truth.

The dialectic can be trying to fit new knowledge into a viable pattern, speculating in unlikely directions about the significance of new knowledge, postulating way-out theory, or simply trying to resolve a common problem. It can be transacted with other people or with oneself. In his adult scientific life, Einstein had a continuing dialectic with his childhood questions of nature, a common element of scientific breakthroughs.[6] Leading to his most creative science, as a youth he puzzled over the behavior of the point of a compass and the thought experiment of riding on a light beam. With the sophistication of his adult knowledge of physics, he was able to solve problems relating to these questions.

Opposed to the eristic and competitive struggle for establishing intellectual turf, a free exchange of ideas between technologists and scientists passionately imbued with a problem can lead to an excitement that can stimulate new ideas. Challenge, controversy, and debate are essential to the efficient evolution of knowledge. If the people in the setting feel a spirit of cooperation and trust, and have the firm belief that such openness will benefit themselves as much as the group, maximum benefit can be achieved from the dialectic. Ideally, it is a setting in which ideas are analyzed with great care, and the paranoia that commonly accompanies perceived ownership of concepts is set aside for a higher intellectual level of debate. Rather than viewing discourse as an opportunity for the self-serving manipulation of one's image, it can be viewed as an opportunity to move a little closer to truth. With a genuine desire to ferret out the truth, the evasiveness of objectivity can be subdued. The short-term benefit of winning the debate without the truth is counterproductive to the long-term benefit of everyone. In such an unrestricted setting, each man becomes stronger than he is in isolation—the group becomes a collective brain of inordinate power.

Such an open, dialectical setting just described is idealistic, but it is a syndrome that every technical group should diligently attempt to achieve. In Lockheed's skunk works, heated debates were not infrequent, but their leader, Bob Taylor, had a unique and effective way of dissipating the an-

ger.[7] He would convince the opponents to change their approach from a
Class 1 debate to a Class 2 level. This entailed each side describing the
other's position. As a consequence, common ground would develop and
the debate was cooled to a level of reasonable exchange. Without collegial,
friendly, honest debate, science progress would be sluggish and more errant.
Undeterred, heated debate can lead to the festering anger of savaged egos
and the loss of objectivity. Such undermining of trust defeats the collaborative process of discovery.

Physicist John Barrow gives added weight to the importance of the dialectic.[8] He points out that in any complex system the size of the components
is far less important than the number of connections between them. This
is exemplified by a network of three points where each point has two connections, but in a network of six points each point has five connections.
He foresees a time when the networking of computers can stimulate and
solve problems of enormous complexity.

The intellectual rewards of successful, revealing debate can be enormous,
but a secondary benefit of great value is the monumental uplift of morale.
This uplift, perforce, accompanies the near perfection of the dialectic. The
achievement of many brains working together harmoniously in a technology group is similar to the superorganism of the entomologist William
Morton Wheeler.[9]

In his study of ant colonies, Wheeler saw this phenomenon in the extensive cooperation of many individuals. All of the specialized actions of the
ants in a colony can be viewed as a unitary organism, performing all of
the requirements for life that a solitary individual does to survive. About
half of the insect biomass is composed of ants which biologist E.O. Wilson
surmised must have something to do with the advanced colonial organization of ants.[10] Superorganisms can control their environment in competition with most solitary creatures, which seems to be why ants live in
abundance over much of the world. Although the members of a creative
technology group are not so specialized, the most successful groups are
generally highly proficient superorganisms.

Philosopher Harold Brown[11] saw discovery as a dialectical process between old and new theories. The new theory develops because of failures
of the old theory, but some degree of commonality is retained. Many presuppositions will be entertained while establishing a new theory, which will
pose many questions. Some answers will be discarded from presuppositions, but at any point the presuppositions can be questioned as well. This
process is distinct from deductive logic in that it is pursued without the aid
of formal rules. It can be used to analyze relations between succeeding
theories and the research process.

Utility of deductive logic occurs largely with the reconstruction of research projects. Without the aid of mechanical rules, dialectical logic involves reasoned judgments in the scientific community to resolve conflicts

between theory and observation. This is the driving force of research: the persistent striving to develop a coherently organized system of observation and theory. Opposed to the existing body of knowledge, the essence of science is leading-edge research, with the dialectic playing a major role in establishing new knowledge.

The ability to question what one has learned in childhood is usually absent without some form of training.[12] Generally, people growing up in a rural area are firmly attached to the socially accepted beliefs of home and community. Only when they contact other communities having different beliefs can doubt flourish. The interaction of communities throughout the world, therefore, is important to intellectual growth.

Continuing this line of thought, the psychologist Jerome Bruner[13] alluded to isolation experiments. He described how it has been shown that sensorially deprived individuals lose control of their mental functions, and that alertness depends on a constant interaction with diversity. The dialectic used in a setting designed for open exchange between people of different knowledge patterns, disciplines, and cultures is a method of tapping diversity.

A marvelous example of diverse environmental influence in nature is afforded by the amphibious plant, arrowleaf. Described by Wilson, on land the leaves are shaped like arrowheads, in shallow water leaves at the surface are like lily pads, and in deeper water the leaves are eelgrasslike.[14] These plants have no apparent genetic differences. As Wilson explains, "they embrace the full variation in expression of the genes in all known survivable environments." These changes are effected by the interaction of genes and environment. In similar fashion, change the environment of researchers, as with new, more stimulating surroundings, such as new scientists on the scene with different backgrounds and perspectives, and the ensuing accommodations to these influences may lead to major discovery via the dialectic.

If researchers closely protect their seeming new knowledge, they run the distinct risk of being grossly incorrect and narrow in their conclusions. If they share their knowledge with other technologists within their laboratory, they increase their chances of being approximately correct. If, on the other hand, they extend their exchange of ideas to the international community, they optimize their chances of discovery and acceptance by the community of technologists and scientists at large.

According to chemist Henry Bauer,[15] "What really constitutes pseudoscience is isolation from the scientific community." Perhaps, then, it is fair to conclude that the obligatory isolation of novel, unpatented technology often leads to pseudotechnology. Continuing this presumed logical path, if the patent system could be abandoned, if company technology secrets could become passé, if there were a free and open exchange of technology and science worldwide, the technical world would undergo a drastic change.

It takes no more than superficial thought to realize that such openness is a utopian dream; but if it were to happen, it is probable that the growth of knowledge would experience a monumental rate of increase. Coincident with knowledge increase, innovation would then have the potential of increasing at a similar rate. Economic well-being of the world conceivably could improve at a rate similar to that of innovative growth. These unconventional thoughts are simply another way of emphasizing the importance of an international dialectic for all scientists and technologists.

To some extent this ideal of knowledge openness is being realized by globalization which is the integration of capital, technology, and information across national borders. It is rapidly creating a single global market. The *New York Times* foreign affairs columnist Thomas Friedman points out that an important reason why the Internet has grown so fast is that it is an open standard, where knowledge is openly shared.[16] Countries and companies operating on an open standard must learn how to be faster, to engineer smarter, to relate to customers better, and to manage knowledge better.

Friedman alludes to Robert Shapiro, the chairman of Monsanto, who says that the culture created around secrecy is slower and suited to a slower world. Your only sustainable advantages are the way you manage and exchange information and the way you learn as a company. What really counts is being a better competitor in a wide-open race.

Perhaps the most impressive example given by Friedman is a study, "Regional Advantage," made by the University of California at Berkeley urban studies expert, AnnaLee Saxenian. She explains that Silicon Valley is so distinctive and creative because the boundaries among technology firms, and between these firms and the venture capital community, the banking community, the university research community, and the local government are open. On the other hand, its twin community in Boston has been dominated by secrecy and risk aversion, and as a consequence has always lagged behind. In a similar vein, Singapore has purposely lured immigration, and this action stemmed from a survey of thriving societies, as the United States and Britain, showing that they prosper because of their openness and diversity.

The greatest danger that potentially could arise from an international dialectic is that such connectedness may lead to a serious reduction in diversity.[17] This potential danger seems even more real with the growth of the Internet where extensive international collaborations could promote approaches to problems via a single paradigm. Multiple approaches are generally essential to find the most creative and favorable result. Although connectedness has many advantages, it is paramount that diversity of style and approach be maintained in the dialectical pursuit of the best science and technology.

# RATIONALISM AND EMPIRICISM

## The Syllogism

Although Socrates described the method of deduction in his *Dialogue*, and Plato contributed further to its understanding, it was Aristotle who gave order and full recognition to the concept.[18] Deduction, embodied by the syllogism, is the reasoning tool of rationalism. Aristotle considered the syllogism to be the fundamental model of all argument. The syllogism consists of a major and a minor premise that have one term in common. *All men are mortal; Socrates is a man; therefore Socrates is mortal*, is an example. If the premises are true, any conclusion correctly derived is true, although true conclusion can be derived from false premises.

Cognitive scientist Massimo Piatelli-Palmarini[19] gave a striking example of a syllogism that creates great difficulty for even the most intelligent people. *All members of the cabinet are thieves; no composer is a member of the cabinet.* Thoughtful people conclude that no logical conclusion can be derived. The British psychologist Philip Johnson-Laird gave a solution: *some thieves are not composers.* Our inability to solve such a syllogism is psychological, not logical. Piatelli-Palmarini refers to this mental block as a mental tunnel, which illustrates the ease with which we fall into error, and the imperfection of the structure of our brains.

Inanity in syllogisms is not difficult to come by: *Where there is smoke there is fire; this man is blowing smoke; therefore he is on fire.* Physicists Tony Rothman and George Sudarshan[20] explain that this playfulness in thought can fit the requirements of a syllogism because the logic, the mathematics, offers nothing to base the statement in reality.

For nearly 2,000 years, from the ancient Greeks to the latter part of the Renaissance during the scientific revolution, this type of argument held supreme and was considered the only valid polemic. Because Aristotle's authority was firmly established in Catholic doctrine by St. Thomas Aquinas, few dared to introduce alternate methods of reasoning.

## Conflicts between Rationalism and Empiricism

Contrasting sharply to the dependence on intellectuality alone for the approach of classical philosophers to truth, the Christian approach in the nearly 1,700 years before the Enlightenment pivoted on the revelations of Jesus Christ.[21] All areas of study were subservient to theology. Not only did science deteriorate in the Roman world, but until the Renaissance, earthly phenomena had little significance in contrast to the transcendent, spiritual "reality." Scripture, prayer, and faith in the teachings of the church were considered the only sources of truth.

In the thirteenth century, Roger Bacon promoted the idea of empiricism by way of emphasizing the need to support convictions by experiment and observation.[22] Not surprisingly, in promoting his contention, he aroused the ire of the orthodoxy and spent fifteen years in prison. This immutable grip on philosophy and science by Aristotle via the orthodoxy persisted until the seventeenth century. At this time Francis Bacon successfully challenged Aristotle's nonempirical approach. Looking for an instrument of discovery to overshadow the limitations of deductive logic, he contended that to understand nature it is necessary to begin with observed fact rather than with prejudice about those facts. The notion of induction, however, was not new as Aristotle had already used it. Rejecting rationalism, Bacon was the first to state explicitly the great need for a new logic. Furthermore, he was a forceful individual, which was required to break the iron grip of the church's enchantment with Aristotelian philosophy.

This limitation to deductive logic for nearly 1,700 years is a tragic example of the great danger of allowing authority to dictate intellectual life. It can only be speculated how much further along civilization would have advanced if both deductive and inductive logic would have been accepted and utilized as methods of science throughout this long period.

George Johnson[23] contended that much of "the history of ideas has been driven by a tension between rationalism and empiricism." Rationalism is the belief that valid inquiry requires beginning with self-evident truths—*a priori*—from which nature's laws can be derived by deductive logic—predictions via general rules. The pure rationalists, therefore, rely solely on deductive logic. Introspective logic, however, is commonly wrong, and is a source of myth and self-deception. Unable to explain adequately the origin of self-evident truths, pure rationalists lose much of their credibility.

Elaborated by philosopher Morris Cohen,[24] all observations contain some assumptions, yet they have been false so often in science that they should always be recognized for what they are. Furthermore, *a priori* truth varies from one philosopher to another. On the other hand, science can never do without *a priori* or unproved universal propositions lest there be no starting point for any investigation nor sufficient basis for hypothesis.

An interesting twist on the nature of rationalism is derived from the enigmatic and close relationship between physics and mathematics.[25] Einstein believed that pure mathematical construction enables an understanding of the laws and concepts that connect these two disciplines. In this regard, he stated "In a certain sense, therefore, I hold that it is true that pure thought can grasp reality, as the ancients dreamed." Mathematics, in this sense, gives some stature to the claims of rationalists.

Empiricists believe that what can be known must come by way of the senses, and, therefore, rely on inductive reasoning, which is deriving general rules from observations. This kind of knowledge is called *a posteriori*. In this view, our brains begin as a blank slate, a *tabula rasa*, and as promoted by the philosopher John Locke, the founder of British empiricism, remain blank until the advent of experience. The concept of empiricism, held by a school of philosophers known as logical positivists or logical empiricists, is much more recent than rationalism.

Described by Johnson,[26] what we perceive may be a peculiarity of the structure of our brains. Science is a description of how the world interacts with the mind. So arises a major philosophical conundrum: "Is science invented or discovered?" Is science a part of nature, or is our idiosyncratic reality improvisation? If the abstract concept of Plato's ideal world of mathematics is equivalent to conditions for science, then it follows that science is discovered (Chapter 15). If the new things that are being created continuously are considered, as in the evolution of life, then some things are invented that are not improvisations of the human mind. Prediction and technology derived from science are consequences that verify some validity to discovery, not improvisation. Indeed, the universe is an ongoing, evolutionary phenomenon. At least to some degree, science is not human improvisation.

Philosophers have been aware since ancient times that our senses can color our observations. This point was used by René Descartes, among others, to defend his firm belief in rationalism and to denigrate empiricism. Our view of the world is but simply our highly limited personal reality. If, for example, we could see by means of the entire electromagnetic spectrum instead of by our limited visual spectrum, our view of the world would be enhanced greatly. On the other hand, our current brains would experience the proverbial, informational overload. Because of these limitations, we have an incomplete picture of nature and our interpretations are perforce distorted.

In addition to sense distortion of reality, early philosophers recognized that inductive inference can lead to erroneous conclusions. Today, philosophers recognize that science cannot be expected to yield flawless results. The shortcomings of deductive and inductive inference, without anything better, can be tolerated.

### More Pitfalls of Induction and Deduction

Induction is laden with even more difficult problems than that posed by the fallibility of our senses. Philosopher Wesley Salmon[27] observed that the most damaging criticism of induction came from the Scottish philosopher David Hume. How do we acquire knowledge of the unobserved? This has been tagged Hume's paradox. Never satisfactorily answered, this classic question is illustrated by observing 100 or more white swans and then concluding that all swans are white. That the next swan observed will not be black, is not a certainty. As a black swan is not inherently illogical, there is not a logical necessity for an inductive conclusion. Absolute empirical truth is myth, and existing knowledge does not ensure its future validity.

Already alluded to in Chapter 8, inductive conclusions are colored by our experience. Hume contended that there is "no idea without an antecedent impression."[28] Knowledge becomes the product of the interaction of our existing knowledge with new perceptions. Sociologist David Bloor[29] gave an example of this paradox by the followers of Ptolemy viewing the relative positions of the sun and earth differently than the followers of Copernicus.

The uncertainty of inductive knowledge is a critical point to remember in all observations and experimental work. Truth, though elusive, is worth pursuing, but its full grasp is beyond our reach. For theories to be acceptable, they must fit observed phenomena and allow successful predictions. They are pragmatically useful and enable further asymptotic strides toward truth. Every inductive conclusion, no matter how much its seeming truth is prized, may need modification if additional progress is to be made.

To the extent that the uncertainty of knowledge is kept in mind, scientists and technologists are less apt to become indelibly sold on a single explanation of a phenomenon. They are more apt to recognize flaws in concepts and to be receptive to change. Although little more than a platitude, it is of paramount concern to good science that there be a constant reminder that mind-sets and dogma are the nemeses of progress in knowledge. French artist George Braque was on target when he said, "Truth exists; only falsehood has to be invented."[30] Even more to the point, American humorist Josh Billings said, "It ain't what a man don't know that makes him a fool, but what he does know that ain't so."[31]

Wesley Salmon[32] made an important distinction between an inductive notion and a scientific inference. For example, we know inductively that the sun will rise and set everyday. This is different from the scientific inference that these events will happen each day. The way the solar system functions is known by the laws of physics, and this enables us to make astronomical predictions by virtue of knowing initial conditions. These physical laws are not experiential generalizations as are our inductive notions of the sun's relation to the earth.

Such inference is known as the hypothetico-deductive method, which is contrasted with induction by enumeration—inductive generalizations from instances. Salmon described the hypothetico-deductive method as follows: "From a general hypothesis and particular statements of initial conditions, a particular predictive statement is deduced. Statements of initial conditions, at least for the time, are accepted as true; the hypothesis is the statement whose truth is at issue. By observation we determine whether the predictive statement turned out to be true. If the predictive consequence is false, the hypothesis is disconfirmed. If observation reveals that the predictive statement is true, we say that the hypothesis is confirmed to some extent."

Philosopher Karl Popper recognized that, sharply contrasting with the uncertainty of inductive confirmation, all it takes for refutation is one negative datum.[33] Concluding that all swans are white, for example, is refuted by the observation of only one black swan. This is known as the method of falsification, but the reality is that very few scientists expedite this procedure. Furthermore, abundant room for speculation usually exists with respect to alternate explanations, making easy refutations a rarity.

Perhaps the greatest difficulty of Popper's approach is the human penchant for confirming a belief rather than refuting it. Neurobiologist Michael Gazziniga[34] saw our propensity for holding on to beliefs despite logical refutation to be astounding. People are prone to discredit methodology before they will discredit their personal beliefs. As Gazziniga explained, "We place a disproportionate amount of belief on evidence that supports an established theory and tend to discredit opposing evidence." This psychological aspect of people, or at least a flaw in our brain structure, like deeply held philosophical beliefs, is a major obstacle to discovery and creativity.

Perception of the world is built over a lifetime and is inscribed in a neural net in billions of cells throughout the brain. Only those new perceptions that fit our pattern of beliefs are apt to be acquired or can find a niche in our knowledge picture. Requiring such long-term effort to construct the neural network, it is imminently understandable that people defend beliefs with ferocious tenacity. They cling to many of their ideas, which may give the illusion of control and may solve some of their problems. Reconstruction of the neural net into a new picture of the world may come, if at all, with enormous difficulty. The result may be a profound loss of control or loss of belonging to a valued social group or superorganism.

A benefit arising from Popper's falsification theory is that it provides a mechanism for distinguishing science from pseudoscience. A theory must be falsifiable in the sense that it must be amenable to tests of validity. If reinterpretation is used as a defense, the theory has been made unfalsifiable and, therefore, unscientific. Astrology, for example, is constructed so as to be unfalsifiable. A theory, according to Popper, must be rejected with the first negative evidence. Because if it is falsifiable, it is still considered scientific. Paradoxically, a failed experiment generally provides a greater certainty of understanding than does a workable hypothesis.

Another aspect of the problem of induction was elaborated by mathematician John Casti[35] with respect to IQ tests. If one is asked the right or natural continuation of {1, 2, 4, 8} the expected answer probably is {16, 32, 64, 128}. It could have been {9, 11, 15} which is derived from the differences in the original sequence. In another sense it could have been {1, 2, 4, 8}, {who do we appreciate?}. Actually, the number sequence generally used is {2, 4, 6, 8} but the former serves the illustration. Clearly the context is essential before a natural sequence can be derived. Casti pointed out that science is directed by the historical and sociological beliefs ingrained in the scientific ideology of the dominant social group.

Illustrating the ease with which socially determined conceptions can influence thought processes is the following exchange of ideas. A man had just given his Chinese servant permission to attend the funeral of a friend, also Chinese. Jokingly, the man said, "I suppose you will follow the old Chinese custom of putting food on the grave."

"Yes, sir," he said.

Still laughing, the man said, "When do you suppose the food will be eaten?"

The servant responded calmly and respectfully, "As soon, sir, as the friend you buried last week will smell the flowers you put on his grave."

The experience of the Austrian physicist, Ludwig Boltzman, offers a dramatic example of how social climate influences scientific paradigms.[36] In the early part of the twentieth century, he attempted to sell his ideas on the atomic nature of matter. His theory of heat required the movement of atoms in accord with Newtonian mechanics. Boltzman argued vehemently with other scientists of the time, namely Ernest Mach and Wilhelm Ostwald. They contended that atoms are intellectual fictions and should be excluded from science.

Because of this demoralizing conflict and his failing health, Boltzman took his life in 1906. With notable irony, his concepts were verified a short time later by J.J. Thomson and Ernest Rutherford. Novelist and existentialist Feodor Mikhailovich Dostoyevski was keenly aware of the pain experienced by a man such as Boltzman, when he said, "If it were desired to crush a man completely, to punish him so severely that even the most hardened murderer would quail, it would only be needed to make his work absolutely pointless and absurd."[37]

### The Utility of Induction and Deduction

Observed by psychobiologist Henry Plotkin,[38] empiricism is not in concert with everyday experience. Common sense, in the short-term, dominates academic logic. One can travel to the same destination for many years by the same means without a flaw. Social relationships, on the other hand, often change rapidly, and Hume's skepticism about induction holds sway. For induction to be generally true, a much larger period is required. Continental drift and biological evolution are examples.

Logically correct, Hume's criticism of empiricism was a denial of the law of causality and of the principle of the uniformity of nature. He showed that these principles are not based on logic but on faith. Plotkin[39] indicated that Hume was saying that nature is never prescient. To some degree science is prescient, and correctness of predictions is fundamental to the quality of science. Plotkin saw science as an uncertainty detector, with degree of validity being measured by the extent to which uncertainty is reduced. All physical systems possess uncertainty, but a good idea can be gained as to the reasons why and to what degree. He concluded that "Such knowledge is an extraordinary achievement, as close to prescience as we will ever come. It is so close that one might want to judge it unnatural knowledge."

The modern conception of inquiry, which began with the scientific revolution, confirms the essential interaction of deductive and inductive reasoning. Science did not really begin until the symbiotic relation of rationalism and empiricism was recognized. Although never without respectability, the importance of deductive logic is emphasized by the perennial concern for making inductive logic respectable. Some have attempted to justify inductive logic by inductive methods, which is a circular argument. Insidiously, at least to empiricists, induction is justified by deductive reasoning.[40] Induction is the only way of obtaining generalizations or tentative facts about nature and is used with the assumption that the world is not deceptive. Despite its many flaws, induction is not discarded for reasoning. It is the most basic tool of the scientific method.

At the very beginning of life, knowledge must have begun with sensory experience. Intellect was long in coming. To this extent, therefore, the empiricists are correct. By virtue of knowledge storage in the gene pool, instincts, much of our knowledge has become innate. Giving credence to the rationalists, we now come into the world knowing what we must learn for survival. Plotkin[41] surmised, therefore, that some degree of truth is possessed by both rationalism and empiricism.

Casti[42] emphasized the importance of observation, and, therefore, inductive reasoning in an example of uncommon sense in science. If we can walk up stairs one step at a time, common sense demands that we can achieve the same goal by walking up a ramp. On the other hand, subatomic particles do not abide by the laws of common sense as witness the change in energy levels occurring in discrete or quantum steps. Most of nature is counterintuitive, and experiment, observation, and mathematics are the primary keys to understanding such unexpected phenomena. Whereas knowledge gained by induction and deduction is only an approximation, Casti points out that the best that scientists can do is to be vigilant, critical, and skeptical. Despite the uncertainty of knowledge, its reliability is increased by the elimination of fallacies.

## Paradoxes of Reasoning

To add insult to injury, physicist and writer William Poundstone[43] describes how the interplay of induction and deduction often leads to paradoxes exposing the defects in our thought systems. Philosopher Bertrand

Russell gave considerable attention to paradoxes and showed how they can arise with seeming correctness of thought. Beginning with two premises in a paradox, the deductive step leads to a conclusion that undermines the premises. The reason for the contradiction apparently arises from mistaken presuppositions.

Poundstone provided a book full of paradoxes, but the "twin paradox" will serve to illustrate the point. According to the special theory of relativity, time passes at different rates dependent on the observer's motion. If one were to travel at the speed of light, the past, the present, and the future would be compressed into an everlasting now, and so traveling near the speed of light, in effect, stops the clock. If one identical twin travels near the speed of light distant into space and then returns to earth, he will be years younger than his twin brother. Mistakenly considering time to be universal, French philosopher Henri Bergson saw this thought experiment as fallacious and, therefore, proof that relativity was wrong.

Today, the twin paradox is accepted. Cesium clocks transported around the world by jetliners in 1972 have shown that human passengers were a fraction of a second younger than they would have been had they not taken the trip. As explained by Poundstone, the unspoken but false premise of this paradox is that time is universal—a commonsense belief. Demonstrating again that common sense can be wrong, the twin paradox shows that this premise is untenable.

As deductive reasoning is common sense, its reliability can be as much in question as is inductive reasoning. The ubiquitous nature of paradoxes is another reason to be eternally alert and skeptical. Furthermore, it illustrates how easily common sense can lead people astray.

Abduction or hypothetical, analogical, and reductionist thinking in the next chapter will complete the processes of conventional thinking.

*Chapter 14*

# Stimulation:
# Conventional Thinking II

Knowledge gain, preparation, the dialectic, and deductive and inductive logic in the model for creativity and discovery can bring the researcher to a high level of understanding about nature. Without other ancillary methods of thinking, however, the advance of knowledge would be stagnant, indeed.

## ABDUCTION

Stagnation in science is often produced by the strict adherence to what seems to be the most likely explanation of a phenomenon. This impasse can be addressed by questioning all tenets and deriving and exploring all seemingly feasible hypotheses. Herculean efforts are made to generate every potentially feasible hypothesis and to explore each, lest the most viable and novel systems be missed. Although perhaps considered as standard procedure in scientific method, this approach is often contrary to practice. This is particularly true in industry in which inadequacy of time and resources and the pressure for immediate results may seem to preclude pursuing anything other than what seems to be the most likely solution. The mistaken notion exists that under the circumstances such a limited procedure will lead to the greatest productivity. This attitude can be a colossal mistake. Exploring all possible solutions, holding out for the most creative, is the best path, at least long-term, to maximum productivity and to creativity as well.

One way in which the most cryptic hypotheses can be stimulated into awareness is through the process of "metaphorming." In his book *Breaking the Mind Barrier*, Todd Siler[1] coined this term, which is simply the process of forming metaphors. As the originator of neurocosmology, he promoted studying the universe by showing the relation of the human brain to the cosmos. As science is the interaction of the senses with reality, special credence is given to such metaphorming.

In neurocosmology, brain processes are considered to be an extension of the cosmos and vice versa. For example, nuclear fusion and fission processes may relate to similar processes in the brain. Creativity may be a fusion process by which both hemispheres of the brain may merge in thought and cooperatively generate a novel idea. Such brain activity, inspiration, has been observed in electroencephalographic recordings as high amplitude alpha waves and lower amplitude theta and beta waves.

In contrast, reasoning may be a fission process representing asymmetrical cerebration where one hemisphere dominates the thought process. Requiring learning a great deal about the human brain, an unusually broad array of metaphors can be established between prospective disciplines and the human nervous system. By this mechanism, probing the abyss of the imagination is made easier, and more insightful hypotheses can be formulated. Everything in the universe, presumably, is connected and interrelated, and the most profound understanding of phenomena comes from understanding their relationships to other things.

Exploration of all feasible hypotheses relates to vertical versus lateral thinking, and these kinds of thinking will be considered in greater detail in Chapter 16. In lateral thinking, which helps to promote creativity, all possible approaches to problems are considered for their relative merits. This is opposed to vertical thinking in which the efforts are concentrated on what at first seems to be the most effective method. The point of the lateral approach is to find the optimum path. It is critical, however, that only those hypotheses are pursued that seem to have a possibility of being true; otherwise the game could be lost to time.

In emphasizing the need to maintain an open mind to a broad spectrum of possibilities, it is helpful to recognize that hypotheses control the nature, direction, and potential success of science as well. If one follows only the approach that seems most viable, more effective and creative approaches often are missed. If all potential solutions are investigated, the probability of finding the best approach is enhanced greatly.

A major problem is introduced in the investigation of all likely hypotheses when one considers the underdetermination thesis.[2] This is the principle that an infinite number of theories can describe a set of experimental data. It creates the greatest problem in fields with little mathematical foundation, such as the social sciences and biology. In physics, mathematics reduces the number of possibilities to a more manageable level. Aesthetics as in elegance, insightful data selection, integrity of explanation, power of prediction, and correspondence to empirical data must all be used to select theory. With these guidelines, the underdetermination thesis can be subdued with insight and objectivity.

Biologist Lewis Wolpert[3] pointed out that psychological studies of Apollo moon scientists have shown that those deemed the most creative were also the most resistant to idea change. All of these scientists found the objective, emotionally disinterested characterization of scientists to be fallacious. This suggests a dilemma where the most creative scientists develop the most resistance to change because of their successes, thus tending to suppress their own innate creativity. On the other hand, such people generally develop more incisive insight and, justifiably, are less willing to change from what they view as a seemingly good idea to less promising approaches. Nevertheless, continued creativity can be promoted by being on guard, and doggedly maintaining the original broad perspective that must have been an essential part of the researchers' creative successes.

Although it had been believed that hypotheses were the result of either deduction or induction, dependent on philosophical bias, philosopher C.S. Peirce conceived that neither view was adequate.[4] To account for hypothetical thinking, he proposed a new process, which he called "abduction." The process is one of finding other potentially viable hypotheses, which leads to the tentative adoption of the most feasible explanation to save an appearance. The validity of an hypothesis is determined by deduction, which is seeing if it fits the facts, but its acceptance is a matter of abduction. Hypotheses are necessarily tentative, and as new facts are garnered, appearances change and new or modified hypotheses can evolve.

Hypothesizing or abductive thinking in science is a primary source of stimulation. Being the vectors of potential progress and, therefore, springboards for action, hypotheses are essential to scientific method whether they lead to verification or refutation. A new fragment of knowledge can be wasted if it is viewed strictly as rote memory, but offers much greater benefit if it is viewed as discovery. What impact does this new knowledge have on existing knowledge? Is a new hypothesis warranted for the sake of appearance? Is more than one new hypothesis justified? For the greatest chance of creativity, pursue all new, reasonable hypotheses in the interest of lateral thinking and its common association with novelty.

For greatest reward technologists can pursue new knowledge from both the standpoints of science and technology. What are the scientific and technologic ramifications? What new questions are raised by this new knowledge, and, therefore, what new research is indicated? What new products might be derived from this new knowledge? How can new application ideas be reduced to practice in the plant? Extensive ideation sessions on the relationship of new knowledge to application can be surprisingly fruitful. Such exercises are essential to discovery and to intellectual growth, and represent prime mechanisms for growing technologically beyond the competition.

## PARADIGMATIC THINKING

Scientists either pursue "normal" or "revolutionary" science. In normal science, investigations are directed to reinforce or enlarge an established body of knowledge. Revolutionary science is concerned with the leading edge of knowledge, largely within the unknown or unexplored regions of nature. Depending on which area a scientist pursues, his state of mind and the way he approaches problems can take on a distinctly different character.

Working within an established paradigm, the normal scientist need not establish new theory. Revolutionary science is replete with uncertainty, and inordinate effort is required to make a significant contribution. New approaches are constantly sought in an effort to penetrate the seemingly impenetrable shell of the unknown.

Generally being developed within an established scientific paradigm, technology is considered to be normal science. If the basic science is understood, technological targeted research becomes feasible and is largely algorithmic. On the other hand, studying the technical obstacles to targeted research may entail basic or applied science. This new knowledge can lead to the reconstitution of existing knowledge into a novel, holistic pattern. Such effort might be classified, then, as revolutionary technology. Certainly invention transcends conventional wisdom and, in that sense, entails a new or modified paradigm of technology.

That scientists work within a distinctive paradigm was a conclusion of philosopher Thomas Kuhn in his work, *The Structure of Scientific Revolutions.*[5] A scientific paradigm, in the broad sense, as defined by psychologist Marc De Mey,[6] is "the whole set of shared beliefs and skills which shape the expectations of a community of scientists and establish a common directionality in their activities." In developing his concept about scientific revolution structure, Kuhn was perplexed that a man of Aristotle's brilliance could be so wrong about nature.[7] By viewing ancient Greece in the context of the time, Kuhn then realized that Aristotle's view was common sense. It was natural thinking to believe that material bodies have spirits such that bodies like air rise and bodies like earth fall.

From this observation Kuhn extrapolated that scientists work within a paradigm derived from their environment. The precise nature of the paradigm is controlled by the dominant scientists within the community. As science is about consensus, to a large extent, publicity and selling of ideas becomes paramount. Therefore, some sociologists characterize science as a social construct.

Neglecting the importance of new tools in promoting scientific revolutions, Kuhn developed his thinking around concept-driven revolutions. Physicist Freeman Dyson[8] points out that most of the recent scientific revolutions have been tool-driven. Examples are the double-helix revolution, driven by X-ray technology and structural models, and the big-bang revolution, promoted by the measurement of the red-shift shown by the Doppler effect.

Concept-driven revolutions are much less common, but an example is the plate-tectonic revolution of the 1960s. Although the German geologist Alfred Wegener presented his evidence in 1915, it was not accepted until there was a conceptual framework in which his evidence could fit. In the new concept, plates of crustal rock were ever so slowly being destroyed and regenerated by being subsumed on one side of mid-ocean ridges and by moving out on the other. In this revolution, the new concept permitted the sudden acceptance of long-neglected evidence that contradicted dogma.

Kuhn's one-sided approach to scientific revolutions left many people to believe that science is a subjective struggle between opposing points of view. The larger picture shows that science is much more an objective struggle among the vicissitudes of nature, the precision of tools, and the development of concepts that fit the data. This precludes science being viewed strictly as a social construct.

Despite its utility for enabling the scientist to know what research to do, the basic problem with a scientific paradigm is that it dictates research direction. It is a tunnel vision that delimits what can be observed. Paradigms are preconceptions that commonly preclude open-mindedness and promote blindness to other possibilities. Thus, the concepts of reality are molded by the idiosyncratic nature of paradigms and are reshaped only by paradigm shifts. Such shifts come about usually with great pain. Sometimes, it requires the death of a dominant scientist before a paradigm shift can occur.

Sociologist David Bloor[9] made an important distinction between the evils of preconception and its necessity to the pursuit of scientific inquiry. In so doing he alluded to Durkheim's discussion of crime in his *Rules of Sociological Method*. Durkheim contended that if we were to exert sufficient pressure to eliminate crime, other problems would become major social problems and would suppress important forces promoting diversity and individuality. Although crime is to be deplored, the effort to reduce it without limits is a misunderstanding of how society functions. Similarly, the misperceptions sometimes created by paradigms are also a necessary consequence for the pursuit of knowledge.

Newtonian gravitation, Darwinian evolution, Einsteinian relativity, and the Watson-Crick double helix model of DNA are some of the classic revolutions of modern science. They altered paradigms and made a mockery of common sense. The old guard accepted these new concepts, if at all, with great difficulty. Discoveries generally arise unexpectedly, and they are commonly resisted if they depart significantly from the conventional wisdom of the scientific community.

Pointed out by chemist Henry Bauer,[10] it is this conservatism that gives credence to the reliability of science. The new concept must be filtered through many different people and experimental situations before it can become established as textbook science. Einstein, in stark contrast, departed significantly from this conservatism and was truly a rebel. He made breakthroughs because he did not accept the paradigms of the time, insisting on going back to first principles and on originating his own ideas. It is this complex of liberal-conservative approaches that enables science to progress with high credibility.

A major paradigm shift or revolution was Copernicus' reintroduction of the heliocentric theory of planetary movement. Howard Margolis described this revolution in science in great detail.[11] Not only did the proposal of heliocentricity have a climactic effect on both the scientific and the clerical world of that time; but for those who saw merit in his concept, a new physics was required. No longer to be considered as static at the center of the universe, the Earth was seen as in orbit around a stationary sun—necessitating the revision of terrestrial mechanics.[12] Why other earthly bodies fell to the Earth, why the Earth did not leave its atmosphere, and why a stone thrown straight up fell straight down were some of the questions to be answered. Such questions, on reflection and attendant with the knowledge of that time, give credence to the pre-Copernican commonsense view that the Earth was fixed in space.

As elaborated by Margolis, "The Copernican discovery was a landmark to the recognition by the masses that radical discovery was indeed possible, and that knowledge held to be sacrosanct could be effectively challenged by the courageous." This was a scientific revolution of major proportions; the explosion of innovation in the seventeenth century, according to Margolis, can be attributed to the demonstration effect by Copernicus and to the printing technology of Gutenberg. Of equal importance, the further development of the scientific method played a critical role in the scientific revolution.

The major work done by most scientists is normal science.[13] This amounts, largely, to data collection and refining the existing paradigm. It is the final stage of scientific discovery. In contrast, significant shifts in theory are a consequence of scientists who have the insight and the perseverance to recognize and explain anomalies from a fresh perspective. In a sense, the discovery picks the discoverer or the revolutionary scientist.[14] Discovery is biased toward the individual who is independent of thought, who is determined to discover, and who is primed with knowledge and ideas. Furthermore, the number of discoveries and inventions is independent of the number of investigators. Increasing linearly, discovery is largely dependent on the number and divergence of concepts and techniques in the field.

The overwhelming majority of scientists follow Kuhnian normal science. They simply increase the reservoir of knowledge within the conventional paradigm, and these data increase exponentially. Professional meetings are generally replete with papers covering similar problems using similar techniques, not only at the same meeting but at those meetings in subsequent years. Such fads, although not entirely without merit, are not only infectious but can be devastating to the cause of creativity and discovery. The publish or perish dilemma of some academicians further accentuates this easy publication track.

In stark conflict with Kuhn's theory of scientific revolutions, psychologist Jean Piaget saw continuity in the growth of science. Philosopher and historian of science Arthur Miller[15] describes Piaget's idea of how new concepts emerge from those already established in the brain. This is the enigma of creativity, which comes about, according to Piaget, by the assimilation/accommodation process. New data can disequilibrate existing data. Metaphorical reasoning enables the accommodation of the new data, which may lead then to a modified hypothesis. The ease with which one can accommodate and assimilate new data is a measure of individual creativity. Permitted by causal theory, this is the concept of continuous change. It is how Piaget believed that new theories evolve from old ones. Miller asserts that historical studies show that scientific progress corresponds most closely to Piaget's explanation.

The creative thinker generally begins his research with an existing research tradition. He then moves away cautiously and incrementally to a complete overthrow of the original paradigm.[16] An example of this process was provided by Kepler when he experimented with ovoids, instead of circles, to explain the orbits of the planets. After extensive failure and mathematical difficulties, he then tried the ellipse with which he finally succeeded. This incremental approach was, indeed, successful in establishing a new paradigm, but the process was one of continuity, not abrupt change. Revolutions in science are generally not sharp demarcations; old concepts usually persist with new meanings.

Also in stark contrast to Kuhn, physicist Alan Cromer[17] saw science as overwhelmingly cumulative. Revolutions have occurred, but he contends that just as Archimedes' principle is still taught today in much the same way it was first stated, some of Greek science is still valid today. He saw atomic theory as essentially complete knowledge, and that there are no new elements to be discovered having fewer than ninety-eight protons. Atoms and genes are certainties as much so as the word processors with which we write.

Most of the established results in science will be around as long as science exists. Further theoretical development will proceed and will enfold existing knowledge rather than replace it. The uncertainty of science, in this sense, is much more a problem of its leading edge.

## ANALOGY

Creative work has its beginnings with what is known and what has been done before. An invention may begin with a retrieval from memory of an analogy that could potentially be modified to solve a problem. It is an extension of the past, but it can become creative through the incorporation of new knowledge that is interacted in novel and useful ways. As the quantity of relevant information is increased, the potential for arriving at a creative solution is also increased. Without cultural antecedents, as similar machines or theories, the natural world may be used, as birds became a model for the Wright brothers in wing-warping.

Analogical thinking, therefore, is a critical aspect of creative thinking. Weisburg[18] referred to this thought process of extending the past as "continuity of thinking." Discontinuities develop with feedback and external stimuli, which can lead to new viable relationships that may result in a change of the solution mode. Those who produce creative works of great distinction do so because of inordinately high levels of knowledge (analogues and associations), mastered skills, both intuitive and logical thinking, external stimuli, and irrepressible motivation. Profound immersion within a domain cannot be emphasized enough as a prerequisite to the creation of novelty.

Analogical thinking is a common method of problem solving, and two examples described by psychologist Keith Holyoak serve to describe the mechanism.[19] You are a doctor for a patient having a malignant tumor in his stomach. Operation is impossible. For the patient to live, however, the tumor must be removed. At high intensity, radiation will destroy the tumor, but the contacted healthy tissue will be destroyed also. At lower intensities the healthy tissue will not be harmed, but the tumor will not be affected either. How can the radiation be used to destroy the tumor without harming the healthy tissue? According to Holyoak, few people solve this problem. The solution is irradiation from multiple directions simultaneously with low intensity rays. By convergence of the rays at the tumor, the additive effect will result in the required high intensity without destroying the adjacent healthy tissue.

Now consider another problem posed by Holyoak. A general was intent on capturing a fortress located in the middle of a country. Many roads radiated out from the fortress, but they were all mined. Small groups could traverse the roads without setting off the mines, but the general wished to use his entire army. Solution to the problem is analogous to the solution for the radiation problem. The general divided his men into small groups dispatching each to the head of a different road, and then had all the groups converge simultaneously on the fortress. Analogy with the radiation problem served to restructure the fortress problem such that solution was easy. And, if one had understood the solution to the fortress problem before hearing the radiation problem, solution could have been assisted. Frequently, problems can be restructured into forms that we know how to approach, or into forms that are solvable by virtue of analogy.

Psychologist Robert Keegan[20] suggested that the acquisition of expert knowledge in at least one field is a requisite for scientific creativity. By this mechanism a thought-form is constructed which is then used in other disciplines—thinking by analogy. This was the method of Darwin who first gained expert knowledge in geology which he used as the foundation for understanding in other areas of science. Darwin patterned much of his thinking after the English geologist Charles Lyell who contended that geological change occurs gradually. Using this concept, Darwin disputed Lyell's contention that different types of coral reefs have different geologic histories. Instead he argued that they form by similar processes but are different by virtue of different degrees of subsidence.

This central idea of Darwin's thought-form, "gradualism," persisted in the development of his theory of evolution. Although this thought-form was notably useful in deriving a theory of evolution, it also promoted a tunnel vision. It precluded, for instance, recognition of the potential merit of punctuated equilibrium,[21] as proposed by Niles Eldredge and Stephen Jay Gould. This concept claims that species do not change very much and that evolution is seen in the sudden appearance of new species, which is empirically shown by some aspects of the fossil record. Sometimes the change is extremely slow, and this inconsistency of change, punctuated equilibrium, led some to believe that it cannot be explained by conventional evolutionary theory. Although now largely discredited as a new theory of evolution, the proposal promoted an invaluable reappraisal of evolutionary theory.

Models of population genetics predict that natural selection can be so rapid that it will appear instantaneous in geological time. Presumably, the rapid change of life forms is not abrupt but occurs over many generations in small increments, which, nevertheless, is fast enough to look like an abrupt change in the fossil record. Equally important, the models allow for long periods of little or no detectable evolution. Such predictions have been upheld by extensive study for a wide range of organisms, and seem to preclude refutation of neo-Darwinian theory (explains evolution by natural selection and population genetics).[22]

Despite the seeming refutation of punctuated equilibrium as a displacement of conventional evolutionary theory, an important point can still be made about the dangers of adhering too closely to a thought-form. Darwin noted this nongradual aspect of the fossil record but considered it to be an imperfection in the record, which in a sense it was. In the interest of considering all possibilities, punctuated equilibrium should have been weighed even in his time. Although discredited as a new paradigm, the idea lead to invaluable research on rates of evolutionary change and by that means has greatly enriched the knowledge pool of evolution. Thinking by analogy potentially can have broad implications in the development of creative concepts. On the other hand, stubborn adherence to one thought-form may preclude even more viable approaches to problems.

Recognition of analogies that may help in problem solution can be tricky. To minimize interference, analogies have similar story lines, the objects in each are similar with comparable roles, and information is extensive. Sluggishness of analogical transfer, therefore, can be the basis of impasses in problem solving. Transfer is enhanced by understanding the role of analogies in problem solving, and by instruction on the use of experience.[23]

Analogical thinking or associationist thinking is problem solving by preexisting responses known as "habits."[24] In contrast, Gestalt thinking (holistic) is the process of interrelating each aspect of a problem. The approach results in understanding how all of the parts fit together to satisfy problem solution. Gestaltists attempt to create novel solutions, whereas the associationists attempt to solve problems based on experience.

Prior experience can simplify but sometimes may even inhibit problem solution. Witness the nine-dot problem in Figures 16.1 and 16.2, in which convention generally precludes seeking a solution outside of the confines of the problem or the area delineated by the outer dots. Psychologists call this block to problem solution, functional fixedness—a mental block against new ways to solve problems.

## REDUCTIONISM

An idea of great import that developed during the scientific revolution was that problems could be made easier to solve by breaking them into their component parts—reductionism. Prior to the time of Galileo, the approach to problems was made extremely difficult, if not impossible, by the effort to solve problems from the view of the whole. Seeking to understand the most elementary subatomic particles rather than studying the whole atom is an example of reductionism. Concepts are reduced to ever deeper explanations via mathematics, with logic being the ultimate reduction. Introduced by the French philosopher René Descartes, this method was named "the method of detail" by British philosopher John Stuart Mill.[25]

Although the reductionist approach does not require a particular philosophy of nature, its development was coincident with the growth of mechanistic philosophy. Problems that seemed otherwise unapproachable were much more readily analyzed and solved by studying the component parts as separate entities. With mathematics, scale drawing, scientific method, and mechanistic philosophy, the method of detail had a monumental influence on the scientific revolution, the invention of new machines, and the development of industry. Today, reductionism is still the primary approach to scientific and technological problems, but holism is making gains (Chapter 14).

Believing that God had created the world solely for man's use in accord with his selfish needs precluded an understanding of how easily the balance of nature could be upset. Viewed simply as a machine, the world could be retrofitted as people saw fit. The relationship of the parts to the whole was usually ignored which, according to Pacey,[26] is the root cause of twentieth-century environmental problems. Reductionism became established as a natural route for progress.

Attitudes toward reductionism are greatly influenced by the underlying science.[27] In the social sciences, as anthropology, sociology, and psychology, reductionism is believed to be powerless to address emergent complexity, as the emergence of life from certain organic systems. In the natural sciences, such as physics and chemistry, reductionism is greatly respected and is a necessary route for establishing systematic relationships between different disciplines.

Sensations such as pain, happiness, or the flow experience of discovery are believed by some to be beyond materialism or reduction. Human behavior is held understandable only in relation to holism, or the nonlinearity of emergent properties derived from interactions within the whole body. The interaction between classical valence chemistry and quantum physics illustrates the importance of holistic approaches to some problem solving. Characterizing the quantum nature of electronic shells around an atom's nucleus and electron-sharing between atoms permitted the reconstruction of the electronic structure of elements, laws of valence-bonding, and the periodic table.

Rarely used to its maximum utility, holism properly carried out often leads to creativity and is classified as unconventional. Its relationship to reductionism is described in greater detail in the next chapter, along with sundry other methods of unconventional thinking—primary pathways to creativity and discovery.

# Chapter 15

# Stimulation:
# Unconventional Thinking I

Conventional, reductionist thinking contributes significantly to science and technology, but it also promotes the status quo. Reaching the modern concept of the scientific method was the product of the Enlightenment and of a consequent revolution in science. This freed Middle Ages Europe from enslavement to mysticism and allowed reason to power intellectual growth. Invention gained a tremendous boost from the newfound rationalism, but unconventionality was the subtle, often hidden, dimension of successful innovation.

Thought processes leading to invention and new viable theory generally deviate from established patterns, and unconventional thought becomes a major conduit for creative illumination. "A man whose only tool is a hammer analyzes every problem in terms of nails." This old expression applies emphatically to the discovery process. As pointed out by psychologist Howard Bloom, "Without the hammer of antidepressants, the doctor once denied the existence of adolescent depression."[1] Without the hammer of unconventional thinking, creativity and discovery, indeed, would be rare phenomena.

Conventional thinking, as deductive and inductive, are used to confirm or reject hypotheses and commonly have little immediate relationship to discovery. Contradictions to conventional beliefs in science are the source of discovery. Not until such conflicts are recognized and explained by hypotheses, however, does conventional thought take a firm grip.

Helping to preserve intellectual purity, the aseptic qualities of scientific articles exclude the chaos, the bias, the serendipity, the intuition, and the sometimes embarrassing mistakes that have led to discovery. Similarly, the esoteric thought processes that have been used are not revealed and are generally hidden from the consciousness of even the discoverer. The interaction of the left brain and the right brain is as important to discovery as are the empirical facts that have led to superior understanding. Revelation of all related thought processes is a potential key to additional discovery.

Each person develops an idiosyncratic paradigm for thinking, and differences are probably as indeterminately varied as are people. It is the belief of some, particularly philosophers, that verbalization is essential to thought. Disputing this idea, mathematician and physicist Roger Penrose[2] noted that his own mathematical thought is nonverbal, largely geometrical. Sometimes when he had been concentrating on a mathematical thought and was suddenly engaged in conversation, several seconds were required to find words. Perhaps he had been thinking with the right hemisphere of his brain in such great depth that seeking verbalization in the left hemisphere caused this delay.

Visual-spatial thinking was essential to Einstein's conception of his relativity theories. Presumably different modes of thinking can achieve similar high levels of intellectuality, which Penrose exemplified by the ideal Platonic world of mathematics. After seeing a mathematical truth, contact with this world is made exclusively via the intellect. Mathematicians use many different kinds of thought processes that enable them to contact this esoteric world. The benefits of diverse modes of thinking are equally applicable to all areas of creativity and discovery.

Several, though not definitive, unconventional methods of thinking used by creative people are shown in Figure 15.1. These methods can be assimilated and utilized to enhance one's ability to conceive in a novel way.

## SYNTHETIC, HOLISTIC, OR NETWORK THINKING

Illustrating the importance of networking in animals other than ourselves, psychologist Howard Bloom appealed to the intelligence relationship between chimpanzees and baboons.[3] Much less intelligent than chimpanzees who can make their own tools, baboons are relatively dumb. Baboons, nevertheless, are a much more successful species. This is shown by their rapidly increasing numbers and their superior adaptation to new environments. Opposed to chimpanzees which are being decimated, baboons are widely spread primates, second only to humans. Having a vastly superior social web over that of chimpanzees, baboons are superb practitioners of group creativity, and in that fashion have outwitted their more intelligent cousins.

This kind of chance occurrence, group creativity, selected by the evolutionary process, has been one of the most progressive and powerful tools for the evolution of life from the beginnings of single-celled organisms to the most complex, multicellular organisms. Networking in the evolutionary process has been transformed by *Homo sapiens* into an equally powerful

- Synthetic, holistic, or network—interaction of knowledge patterns
- Pyramidal—exhaustive approach to problem solving
- Elegant theory—may preclude empiricism
- Fuzz—multivalent logic, true, false, and indeterminate
- Lateral—searching many paths to find the optimum
- Knowledge-based—broad knowledge-based approach to problems
- Heuristic Search—establishing rules of thumb for problem solving in systems having countless solution possibilities
- Janusian—showing that opposites can be true simultaneously in the same space
- Visual-Spatial—mental imagery
- Homospatial—synthesis of simultaneous perceptions
- Metaphorical—establishing similarities, character, and limits to problems via different phenomena
- Hemispherical—thinking influenced by brain asymmetry

**Figure 15.1.** Some unconventional thought processes.

thought-form for the advancement of knowledge. Such thinking involves the interaction of multiple patterns of knowledge and is variously referred to as synthesis, network, or holistic. In such systems the parts are interacted such that their collective behavior is more complex than the noninteractive sum. This kind of thinking is one of the most powerful tools of science. Reduction of phenomena to their elements is generally how science advances, but it is only the first phase of science. Reconstitution of these elements to understand the working of the whole, for example, ecosystems, is perhaps the penultimate goal of science. Perhaps the ultimate goal of science is the reduction of knowledge to the laws of physics.

As reasoned by German philosopher Georg Wilhelm Friedrich Hegel, progression of concept understanding eventually ends, which is the Absolute. This, Hegel believed, to be the only reality from which it follows that no portion of the whole has any meaning.[4] Even found among the pre-Socratics, this concept of synthesis recurs throughout history and is a common interpretation of quantum mechanical theory. In Einstein's general relativity ($E = mc^2$) neither the energy nor the mass of a system can be characterized at any particular location, thereby becoming a synthetic concept.[5] Mass can become energy and energy can become mass.

Physicist Fritjof Capra,[6] in his systems approach to reality, promoted the holistic concept—the essential interrelatedness and interdependence of all phenomena. Such a concept stems from the strange behavior of subatomic matter that cannot be understood as isolated parts. Quantum theory has shown that subatomic particles are probability patterns, which are interconnected inseparably throughout the universe. At this fundamental level, things do not have intrinsic properties, and all properties are about relationships between things. This includes the consciousness of the human observer. For example, according to Capra, the electron does not have properties independent of investigators' minds. If they ask a wave question, they will get a wave answer, and if they ask a particle question, they will get a particle answer. Both the systems theory of Capra and Hegel's concept of the Absolute have obvious limitations in application.

The ultimate concept of holism, the interdependency of everything within the universe, suggested by quantum mechanics, seems to be made meaningless by Einstein's speed limit, the speed of light. Such all-inclusive holism necessitates infinite speed and simultaneous action throughout space. Unless tachyons (Chapter 6) can be demonstrated to exist or some other demonstrable explanation can be derived, infinite speed has no substantiation. Physicists Tony Rothman and George Sudarshan explain this paradox by the observation that correlated subatomic particles are nondecomposable (Chapter 6), which precludes the necessity of subliminal speed. At least in the macroscopic world, holism must be considered within the practical limits of inclusion. Some metaphysically inclined people transmogrify quantum holism into mystical notions of the universe which have never been demonstrated to exist.

Because what we investigate is always finite, our interpretations of natural phenomena are necessarily provisional.[7] Our world is nonlinear, but we study it by linear methods, which is the fundamental basis of uncertainty principles. The noninteractive sum of the parts behaves differently than the interactive whole. Making ultimate truth inaccessible, it is a convenient but essential simplification to study an isolated phenomenon and to consider everything else to be irrelevant. Simplification is a restructuring process that simplifies problem solution, which is seemingly out of reach by any other method. Reductionism, therefore, is a necessary simplification, and this distortion of reality enables us to gain at least a pragmatic approximation of how nature functions. After the parts are understood, it is easier to study the interrelationship of all of the parts.

In support of synthetic concepts, science has shown that nature is understood from an ever expanding framework, and new relationships are continuously being discovered.[8] Enzymes have been shown to be effective catalysts in some heavy chemical plants. Computer programs developed for X-ray scanning of the brain were later shown to be useful for seismic prospecting of oil fields. Microscopic study of radiation damage in plastic films was subsequently found applicable to the detection of cosmic radiation, among many examples. It is in interdisciplinary areas that science experiences the greatest vigor.

According to philosopher Bertrand Russell,[9] everything is related to everything else, but he did not believe that things necessarily change by being connected to something else. "You can know something without knowing everything about it; you can use a word intelligently without knowing the entire vocabulary." Thus, to conclude, as did Hegel, that no portion of the whole has any meaning is to deny the seeming correctness of Russell's rationale. Furthermore, such holistic concepts negate progress in science and proclaim its futility. Great progress in technology and predictive science refute such pessimistic notions.

David Bohm and David Peat,[10] both physicists, deplored fragmentation in science, the increasing isolation of developing disciplines, and were strong proponents of holism. Fragmentation causes an ever increasing confusion of communication making the viable interaction of different disciplines more difficult. As this difficulty increases, the potential for creativity decreases.

This brings us to the practical problem of reductionism versus holism. If the parts are understood, a limited form of holism can be an invaluable approach to creativity and problem solution. Bohm and Peat illustrated the concepts of reductionism and holism by the example of a smashed watch— the study of the isolated parts has little to do with the synchronized working of the whole. The assembly of the parts leads to an emergent property of timekeeping. This is what British philosopher Gilbert Ryle[11] called Ghostly Emergence—a property that cannot be understood by knowledge of the pieces alone. He made this reference, however, to ridicule dualism— the belief that the brain and mind are separate entities.[12] All machines, all life, and most phenomena in nature have this nonlinear property of emergence. It is a synergistic property where the interaction of the parts creates a whole that is greater than the sum of the parts. Nonlinearity is a dominant principle of creativity and a dominant theme in the new science of complexity.

A close relation exists between chaos and complexity, and these areas of science are often referred to collectively as chaoplexology. In this science, emergence of order, exclusive of vitalism, is considered a fundamental internal property of complex dynamical systems—as the emergence of cities and states from social groups or the emergence of an inspiration from a chaotic complex of thoughts. Chaoplexologists characteristically argue that traditional reductionism cannot solve complex problems. Both approaches are important, and there can be a judicious balance in their use.

Suggested by visual artist and neurocosmologist Todd Siler,[13] the level of fragmentation in science may reach a point where reductionism no longer produces coherent results. Reductionism does seem to have a lower limit—quarks, neutrinos, and electrons, for example, presumably cannot be reduced to smaller particles. The only alternative to their characterization seems to be to determine their relationships with other things and their consequent behavior. If this, indeed, is the case, then, as conjectured by theoretical physicist Lee Smolin, infinitesimals may have several potential properties as influenced by their nearest neighbors.[14] Although there is no evidence to draw this conclusion, synthesis seemingly would become the only route to greater understanding. "If elementary particles are so influenced, then perhaps their properties are not absolute and eternal. Instead, to understand a quark or an electron, we may have to know something about the history or organization of the universe."

Although the holistic approach cannot always be achieved practically, it can be used effectively much more than it is. Despite the fact that most of nature is more than the sum of the parts, reductionism implies that the parts are all that can be. Characterizing isolated phenomena without considering their relationship to other things trivializes the significance of research investigations and excludes recognition of important connections.

The late Senator William Proxmire's "Golden Fleece Awards" of the 1980s for what he considered to be trivial, inane research seems to have arisen largely because of his poor understanding of the complexity of the scientific process. Perhaps some of this poor understanding could have been averted by virtue of more holistic considerations by the researchers. Molecular biologist Seymour Benzer was nominated for the "Golden Fleece Award" and the Nobel Prize in the same year.[15]

Society, on the other hand, could not function efficiently without reductionism. For example, the field of medicine is so vast that it would be impossible, often, to obtain efficient care without the knowledge of specialists. Unless the parts are understood first, it would not be possible to treat the whole with efficiency. The necessity of specialization is generally true throughout the sciences, and becomes increasingly true with increase in complexity. To effectively use the holistic approach, one must have learned the basics associated with a broad range of knowledge, especially scientific. Until the advent of such a broad perspective, understanding the components of the whole, holistic approaches to problems can be futile.

Overemphasis of reductionism, however, is the rule rather than the exception, particularly in universities where students are trained within the narrow perspective of a confining discipline. Despite the necessity of this approach to address highly specific problems, such as in medical practice, efforts to greatly broaden scientific training would help deepen perspective. Knowledge depth in many areas is sufficient to begin the onerous but potentially highly profitable exercise of integrating all scientific endeavor. Although of great difficulty, such an approach, according to neurobiologist Robert Ornstein and biologist Paul Ehrlich,[16] would have the greatest potential for advancing civilization. As emphasized throughout this book, it is the interaction of a broad range of knowledge patterns that is fundamental to invention.

Industrial research, by necessity, usually approaches problems more holistically than does academe. For example, assume that an industrial minerals company has just discovered some important new knowledge about an industrial mineral. This new knowledge gives them the opportunity to develop new products. To understand how the potential new product technology can be used to enhance profit, it would be interacted not only with much of that mineral science but with much of the knowledge associated with many potential areas of application. Additionally, it would be interacted with the nature of the available crude mineral, plant logistics, customer needs, and cost-effectiveness. The common difficulty in industry, however, is that this process of diverse knowledge interaction generally becomes highly fragmented as well. Fundamental scientists may do the initial work to delineate the useful knowledge. Applied scientists may interact the new knowledge with different areas of application. Engineers and accountants may evaluate plant logistics and cost-effectiveness. Marketing specialists may evaluate market potential.

Although one individual may not have the time nor the resources to carry out all evaluation, to gain the greatest benefit, he or she would follow each investigation in-depth. This would be done to understand the impact of the new concept both technologically and scientifically. Potential technological problems that invariably arise with the process of innovation would be considered as well. Individuals who assume this responsibility grow holistically and cultivate the broadest and most fertile field of knowledge for the growth of creative ideas. Such individuals may be thought of as champions, but their responsibilities would go much deeper than in the conventional sense. By analogy they would be the Leonardo da Vincis or the Renaissance people of modern industry. They would have the responsibility not only for expediting new product development but for understanding, in-depth, all parameters of the knowledge interaction. This means that such people, preferably, would be experienced technologists who would explore, with broad brush strokes, new product concepts scientifically, technologically, logistically, and economically.

Individuals who develop into such broad company experts become the people most capable of originating and developing new products. They are not only the Renaissance people but the most probable creators and developers of other new concepts. Appropriate people would not be the type who become lost in the obscurity of detail, and they would have the knack of filtering out the most important concepts. Such abilities are essential to the balancing and interacting of a broad range of knowledge patterns. This holistic approach can be a premier way of cultivating creativity within a company.

Thus, the range of knowledge patterns that are interacted in new product development can be quite large, taking on a more holistic flavor than, for example, the study of a specific industrial mineral parameter. Unfortunately, companies rarely practice holism with all of its necessary ramifications. Its practical implementation could be the giant step that is needed to address the perennial problem of how to achieve innovation.

It is only through extensive, reductionist study to understand the parts that the holistic approach to problems can be expedited with efficiency. The primary point is that knowledge-based holism has the greatest potential for exploiting creativity and discovery. It may be the secret weapon that will do the most to promote industrial innovation.

Theoretical physicist Michio Kaku suggests that reductionism is past its heyday and that the next century will be a time when we become the masters of nature.[17] Physics, chemistry, and biology have attained their current high achievements by the reductionist approach. This has led to the quantum revolution which promoted the computer and the bimolecular revolutions. Emphasized by Kaku, "Already, scientists who do not have some understanding of these three revolutions are finding themselves at a distinct competitive disadvantage."

Even in foreign affairs, holistic considerations are being recognized as critical to understanding. In his book *The Lexus and the Olive Tree, New York Times* foreign affairs columnist Thomas L. Friedman explains how the traditional boundaries between politics, culture, technology, finance, national security, and ecology are disappearing.[18] Thus, he saw the most insightful approach to foreign affairs to be six-dimensional, and new dimensions may arise at any time. As he pointed out, "If you don't see the connections, you don't see the world."

Holistic considerations are becoming ever more important as a consequence of globalization, the integration of capital, technology, and information across national borders, which has become the international system replacing the Cold War system. Creating a single global market, globalization is a rapidly changing and evolving system that poses a major new challenge to technology. New more efficient technologies are emerging more rapidly than ever, and they must be anticipated with other more viable technologies if companies are to maintain a competitive edge. The high velocity of change is the essential ingredient of globalization that must be addressed with a technological sense of urgency. This high rate of change demonstrates how dynamic and influential holistic systems can be. Holism, synthesis, or network thinking seemingly will be the dominant pathway to discovery in the twenty-first century.

## A Challenge to Holism

In biologist E.O. Wilson's book *Consilience*, he promotes the concept of linking all of human learning, which he sees as the greatest enterprise of the human mind.[19] Although fundamentally a reductionist concept by envisioning the explanation of everything by the laws of physics, it has holistic flavor as well by envisioning a seamless web of cause and effect across disciplines. This would entail the interaction of the disparate areas of science, the humanities, and the social sciences.

"The central idea of the consilient world view is that all tangible phenomena, from the birth of stars to the workings of social institutions, are based on material processes that are ultimately reducible, however long and tortuous the sequences, to the laws of physics." Underlying the explanation of everything, including life, are the atoms of which they are composed, all of which obey the same laws.

This reductionist view is supported by theoretical physicist Lee Smolin,[20] who contends that to understand the origin of life, a general theory of how self-organization can arise from a random starting point is essential. He saw the mechanism for the origin of life to be grounded in physics, a thermodynamic process whereby a system is far from equilibrium because of steady infusion of energy. In accord with the science of complexity, this process can lead to self-organization by virtue of internal dynamics. Without the loss or gain of energy, increasing entropy or disorder is applicable only to closed systems, or systems that are isolated from the rest of the universe. Isolated systems, without a flux of energy, are condemned to randomness and equilibrium. Because energy enters the biosphere constantly via the light from the sun and then exits in the form of heat, the Earth's surface is not a closed system. With the right ingredients, then, self-organization can lead to such things as crystals and life. By this reductionist observation, it does seem that there is potential for eventually reducing every niche of nature to the laws of physics.

The idea of consilience originated during the Age of Enlightenment, but was lost in the deluge of specialized knowledge that developed in the ensuing centuries. The ultimate hope for the reduction of all knowledge to a few unifying principles may never materialize, but the effort to do so should enhance immensely our understanding of reality. If the twenty-first century is to be the age of holistic problem solution, then the ultimate goal of consilience, reduction of everything to the laws of physics, if possible, will be much further into the future.

## PYRAMIDAL THINKING

Pyramidal thinking is as much a state of mind as it is a way of thinking. Although the term is new, the idea is not. It is an aspect of scientific method by which hypotheses are generated persistently and discarded until the process peaks at a creative solution. The key to pyramidal thinking is positivism, introspectively asking oneself how to solve the problem if the alternative is dire, perhaps even unemployment. For example, if a new product satisfies a major segment of industry but is too costly, an Herculean effort is then made to reduce production costs. It is always easier to explain why a system will not work than to find a way to make it work. Far too many people opt for the easy way out.

Many people become involved in the innovative process all of whom can be critical to the program's success. Some of these people may not have sufficient motivation to put forth the extra effort. Such weak links can destroy the noble efforts of others, despite their determination to make the system work. Worthwhile innovation is rarely easy, and its success generally requires an extraordinary effort. It is the job of the technology manager to cultivate a pyramidal atmosphere within the technology group, but it is the job of all of management to provide the motivation commensurate with the difficulty of the innovative task. On the other hand, the danger exists of studying a problem beyond a reasonable limit, or of competing against a new technology that makes yours obsolete. Project termination is a judgment call, and the wisdom of knowing when to quit generally evolves, begrudgingly, with knowledge and experience.

Psychologist Robert Weisberg[21] contended that creativity derives from ordinary thinking. From his perspective, extraordinary thinking is fictional. For example, analogical thinking, which is generally ordinary, occasionally leads to creative results. Darwin's use of the thought form "gradualism" in both geological and evolutionary theory is a prime example (Chapter 14). That creativity can develop from ordinary thinking seems to be valid, but it seems equally valid that extraordinary or unconventional thinking generally plays a dominant role.

To accommodate the idea of ordinary thinking in creativity, the term "pyramidal" has been introduced. Seemingly, no kind of thinking leads to creativity without extraordinary dedication. Thus, the greater the dedication, the greater the opportunity for creativity to result from conventional thought processes. Enter pyramidal thinking, often producing novelty and sufficiently rare to be classified as unconventional. It is a method for transforming the conventional into the unconventional. In the extreme this concept invokes a new meaning to conventionality—inadequate effort gives rise to conventional thinking. Adequate (Herculean) effort transforms conventional thinking into unconventional and thence to novelty.

The convergence of inductive, deductive, abductive, and dialectical thinking, all ordinary, can lead to hypotheses. With the introduction of pyramidal thinking, this complex of thought processes, even exclusive of induction, can lead to elegant theory, which is, indeed, extraordinary. Ultimately, creativity results from the appropriate combination of thought processes and knowledge patterns, coincident with opportunistic social conditions.

## ELEGANT THEORY

Although induction has been alluded to in the previous chapter as the primary process of science, there can be a major exception to this generalization. It is an exception that usurps empiricism and demonstrates the flexibility of science. Namely, elegance, simplicity, and appropriateness of a theory can play supreme, even without supporting empirical evidence. Just as Newton's gravity seemed—and still does—a preposterous suggestion, it supported predictions so well that it could not be discredited.

Theoretical physicist and author Richard Morris[22] gave examples of important new concepts in science that thrived without the support of observation, and sometimes even when confronted with contradictory evidence. Galileo's promotion of Copernicus' heliocentric theory of planetary movement was done in spite of the absence of empirical proof. Such proof, however, did not come forth for more than 200 years after Galileo's death. Galileo was so convinced of the theory that he was willing to risk the wrath of the Inquisition.

Einstein's general theory of relativity, similarly, had wide support many years before supporting evidence was garnered. The logical simplicity of a theory, its clear explanation of cryptic phenomena, in Einstein's view, had greater significance than laboratory results. He was in concert with the ancient Greeks in the belief that creative imagination is essential to the understanding of nature. Experiment that contradicted elegant vision, as Einstein was prone to believe, was necessarily wrong.

Even Charles Darwin attempted to rationalize the validity of elegant theory without justification from empirical evidence.[23] Although he used the analogy of artificial selection to argue the rationale for natural selection, his critics were loud in their skepticism. Finally, Darwin argued that empiricism is not the only criterion of good science. He believed that if a hypothesis fit the facts, it deserved the rank of well-grounded theory.

A modern example of elegant theory, which Morris described as the most important theory in cosmology, is the inflationary universe theory of MIT physicist Alun Guth. Proposed in 1980, the Guth theory ascribes a very rapid expansion of the universe when it was about $10^{-35}$ seconds old or post–big bang. During this enormous inflation, the universe could have expanded by a factor of as much as $10^{50}$. The cause was an antigravitational force lasting until the universe was about $10^{-32}$ seconds old, after which the universe expanded at the much slower rate observed today. According to this theory, what we can observe with telescopes is only an infinitesimal bubble of a much larger universe.

Guth's original version postulated that expansion would have taken place in many isolated domains. These domains, with expansion, would have coalesced into a universe having the appearance of soap bubbles. Within the observations at that time the universe did not have such an appearance, but it was concluded later that such bubbles would necessarily be so large as to be unobservable. Although falsified in Popperian mode, Guth's theory, by the alternate explanation, was saved.

In 1986, Valerie de Lapparent, Margaret Geller, and John Huchra[24] of the Harvard-Smithsonian Center for Astrophysics showed that the visible universe is constructed in the form of soap bubbles. From their data, they concluded that galaxies are arranged in regular patterns having the appearance of foam. Subsequent studies of other slices of the universe confirmed their studies, and showed that galaxies occur in large clumps separated by gaps about 400 million light-years in diameter. Although this confirmation applies only to a minute portion of the universe, it suggests that the remaining portion of the universe may be constructed similarly and perhaps on the larger scale as well, as suggested by Guth. Inflationary theory will be rejected only if a theory of greater elegance is developed, or if overwhelming data is collected to reject inflation.

The heliocentric theory of Copernicus, Einstein's theory of relativity, and the Guth theory of the inflationary universe all demonstrate that elegant explanation of phenomena can supersede experiment and observation. This can be true even if a theory is falsified in Popperian mode. Darwin's theory of evolution and Mendel's theory of heredity did not have firm empirical evidence until it was shown by Francis Crick how genetic information is encoded in DNA. Giving great emphasis to the importance of acute hypothesizing, the development of elegant theory of great simplicity can be a beneficent goal of all who seek discovery. It is, perhaps, the highest level of thinking and achievement in the complex and dynamic discipline of science.

Superstring theory is a current and prime example that loudly calls for understanding the significance of beauty to correctness of theory.[25] This theory contends that the unification of all of nature's forces, a theory of everything, occurs at the Planck energy, which is about one quadrillion times larger than the energies currently available in accelerators. Testing this theory, which in esence is a theory of creation, is a test of a minute portion of the big bang. Such enormous energies will not be available in the forseeable future, and so a resounding question arises: Is beauty a substitute for empirical proof?

It is not clear that this question is fully answerable, but neuroscientist and Nobel Prize winner Gerald Edelman[26] gives an example of an exception to elegance and simplicity. If a foreign protein is injected into an individual's body, lymphocytes produce molecules called antibodies. The antibodies bind to the foreign molecule at specific sites. In subsequent encounters the antibodies bind even more effectively to the protein. This kind of a recognition system exists even for molecules that have never existed before, such as those synthesized by organic chemists.

One explanation for this unique system of recognition has been the theory of instruction. This theory assumes that in the immune system foreign molecules transfer information about their structure and morphology to the reactive portion of the antibody. In this fashion, it is believed that the immune system is instructed how to form the appropriate antibody protein.

Although the instruction theory is elegant and simple, the new more workable theory of clonal selection is more complex. Our bodies have the capacity to manufacture a huge spectrum of antibody molecules, each with a different shape at its binding site. When they encounter a foreign molecule, the antibody with a close fit binds with the invader. This stimulates the lymphocyte bearing the correct antibody to divide repeatedly, forming clones of identical shape and binding character.

Elegance, therefore, is not always the theory of greatest simplicity, but the generation of such theories can give a tremendous boost to progress in understanding. Elegant theories that support predictions will continue to have merit in scientific circles, even without empiricism. Despite the great utility of elegance, it does not become true science until after empirical substantiation—essential to the establishment of reliable knowledge.

## FUZZY LOGIC

Although fuzzy logic is not generally accepted and is highly controversial, it is perceived by its supporters to be a new and potentially profitable way of thinking about philosophy, science, and technology. Fuzzy thinking is grayness, multivalent logic—true, false, and indeterminate. Bivalent logic—true or false—had its beginnings with Aristotle and is still used by scientists and mathematicians today.

In fuzzy logic light is both wave and particle, but in bivalent logic it is either a wave or a particle, not both. Matter obeys Newtonian mechanics and general relativity for large objects and the laws of quantum mechanics for extremely small objects—molecules and below. Between is uncertain and fuzzy. In Aristotelian logic, bivalency is stated as A or not-A, where the grass is green or not green. Fuzzy logic is A and not-A, where the grass is both green and not green. Although a concise description will be given for this kind of thinking, further reading will be essential to gain an in-depth perspective.[27]

### The Origin of Fuzzy Logic

Fuzzy logic had its beginnings in two major events in the early twentieth century. First, Bertrand Russell saw that the classical Greek paradoxes are a fundamental basis of modern math. Second, Werner Heisenberg discovered the uncertainty principle of quantum mechanics. Ending the certainty of math, Russell found a paradox dealing with sets of all sets that are not members of themselves. He found a set where things are in it and not in it.

Boxes full of boxes are not fuzzy sets. Every box is either in or out. Membership is true or false. A set of apples is not a member of itself. Apples and not the set are members. The set of all sets is a member of itself simply because it is a set. By definition, a set of all sets that belongs to itself does not because the sole criterion of membership is that it does not belong to itself. If, on the other hand, it does not belong to itself, it does because it satisfies the membership criterion. It is fuzzy logic, A and not-A. It cannot be explained by bivalent logic, A and not-A. This was a momentous blow to the field of mathematics, and no one knew how to avoid paradoxes.

Heisenberg made doubt scientific and showed that there are some things that we can never know. He established the principle that it is impossible to determine position and momentum of a particle simultaneously within an atom. Bart Kosko pointed out that there are many uncertainty principles exclusive of quantum mechanics (e.g., signal processing that operates televisions, telephones, and human eyes). Uncertainty principles are artifacts of a linear view of a nonlinear world, which is the basis for many scientists having limited faith in quantum mechanics. Linearity, as does quantum mechanics, assumes that the whole can be determined from its parts. The truth of nonlinearity is that groups behave differently than their members. This creates a mismatch problem—linear math applied to a nonlinear world.

Aristotle said that extremes cannot be united through an excluded middle. Bivalent logic was established by both Aristotle and Plato, and Western thought has been emphatically dualistic ever since. Manichean good and evil duality has been a firm foundation of Christianity. In a similar fashion, Descartes differentiated the "in here" from the "out there." Refuted by Einstein's special theory of relativity and Bohr's theory of complementarity, modern physics has defused these absolute bivalent notions.

As opposed to Euclidean, three-dimensional, rectilinear space, in Einstein's curved space-time continuum time becomes the fourth dimension. Curved time and space are interdependent. If time dilates, space contracts and vice versa. These parameters merge imperceptibly, refuting the uniqueness of bivalency. In a like manner, Bohr's theory of complementarity states that light is both wave and particle, absent an excluded middle.[28]

The laws of science are aspects of nature that we have observed from our limited view. Perhaps, only tautologies are 100% true, as green is green or 2 + 2 = 4, which are true only by definition. Although proponents believe that fuzzy logic would produce greater degrees of truth than bivalent logic, the general problem of definity in science would still be at issue.

In the parlance of modern science, events are characterized by probability, the mathematical theory of chance or randomness, a special case of bivalent logic. Probability is indicated by a number where the probabilities of occurrence and nonoccurrence add up to one. It is still a black and white concept, where events occur or do not occur. In spite of this, critics contend that fuzziness is probability in disguise.

Described by Kosko, probability disappears with increased information.

If our information were of sufficient magnitude, probability would become illusion. In this sense, a coin comes up heads or tails as determined by the laws of physics, not by chance. The mismatch problem, where the fuzzy or multivalent world is described by the bivalency of mathematics, according to Kosko, is not resolved by probability. Logical positivism contends that if you cannot test or mathematically prove what you say, you have said nothing. In the parlance of fuzzy logic, this contention leaves bivalent science in a very "fuzzy" state of affairs at best.

Fuzzy logic, also based on percentages, describes events happening to some degree, not all or none as in probability. If we observe a number line, the concepts of probability and fuzzy logic are clearly contrasted:

$$0 \text{———} \tfrac{1}{2} \text{———} 1$$

Multivalence is represented any place between 0 and 1, where the opposite of 1 is 0, the opposite of $\tfrac{1}{2}$ is $\tfrac{1}{2}$, or the opposite of $\tfrac{1}{4}$ is $\tfrac{3}{4}$. In bivalent logic the midpoint of the line is a paradox of self-reference. In probability, it means that the event is as apt to happen as not. Fuzzy logic contends that the event is a matter of degree. Kosko gave the example of a bumper sticker that says, "Don't trust me." Do we then trust the driver? If the answer is yes, then by the driver's instructions, we should not trust him. If, on the other hand, we don't trust the driver, then similarly, we do not by his instructions. We, therefore, both trust and don't trust the driver simultaneously. Bivalent logic, A or not-A, is believed by fuzzy logicians to be powerless in resolving this paradox. Such an event can be stated by a multivalent equation:

$$A = \text{not-}A$$

Bivalent math denies this relation, but Kosko calls it the yin-yang equation, which resolves the paradoxes of bivalent reasoning. Fuzzy logic contends that paradoxes of self-reference are half truths and are represented at the midpoint of the number line. Although the word "paradox" suggests exception, fuzziness shows that paradoxes are the rule. Black or white outcomes are the exception. The liar paradox (e.g., a Cretan states that all Cretans are liars) in fuzzy logic is simply half true and half false, $A = \text{not-}A$.

The ancient Greek philosopher Protagoras believed all knowledge to be illusion, that truth is a myth. Aristotle seemingly refuted him by bivalent logic, "Your position is true or false; if it is false, then you are answered; if true, then there is something true, and your proposition fails." Multivalent logic, in contrast, assigns some truth to the contention of Protogoras. It is, at once, true and false.

## Making Machines Smarter

Described by Kosko, fuzzy logic can be used to make smarter machines, which think more like humans. Fuzzy logic has extensive application and is being used in Asian countries. Japanese and Korean companies use fuzzy logic, for example, to control air conditioners, where adjustments are not all or nothing, but constantly adjust the air emission temperature to the desired room temperature. Similarly computers, cameras, camcorders, auto engines, brakes, transmissions, cruise controls, among many things, are controlled by fuzzy systems.

Opposed to the Christian world, the Buddha saw the world as full of contradictions, not as black and white. Such a theme is found generally in Eastern belief systems and accounts for the unique application of fuzzy systems in Asian countries.

## The Uncertain Future of Fuzzy Logic

Martin Gardner[29] points out that opposition to fuzzy logic is often fierce and detractors claim that probability theory can operate machinery just as efficiently as fuzzy theory. The strong proponents of fuzzy logic believe that it is a new, revolutionary paradigm that will replace bivalent logic. In a response to Gardner's column in the *Skeptical Inquirer* about fuzzy logic, William Dress of Knoxville, Tennessee, observes that "Kosko forgets that fuzzy logic was created to allow a consistent mathematical treatment of fuzzy and ambiguous linguistic terms, not objective behaviors of physical reality. Indeed quantum electrodynamics has shown us that the physical reality is crisp at least to a part in $10^{16}$—not even remotely fuzzy on a human scale." Dress believes that fuzzy logic is a useful tool in expressing linguistic concepts in a machine or a computer environment. But, with the exception of the human mind and cultural concepts, he believes that it is off base with respect to objective reality.

Physicist John Barrow disparaged the logical inconsistency of statements supposedly containing both truth and falsity.[30] Conventional wisdom holds that no statement can be both true and false. If statements could be true and false, the logical system in use would collapse in that there would be no restrictions on what could be true or false. Barrow gave the striking example of the philosopher Bertrand Russell who made this claim in a public lecture. He was challenged by a skeptic to prove that the questioner was the Pope if twice 2 were 5. Russell said, "If twice 2 is 5, then 4 is 5, subtract 3; then 1 = 2. But you and the Pope are 2; therefore you and the Pope are one!"

Barrow describes the solution to the liar paradox attributed to the sixth century B.C. philosopher Embulides of Megara:

His original version of the paradox required the liar to answer the question, "Do you lie when you say that you are lying?" If the liar says "I am lying," then clearly he is not lying, because if a liar says he is a liar when he really is a liar, then he is speaking the truth. But if the liar says "I am not lying," then it is true that he is lying, and, consequently, he is lying.

The liar paradox, in fact, is not a paradox.

Fuzzy logic may or may not offer some value to the evolution of knowledge. Although it probably will not replace bivalent logic, it can be used as an adjunct, especially in computer environments involving linguistics. To the extent that fuzzy logic is useful over and above probability—and this is still under hot debate—it could change our approach to some problems in ways that may lead to new more viable methods—even if the concept of fuzzy logic is wrong!

The next chapter is a continuation of unconventional thinking, which will conclude the consideration of thought processes behind discovery.

*Chapter 16*

# Stimulation:
# Unconventional Thinking II

From the beginning of abstract thought with archaic man, unconventional thinking has been the lynchpin of creativity. Other kinds of unconventional thinking, other than those described in this and the last chapter, exist or can be created by the researcher. From conventional thinking comes reliable knowledge, but from unconventional thinking comes inspiration and unexpected pathways to discovery.

## LATERAL THINKING

Edward de Bono,[1] a leading authority on creative thinking, promoted lateral thinking as a highly productive method. He pointed out that lateral thinkers thoroughly explore all of the different ways of looking at a problem, commonplace, devious, and otherwise. This is opposed to vertical thinkers who singularly accept what seems to be the most promising method. The rewards of thinking laterally are consistent with the observation that the most able students spend more time selecting a set of steps to solve a problem.[2]

A worthy example of lateral thinking is afforded by a young man and his lady friend who one Friday afternoon in New York City entered a chic fur shop on Fifth Avenue. The young man asked to see the best fur coat in the store. Eventually the manager brought out an exquisite, mutation mink with which the young man was pleased. He said to his lady friend, "Try it on and see how it fits." She was immediately and exquisitely enamored. Then the young man said, "Yes, this will do. Please lay it away. I will pick it up Monday, and meanwhile you may check my credit."

The manager said, "Yes, sir. Anything you say, sir."

**Figure 16.1.** The nine-dot problem.

Monday, the young man returned to the store and the manager greeted him coldly, "You are most certainly not welcome in this store. Your credit is the worst we have ever had the misfortune to check."

The young man responded sheepishly, "I apologize for that, but, actually, nobody was hurt. I just came in to thank you for a wonderful weekend."

In the true spirit of lateral thinking, it is safe to assume that the young man toyed with many different approaches to address his apparent goal before hitting upon this unusually clever and devious solution.

A visual example of both vertical and lateral thinking is the nine-dot problem shown in Figure 16.1. The problem is to connect all nine dots with four line segments without lifting your pencil from the paper. The solution is shown in Figure 16.2, and as described by psychologist Robert Sternberg,[3] most people are unable to solve the problem. Although there is nothing in the stated problem that hints of boundary constraints, an implicit assumption usually is made that the lines cannot be drawn outside the framework delineated by the outer dots.

Prior experience in the use or interpretation of phenomena can impose a mental block to their use and perception in new and novel ways. This mental block is what psychologists call functional fixedness[4] and is a plague on creativity and discovery. Not only does this example emphasize the need to clearly define the problem, it demonstrates the need to approach problems from as many different perspectives as possible.

Conrath[5] showed how the nine-dot problem can be solved with three lines or even one line. Using three lines, start one line at the extreme left of the upper left dot. Then go through the middle of the left middle dot and through the extreme right of the lower left dot. This line must be extended for an inordinately long distance. Return through the middle row of dots similarly, again extending this second line a considerable distance and returning with the third line. With one line, a paint brush can be drawn through all nine dots with one swish. Alternatively, cut the paper and line up all of the dots. These approaches embody the underlying principle of

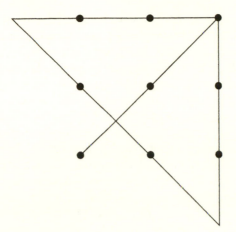

**Figure 16.2.** The nine-dot solution.

the lateral thinker. In his summary statements, de Bono concluded, "There is no sudden conversion from a belief in the omnipotence of vertical thinking. Lateral thinking is a matter of awareness and practice—not revelation."

Another aspect of lateral thinking is "knowledge-based thinking," with its antithesis being "object-centered thinking."[6] An example of the latter is the American automobile industry's past mindset on large luxury cars instead of small energy-efficient cars. Or to make an advance in lighting, the knowledge-based approach can entail the most energy-efficient method of producing light. The object-centered approach, on the other hand, is limited to enhancing energy-efficiency of the incandescent light bulb. The nine-dot problem elicits object-centered thinking by the involuntary imposition of boundary constraints. If one's thought processes can be untethered, a much broader scope of knowledge can be made available for knowledge-based thinking.

## HEURISTIC SEARCH

Problem solving can be viewed as search within a metaphorical space. Algorithms provide a method for investigating all of the paths in a problem space and of finding the correct path. Problems in such areas as checkers and chess are so complicated and the space so large that algorithms are not viable. For example, in a typical game of chess a total of 60 moves might be involved with the potential of 30 alternate moves for each. Astronomic in size, the total number of alternate paths for the game is $30^{60}$, which is called a combinatorial explosion.[7] Here, the fastest computer could not explore every alternate move. Such problems are referred to as intractable. Although human players can look ahead no more than three or four moves, a grand master until recently could play better than any computer program. Computers, however, have been able to defeat a grand master if a time limit of a few seconds is imposed. Given that computers and software evolve at a far greater rate than humans, it seems only a matter of time until computers will defeat grand masters even without time limits. The IBM computer, Deep Blue, in 1997 narrowly defeated the world champion, Garry Kasparov, and, although a likely event, it remains to be seen if computers will dominate grand masters in the future.

In these areas of inordinately large problem space, the method used is called heuristic search by which only a few alternates that seem most likely to provide a solution are considered. General rules gained by experience enable experts to make moves that generally will enhance their position. For example, they may make a move that will help them control the center of the board. Such a move is better than one that does not. This heuristic approach is feasible as long as the best possible solution is not required.

By virtue of the development of expertise, the extent of the search for finding a reasonable solution can be reduced to an acceptable level. If problem solution requires finding the optimal path, heuristic search is futile and brute force is the only alternate. The heuristic approach gives great credence to the importance of knowledge and experience, not only to simplify thought processes in chess but in all areas of thinking.

## JANUSIAN THINKING

Psychiatrist Albert Rothenberg[8] found that janusian thinking is common to many creative people. Named after Janus, the Roman god of beginnings, who is represented with one head and two bearded faces set back to back, janusian thinking occurs early in the creative process. It is a thought mechanism for showing that two opposing ideas can seem to be true simultaneously in the same space. Oxymorons, as bittersweet or violent quiescence, and fuzzy logic with respect to paradox are janusian concepts. Such ambivalence is fundamental to the conflicts, ironies, and ambiguities found in poetry and prose. As opposed to conventional wisdom, it is possible, through illusion, to have it both ways, perhaps more.

Einstein's general theory of relativity was derived partly with the help of Janus. He found Newton's concept of gravity to be flawed, largely because the concept required subluminal speed, which was in conflict with special relativity—that nothing can exceed the speed of light. Newton believed that all matter, like the earth, produces a gravitational field, a force that attracts other matter to it. He accepted the existence of gravity and developed equations that accurately describe its effects, but he did not offer ideas on its cause.

Einstein, in an observation of great insight, concluded that gravity and accelerated motion are equivalent, which in a closed, windowless compartment an observer would find indistinguishable. This was what Einstein declared to be the happiest thought of his life, and it became known as the equivalence principle.[9, 10] By dropping a stone on the floor of an accelerating spacecraft, it can be concluded that it is the floor that is accelerating up. Gravity is experienced by individuals as a force pressing them up. Much less obvious, on earth the effect of gravity is the ground accelerating up. If the acceleration of a spacecraft is stopped, astronauts experience no gravity. This illustrates the equivalence of accelerated motion and gravity, which is a principle element of general relativity.

Einstein conceived that the gravitational field has a relative existence—that an observer in free fall has no gravitational field in his immediate vicinity. If the falling observer releases an object, the object remains at rest relative to him (assumes no air resistance). Similarly, if two stones of different weight are dropped in a spaceship, they will fall at the same rate. At the instant of release, the stones are no longer accelerated by the spaceship; they are in free fall. Einstein stated almost with unbelief that, "The extraordinarily curious law that all bodies in a gravitational field fall with the same acceleration immediately took on, through this consideration, a deep physical meaning." Just one thing that would fall at a different rate would allow observers to recognize that they were falling in a gravitational field. And so in a janusian sense, the observer is falling and at rest at the same time. Such insightful thinking—the equivalence principle and the relative nature of gravity—permitted Einstein to transcend nearly 200 years of Newtonian supremacy. Explained later in this chapter in the section, "*Anschauung, Anschaulichkeit,* and Intuitive Thinking," Einstein conceived, in dramatic contrast to Newton, that gravity is not a force, but is the curvature of space.

An incisive example of janusian thinking was provided in the sixth century B.C. by Chinese philosopher Lao-tzu, who said,

We put 30 spokes together to make a wheel, but it is on the space where there is nothing that the usefulness of the wheel depends. We turn the clay to make a vessel, but it is on the space where there is nothing that the usefulness of the vessel depends. We pierce doors and windows to make a house, but it is on the space where there is nothing that the usefulness of the house depends. Therefore, just as we take advantage of what is, we must recognize the usefulness of what is not.[11]

Poignantly demonstrated is the unholiness of Janus and the utility of unconventional thought. Persistent probing of multiple hypotheses for what seem to be simultaneous truths, may lead to problem solution that could not be derived by conventional methods. It is a clever way to arrive at better perspectives of reality.

One might conclude that janusian thought is in conflict with the logical principle that a statement cannot be true and false at the same time. In fact, a falling observer is not really falling and at rest at the same time. This is simply a relative perception influenced by the observer's environment. Similarly, although the speed of light is a constant, the relative speed of traveling observers can make light seem to be moving at different speeds.

## VISUAL-SPATIAL THINKING

Visual thinking for problem solution is most useful where shapes, forms, or patterns are involved.[12] Our conscious as well as our nonconscious minds are concerned with mental images more than any other tool for thinking.[13] Formation of vivid mental pictures simplifies memory,[14] which is an important aspect of good science. Visual thinking is an essential ingredient to much of problem solving and to creativity. This notion is reinforced by the observation that blind children find difficulty in problem solving although they can speak. In contrast, deaf children without verbalization can visualize and solve problems.[15]

The importance of visual thinking is illustrated by a problem concerning visual memory.[16] The legal system has shown that our memory of faces is frequently flawed. A major reason for this is that we are not equipped to describe faces verbally, and our descriptions for reproduction by artists are notably imprecise. Facial recognition is a special kind of visual-spatial comprehension that eludes adequate descriptive terms.

Mental imagery seems to have unlimited potential, which may lead first to phantasy, thence to potential reality, and, perhaps, if we are persistent, to novelty of great value. On the other hand, as explained by physicist Erich Harth,[17] our perceptions are often different from that sensed, and what we remember is often skewed. We do not necessarily see the irrational as impossible, and we lean toward the fantastic. Occasionally, a visionary alone will see a potential, which will be of great benefit to society. Most such visions are without value. Invention can arise, however, from the interaction of the fantastic with the practical.

Neurologist Richard Restak[18] described an account of visual exercises carried out by oriental children years ago. Sitting before a bonsai tree, they would observe every branch and leaf in detail. Eventually they would close their eyes maintaining a mental image of the tree's pattern. Only after being certain of having captured fully the details of the tree, would they again open their eyes. The image that they had developed in their mind's eye was then compared to the actual image.

Such exercises are invaluable for improving powers of observation, mental imagery, and of clearing the mind of unwanted static. As Restak analogized, those who have made historical discoveries of great merit, ruminated until their theories were so clear that they were presented with indelible confidence.

### *Anshauung, Anshaulichkeit,* and Intuitive Thinking

According to German philosopher Immanuel Kant,[19] visualization (*Anshauung*) was an abstraction of a phenomenon that has been witnessed, as the phenomenon of water waves used to explain light waves. Visualizability (*Anshaulichkeit*) was exemplified by the demonstration of magnetic lines of force with iron filings. It can be the demonstration of the existence of an unseen phenomenon with an intermediary, as iron filings, or visual imagery extrapolated from scientific theories. Subatomic particles cannot be seen but can be abstracted from the mathematics of related theories. This is visualizability.

Arthur Miller[20] described the evolution of thought in physics using visual images and how it has become progressively more abstract and intuitive from Aristotle to the present. This is illustrated by a range of ideas from Aristotle's commonsense intuition, through Galileo-Newton vacuums, inertial motion, absolute time, the velocity addition law, to Einstein's relativity of time and the new velocity addition law. With Einstein's hypothesis of the particle nature of light in 1905, scientists began to struggle with the representation of unseen phenomena. Bohr's atomic theory of 1913, represented as a planetary system, provided a momentary reincarnation of visual representation. Such visualization turned out to be incorrect. Until the advent of atomic physics, theories were based on visual imagery abstracted from the world of sense perceptions.

With atomic physics, visualization lost utility and intuition became a primary mechanism for building theories of the unseen.[21] Excluding intuition from the process of science, logical positivists take seriously only what can be known through direct measurement. Making experiment essential to meaningful ideas, reality to the positivists is uniquely defined by empirical operations. This was the position of Ernest Mach, who strongly influenced Einstein's method of thinking. Later Einstein modified his thought process, which he described in a letter to philosopher Maurice Solovine.[22]

Beginning with extensive experience and experiment, the scientist may use intuition to leap from experience to the abstraction of a postulate. This is counter to the positivist method and transcends experience. A prime example is Einstein's contention that gravity is geometry. Opposed to Newtonian mechanics, which assumes that gravity is a force, Einstein intuited that gravity is not a force. Any mass curves the space nearby altering its geometry. The sun curves space around it, thereby entraping the revolving planets. Thus, gravity can be thought of as entrapment as well. That gravity is geometry or the curvature of space is the central conclusion of general relativity. As no physicist had ever contemplated such a relation between gravity and geometry, Einstein's thought was clearly intuition.

From an intuitive postulate the scientist may deduce potential results that may be experimentally checked. Experiment and data alone often are inadequate for the creative leap to new, revolutionary ideas. Although intuition by itself is irrational, it must be either verifiable or falsifiable, which permits the nullification of irrational conclusions. Scientific creativity often proceeds via intuition followed by experimental substantiation.

Since 1923, visual imagery disappeared in atomic physics and was replaced by nonvisualizable mathematical formalisms. Only the mathematics of a related theory could enable a glimmer of what an event might look like. There are many things in mathematics that cannot be visualized but that can be shown to exist.

The late physicist Heinz Pagels described the drastic change in our perception of reality promoted by the quantum physics interpretation of the atom and subatomic particles.[23] This new vision of reality demands an entirely new approach to understanding the universe. Quantum reality is statistical, not a certainty as in Newtonian physics. A quantum property is measured innumerable times for statistical verification. A single measurement is meaningless. Attempting to form a mental picture of the position and momentum of an electron from these measurements gives a fuzzy image.

The position and momentum of a particle have no meaning until they are measured. Paradoxically, reality is observer-created in that the simple act of observation changes quantum reality, which is not true in classical physics. In Heisenberg's uncertainty, a subatomic particle cannot be measured for position and momentum at the same time. The act of measurement changes the status of the particle.

Pagels gave an example in ordinary life. Studying a small village isolated from modern life, an anthropologist by his presence necessarily alters life in that village. People's behavior change when they are aware of being observed. It follows that quantum mechanics rejects the determinism of Newtonian physics and emphasizes the statistical nature of reality. It rejects objectivity as well, showing that reality is dependent on how it is observed. The atomic world does not have a definite state of existence independent of our observing it. This is shown by Bohr's principle of complementarity, which is the consideration that light is both wave and particle. Depending on experimental method and choice of description, light can be either a wave or a particle.

Although the quantum world is a weird world by our standards, it is mathematics that permits an indirect understanding of the physics of atoms and subatomic particles. Our minds, conditioned to a Newtonian world, have great difficulty in comprehending the strangeness of quantum randomness. Thus, the great power of mathematics has become the primary tool for unlocking the most intransigent mysteries of the universe. An ordinary, intuitive image does not permit visualizing the inner domain of the atom.

Replacing the visualization, planetary notion of an atom's structure, physicist Richard Feynman in 1949 developed diagrams showing how electrons interact with light.[24] Feynman diagrams were derived from the mathematics of quantum mechanics and represented visualizability, not visualization. The Feynman diagram shows an interaction between electrons by exchanging a light quantum. This representation is realistic in the sense of an interaction that does occur, yet it does not reflect an actual image. It is visualizability.

Miller considers extreme abstraction to be the essence of theoretical physics. In quantum theory vacuums are replete with particles and antiparticles constantly being destroyed and created. The extreme speculation is that the cosmos is a result of such a fluctuation, where energy is created from nothing. Part of this energy is transformed into mass. Miller pointed out that Einstein believed that daring speculation is a primary mechanism for advance in knowledge. Thought experiments constituted Einstein's laboratory, but he believed that the most basic creative principles are derived from mathematics. Miller attributes Einstein's lack of contribution after 1907, to his inability to alter his mode of visual imagery. That is, Einstein does not seem to have been able to replace his visualization thought process with visualizability.

### Gestalt Psychology

As for all thought processes, imperfections can be associated with visualization. Lawrence Slobodkin[25] emphasized that in the complex world of nature, illusion can be difficult to recognize. This makes empirical cross-checking of hypotheses derived from visual imagination even more important.

Gestalt psychology is the holistic concept of the social sciences. It is a concept where the parts of perception are not treated as separate entities, and the perceptual whole is more than the sum of the parts. Even if some parts of the whole are missing, as in the drawing of a human face, it can still have meaning, but individual parts in isolation have no meaning. Abraham Maslow[26] said that if he wanted to learn more about an individual, he must study that person as a unit. In many respects, reductionism in the inorganic world has been highly successful, but it has much less utility in the study of human beings.

Discovery arises from the rare ability to arrange knowledge such that order is fashioned from chaos. A major weakness of induction arises from its tendency to minimize this inventive genius. Its ready reference to empirical facts implies, as opposed to creativity, that therein lies the answer to a phenomenon. The approach of the Gestalt psychologists assigns credence to the esoteric process of fashioning order from chaos. By allowing for the *a priori* element, they explain how this insight is not only rare but possible.

Phenomena are perceived as wholes—not as color, size, and so forth, but as larger organizations of many parameters, as buildings and cities, for example. The organization of patterns depends on the emotional and intellectual makeup of the observer, sociological influences, and the environment. This accounts for how the artist, the scientist, and the politician see the same phenomena in a totally different light. It also accounts for how the prepared scientists can make the most of serendipity, how with the same information available to everyone, highly intelligent people can arrive at categorical but contradictory conclusions (see Chapter 8 and Figure 8.1).

### Enhancing Mental Imagery and Intersubjective Validation

Mental imagery can be enhanced by practice in imagining many different objects that have been seen in the past or of things that have never been seen but about which there is some notion of appearance. With practice in imagining a variety of images, both still and action, visual imagery can be enhanced. Graphic imagery practice involves both communicative and thinking sketches. Architectural design is an example of communicative drawing. Thinking sketches simply involve the drawing of images that go through one's mind in attempting to work out a problem. Such exercises in enhancing visualization, if not already well developed, can be invaluable to research.

Visual imagery, like the verbal thought process, is replete with potential pitfalls and distortions that can defeat the lofty intentions of science. Yet scientific knowledge is largely dependent on observation. For observations to be accepted in the scientific community, however, other competent observers must give confirmation. A basic principle of Einstein's special theory of relativity is that all observers are equivalent. John Ziman[27] describes this principle as "the foundation stone of all science." Without intersubjective validation, science could not possess the high level of objectivity necessary for continuous progress in knowledge.

## HOMOSPATIAL THINKING

An important variation of visual thinking is what Rothenberg[28] called homospatial thinking. He found that this type of visual-spatial thinking is commonly associated with the latter part of the creative process. It entails conceptualizing two or more discrete entities occupying the same perceptual space that then evolves into a new identity. For example, components of a landscape may be merged and interacted with human faces, written words, and so forth.

Rothenberg gives the example of the metaphor, "The tarantula rays of the lamp spread across the conference room." The poet who created this was sitting at a desk thinking about a vacation in the tropics. But he was thinking about sound similarities as well—the central "a" assonance in the words ta-rantula and lamp. Then transposing his thought to images of a spider and a light source superimposed on the letters in the words, he found a metaphor encompassing all components. First visualizing spidery light radiating from the entangled images, he extrapolated, "tarantula rays of the lamp." Then he elaborated by adding, "spread across the conference room."

## METAPHORICAL THINKING

We humans have the ability to imagine and to notice when things are like other things and use these relations as a springboard for other thoughts and inspirations. Such thoughts are metaphors but are called similes when introduced by "like" or "as." Metaphors and similes can help transcend conventional thinking. By viewing things in new ways, the shackles of notions that inhibit creativity can be broken. Visual-spatial and janusian thinking help to create these relations, which are not only useful in the arts but in science as well.

Among many examples of metaphor are Newton's analogy of the moon as a "thrown ball" leading to his formula for gravitation, and the dream of atoms as hoop-like snakes which the German chemist Kekule claimed led to his discovery of the ring structure of benzene. A classic example of metaphor is "stream of consciousness" used by psychologist William James in his treatise on human consciousness.[29] Helping to clarify and to establish limits, metaphor is a mechanism for finding unsuspected connections and a primary fuel for establishing new hypotheses. Such unconventional thinking can create intellectual and emotional strain giving a strong motivation to resolve the tension.[30] Tension resolution is often creative.

As information is gained, relationships between different patterns of knowledge become ever more apparent. Such relationships are building blocks of creativity. These building blocks can lead us to new understanding that can spawn inspiration, new approaches to problems, alternate hypotheses, and finally novelty.

Modeling is a metaphorical process, an essential step in the use of scientific method. Theories change gradually by means of metaphor, but the reality basis or ontology remains the same.[31] Atoms are real but, through metaphor, the theory behind their structure may change. Major discoveries often arise from creative interaction among intuition, imagery, and metaphor.

## HEMISPHERICAL THINKING

Visualization is a thought process that in most people originates in the right hemisphere of the brain. Different thought processes arise in the right and left hemispheres in ways that seem to shed some light on the origin of creativity. If one hemisphere of the brain is damaged or removed in child-

hood, the other hemisphere takes over without impairment. High specialization precludes such compensation in adults.[32] Due to this specialization,
the asymmetry of our brains and our hands is the natural order of things.
As the right hemisphere controls the left side of the body and the left hemisphere controls the right side of the body, the thought processes of each
are sometimes called left-handed or right-handed thinking, respectively.

The right side of the brain is older than the left. It is the holistic side of
the brain, synthesizing information simultaneously in gestaltic fashion.
Thinking in three-dimensional images, the right brain is the visual-spatial
center for the processing of information. Examples of its talents are face
and pattern recognition, athletic skills, metaphorical thinking, imaging, perception of proportion, and music appreciation.

This is in sharp contrast to the left brain, which perceives information
sequentially. Relating to an understanding of causality, sequential thinking
is essential to the development of logic. Letters, words, and sentences are
sequential and are abstract representations of images. It was such logic and
abstract thinking that permitted the unique development of foresight in
*Homo sapiens*. If-then syllogisms have become the primary means of predicting the future and have replaced omens, oracles, and portents.[33] Giving
people a sense of time, sequential thinking is essential to strategic thinking,
where past, present, and future are considered.

Generally the left hemisphere controls language, logic, orderliness, arith-
metic, and certain motor skills and is essential to the rigorous logic and
mathematics of science. Often visual-spatial thinking leads to discoveries
(Einstein's dream of riding on a light beam) which are then reduced to logic
by the agent of mathematics (special theory of relativity). Right brain, synthetic thinking for intuition, and left brain, sequential thinking for reduction of ideas to logic are critical components of discoveries.

Surgeon Leonard Shlain[34] described the evolution of the human intellect
as corresponding to a gradual empathy for the three dimensions of Eulidean
space and to three states of time—past, present, and future. The seventh
dimension is Einstein's spacetime continuum. Such types of perception require the cultivation of thinking cooperatively between both brain hemispheres. Broad, general knowledge and skills can be cultivated for the
emergence of the Renaissance psyche.

### Gender and Cultural Differences in Brain Functioning

Neuroscientist Kenneth Klivington[35] described certain gender differences
in brain functioning. Complex motor skills are worse and spatial skills in
women are better when estrogen levels are low. Suggesting that there is less
specialization in the hemispheres of women, some research shows that the
female brain is more symmetrical. In females the corpus callosum connecting the two hemispheres is larger, which is related to greater verbal intel-

ligence.[36] The part of the left hemisphere responsible for language in females is smaller than for males, but female brain cells are more densely packed, which may compensate for the larger size found in males.

Klivington emphasized that experience in early life affects the organization of the brain such that cultural variations may influence minor differences in male and female brains. To the extent that these differences between male and female brains are valid and significant, the complementarity of the sexes is further emphasized. Just as interaction of different knowledge patterns can lead to unsuspected connections of great utility, the interaction of different cerebrations contributed by culturally different brains may lead to new concepts of great value.

Cultural influences on brain functioning are emphasized further by the contrast between the brains of people raised in and out of the Japanese culture.[37] The differences between the cultures are not racial but environmental and are affected by language differences. Emotion is centered in the left hemisphere for the Japanese, and in the right hemisphere for non-Japanese. Similarly, because of its highly emotional nature, sexual functioning is located in the left hemisphere for the Japanese and in the right hemisphere for non-Japanese. These differences in hemispherical dominance are instilled up to the critical age of nine. Raised elsewhere up to the age of nine, a Japanese child returning to live in Japan will continue to perceive his or her emotions like a non-Japanese.

Examples such as this are strong evidence that environmental influences play an important role in brain structure and functioning. On the other hand, abundant evidence also exists for evolutionary-genetic influences independent of the environment. Environmental and genetic influences on the human psyche apparently are intimately intertwined.

## Using Both Hemispheres in Thinking

The ability to alternate between both modes of thought is rare but was a process extensively used by Einstein.[38] His laboratory was largely within his mind. His approach began with visual thinking after which his understanding was reduced to mathematics. Only then would he check the literature for confirmation.

Physics professor Thomas West[39] suggested that Einstein's work be "black magic," as he did not have enough data to develop his theories. He deviated significantly from scientific method, but his approach precluded the establishment of the potentially debilitating effect of preconceived notions. Nevertheless, most scientists seem to study pertinent literature at the beginning.

Described by design engineer James Adams,[40] Robert McKim delineated three essential kinds of visual imagery. Perceptual imagery is what we see and record in our brains; mental imagery is a construct of our minds derived from recorded perceptions; graphic imagery includes drawn or written communication. Perceptual imagery can be improved by first recognizing that people generally only see what is important to them, and then not always as well as they would like. This ability can be improved by drawing things that are seen, especially those things that are considered most important.

By fusing right-handed and left-handed thinking, by purposely generating contradiction and conflict in perceptions, the thought process can be activated and teased into peak performance. This is what journalist Arthur Koestler[41] called a bisociative shock, which he exemplified with a game of definitions: "What is a sadist? A sadist is a person who is kind to a masochist." Bisociated with two opposite meanings, they are linked by the word, 'kind.' Two different meanings can be derived from the definition. The sadist does a kindness to the masochist by torturing him, or the sadist is torturing the masochist by being kind to him.

The sadist goes against his nature in both situations. This paradox can be resolved by recognizing that in either case "kind" must be understood "literally and metaphorically at the same time." The resolution can be understood in the true sense of fuzzy logic and janusian thinking. Koestler emphasized that reversals in logic and the consequent shattering of unimaginative thinking are integral to many discoveries. Creating such anxiety can be risky to one's mental health. But it can lead to titillating prose, bittersweet poems, Nobel Prize–winning theory, and breakthrough inventions, all of which are tension reducing.

## SUMMARY

Because it is important to discovery, visual-spatial thinking has been considered from many different angles. To complement verbal thinking, we can develop our ability to think visually. This can be done by appropriate exercises and awareness of the importance of vivid visualization. Visual, janusian, homospatial, and metaphorical thinking can be incorporated into our thought paradigms as well. Helen Keller summed up the importance of vision and visual thinking in one all-embracing statement, "Use your eyes as if tomorrow you will have been stricken blind."[42]

Because of the uncertainty of knowledge, researchers are forced to be pragmatists, to follow the path of whatever works. On the positive side, the uncertain, dynamic, and evolutionary nature of knowledge suggests an enormous potential for discovery—a veritable utopia for scientists and technologists. The key is persistent, broadly based, open-minded, critical probing. Indeed, it is only by practice and experience that a significant empathy is acquired for the heuristic of discovery. For those who have discovery as their goal, research is not only a vector but an essential, ongoing training ground.

To think with as much clarity and depth as possible and to carry out the best possible research, it is important to have a good working knowledge of as many viable thought processes as possible. Conventional thinking is indispensable to good science and technology and for best results can be thoroughly ingrained into one's thought paradigm. Without taxing and expanding thought processes with unconventional thinking to transcend the mundane, however, progress can become dangerously limited.

The highlights of both conventional and unconventional thinking are summarized by eleven critical considerations to facilitate thought processes that can lead to discovery.

- Be intimately familiar with the essential thought processes involved in scientific method—deduction, induction, and abduction, and invaluable adjuncts such as dialectic and analogical reasoning.
- Allow inductive and deductive reasoning to be the final arbiter in the study of nature, not common sense. Sometimes, elegant theory may displace empiricism temporarily.
- Be constantly aware of the uncertainty of presuppositions, not only to help inhibit mind-sets but to be more alert to flaws in concepts and to be more receptive to change.
- To gain the favorable effects of the interactions of different knowledge patterns, incorporate the dialectic into the scientific process as extensively as possible.
- Find the optimum solution path by exerting a major effort to generate and to explore experimentally all feasible hypotheses to account for a phenomenon.
- Be aware of the relative advantages of reductionism and holism. Practice holism where feasible to promote disparate knowledge interaction and a greater potential for creativity.
- Be aware of the power of scientific thinking, but recognize the importance of transcending conventional methods.
- Develop a working knowledge of as many unconventional methods of thinking as possible. Insert curiosity and intuition when possible.
- Tease the thought process into peak performance by purposely generating conflict and contradiction in perceptions. Think of similarities, opposites, and what-ifs; create paradox, oxymorons, and reversals in logic; visualize via *Anshauung, Anshaulichkeit*, homospatially, and by any other viable method.
- Where knowledge growth is restricted largely to mathematical formalisms, use intuition and visualizability (*Anshaulichkeit*) to enhance the thought process.
- Be aware constantly and optimistically of the tremendous potential for discovery.

The next chapter is a general essay on the problems of accuracy in discovery, the elusive truth, and the enhancement of scientific method. It concludes with a brief statement about the difficulty of transition from discovery to commercialization.

*Chapter 17*

# Illumination

---

After a vast accumulation of knowledge, the intense research of a problem, and adequate time for incubation and stimulation, an *aha!* may emerge (see Figure 6.1). Unfortunately, many *aha!*s are like Bidwell's ghost, the positive afterimage that one sees after being exposed to a flash of light in a dimly lit area. Within a short time the ghost, like many *aha!*s, disappears. Occasionally, an *aha!* remains lucid even after analysis and has sufficient new concept or new product potential to be run through the gauntlet of verification and critical development.

## EXPERIMENTER AND OBSERVER EFFECTS

False illuminations, or Bidwell's ghosts, can arise from observer or experimenter effects. Historian of science Horace Freeland Judson[1] described the observer defect in Sir Isaac Newton's light experiment. When a prism separates sunlight into its component bands of color, the bands are striped with dark lines. These lines represent the wavelengths at which light is absorbed by elements in the sun. Newton based his theory of color and light on this spectrum, but he did not give consideration to the absorption lines. Described by Judson, exact replication of the original experiment by William Bisson at M.I.T. showed that the absorption lines would have been visible to Newton. Arguments have been put forth that Newton's theory simply had no place for these lines. His theoretical assumptions eclipsed the otherwise clear evidence.

Observer effects are similar to experimenter effects where, unintentionally, expectations shade results. Despite lack of empirical evidence, subjective experiences sometimes can convince researchers that something is true.

Such unsubstantiated, intuitive persuasion can be the source of pathological science and false beliefs. The extent to which experimenter effects occur in research is not at all clear, but logic and introspection demand a higher level of incidence than many of us are willing to admit. Verification and consensus in the scientific community, therefore, are the most effective ways and last refuge for objectivity in science.

Being deeply aware of the ease with which error can occur in science and technology, researchers can become more adept at avoiding problems of observation and experimentation. This can occur by reviewing, repeatedly, quality of data and interpretations for accuracy. Despite the desire for objectivity, the framework of science is far more than disembodied theories. It also reflects, to a variable extent, the speculation, the idiosyncrasies, and the biases of people. Scientific method and its variants and the people who carry it out, despite their flaws, are the agencies by which growth in science and technology occurs. Generally these systems provide for significant progress, as witness the current state of science compared to the beginning of the twentieth century.

## PATHWAYS TO DISCOVERY

Science writer John Horgan[2] described an observation made by physicist David Bohm. If a glass barrier is placed in a fish tank, the fish stay clear of it. If it is removed, the fish continue to stay clear of where the barrier had been. By this illusory means, the limits of their world have been defined. Researchers may, in some related fashion, subconsciously define the limits of their world, thereby limiting their ability to discover.

Perhaps the most common way that ability to discover is limited is by the premature narrowing of approaches to problems. Emphasized throughout this book, discovery is achieved by following many different avenues, and the recognition of a new avenue, right or wrong, can become useful to discovery. Root-Bernstein[3] pointed out that Edison's inventions were founded using incorrect electrical theories. Nevertheless, the inventions worked. Edison found reasons, no matter how wrong, to try something that had never been tried before. Even by falsity, novel and useful discoveries can be achieved.

Einstein relied on the elegance of theory, laughing in the face of empiricism, to lead him to the most outstanding of discoveries. Einstein's superb brain was highly instrumental in his success, and not everyone could derive theories so elegant as relativity. The approach, however, is worth trying if one has such a predisposition. Conventional approaches, as embodied by the scientific method, are unquestionably of great value but usually do not lead to novelty. Any unconventional approach that will facilitate new ideas should be an adjunct to the scientific method. Pragmatism, besides life in general, has its place in science and technology.

Develop processing systems, which will reduce operational cost such that all competition is negated, and develop unique new processes on demand that can be utilized at nominal costs.

Develop a paper coating clay, which can be applied easily at high solids and top coating speeds, which will give total opacity brightness, and gloss, and which will give perfect printability, all at nominal cost.

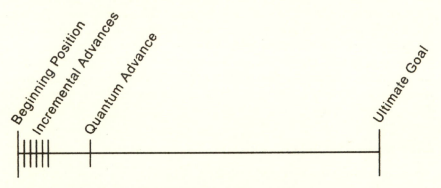

**Figure 17.1.** Examples of ultimate goals: Modern alchemy.

Although major discoveries are the goals of most creative scientists and technologists, incremental advances are the rule rather than the exception. In Figure 17.1 two goals are described, which are reminiscent of the alchemists, but which exemplify the ultimate directions in which technologists strive. Both goals have about as much credibility as the young engineer who thought that steel wool was the fleece of a hydraulic ram. Incremental advances are overwhelmingly the result of attempts to achieve greater goals.

The Japanese face this reality of incremental advance and do an outstanding job of capitalizing on small improvements. Many creative people in Japan devote their efforts to perfecting concepts resulting in extraordinary new products.[4] Cultural in origin, it is a method of creation distinctly different from what has been the custom in the West. This is exemplified best by miniaturization: bonsai trees, recorders, and hand-held video cameras.

## THE VENERABLE *AHA!*

An *aha!* may be only a new fragment of knowledge or, in the ultimate sense, a new viable combination of ideas or patterns of knowledge. An *aha!*

may be the discovery of something that has always existed, such as a nuclear energy. It may be the creation of something that has never existed before, such as a Shakespearian play. Serendipity, an unplanned result, is also an *aha!* but because it is the common result of carefully planned research, it is not strictly dumb luck. A good visual definition of serendipity of unknown origin is looking for a needle in a haystack, but instead coming up with the farmer's daughter.

Described by Root-Bernstein,[5] Horace Walpole coined the name "serendipity" in 1754. Reading the fairy tale of "The Three Princes of Serendip," Walpole noted that "as their highnesses traveled, they were always making discoveries by accident and sagacity, of things they were not in quest of." Serendip was formerly the name of Ceylon, which is now Sri Lanka.

Achievement of an *aha!* is, to a considerable extent, dependent on one's state of mind. It requires a sense of purpose, insatiable desire, and the propensity to explore many different avenues. Howard Gardner[6] referred to the accumulation of the "capital of creativity," which arises from a childhood in which learning about the world takes place in "a comfortable and exploring way." Great harm is done to the creative ability of children when information is conveyed as singularly correct and absolute.

Just how incorrigible wrongheaded conditioning of youth is to creativity is not clear, but it is never too late to improve one's creative outlook. Encouragement by a mentor to view the world in an adventurous, exploratory style can be highly conducive to the accumulation of creative capital. Gardner contended that the creator is one who interacts the most sophisticated understandings of his professional domain with the innocent excitement about nature that characterizes childhood. Cultivating an exploratory attitude can be helpful not only in one's professional domain but in life generally.

A closer connection exists between scientific creativity and scientific writing than is readily apparent.[7] Collation and writing are important components of the creative process and commonly bring observations to light that otherwise may be missed. It is a time, perhaps, when more attention is directed toward the interrelation of phenomena than at any other time during the entire investigation. Writing for publication and preparation for presentation before critical peers promotes more penetrating thought designed to preclude embarrassment and to further reputation. It is a process that is promoted beyond a reasonable limit by the publish-or-perish credo of academe. On the other hand, it is greatly underdone in industry, where an obsessive fear often exists that secrets will be revealed. Additionally, management often fails to recognize the priceless benefits of maintaining a worldwide dialectic.

## THE MOMENT OF DISCOVERY

If one were to emulate all of those actions attendant with creativity, there is no guarantee that historic cognition would come about, but the odds of success would be greatly enhanced. At the minimum, the results should give rise to a profound understanding of the matter in question. Some chance is involved in the creative process,[8] and so the player of the creative game is at the mercy of probability. Social conditions must be ripe for the invention. Discovery is made more probable and the possibilities riper by the development of expertise, which is a major reason the same discovery can be made at the same time by different people.[9] Chance, in the sense of serendipity, however, is probably a misnomer. As Pasteur explained, chance favors the prepared mind.

In his book *In the Palaces of Memory*, science writer George Johnson[10] described the moment of discovery as "that rare existential moment, when, by the very act of observation, subject and object fuse in a jolt of recognition." Johnson continued by describing some observations of the neurobiologist Gary Lynch, still about discovery:

It is an experience that remarkably few people have. You'd think that it is part and parcel of the scientific process, but it is not. Once you've had the feeling, it is like trying to tell people what it is like to see color when they don't see color. It is not even a level of intellectual understanding; it is a level of emotional understanding.

If only the intoxication and the thrill of discovery could be taught, the intellectual level of science would advance at a much greater pace. The business management of the world, perhaps, would have greater empathy for the needs of science and technology. Unfortunately, a significant empathy for the heuristic of discovery comes only after much experience.

## THE ELUSIVE "TRUTH"

Despite the power of scientific method for gaining new knowledge, researchers are still left with an uncertain understanding of reality. Uncertainty persists despite deductive logic derived by the ancient Greeks, Descartes' analytical method of reasoning, Francis Bacon's inductive logic via experiment and observation, Galileo's controlled experiment, and by mathematics promoted by Sir Isaac Newton for precision language. Uncertainty is most pronounced in the area of frontier science.

Inductive logic, which, along with deduction, is the basic substance of scientific method, is plagued with a lack of finality. All conclusions drawn from inductive logic are limited and tentative. Even when verification and peer review are added to this process and a consensus in the scientific community is obtained, the uncertainty remains. The mathematician Jacob

Bronowski indicated that since 1867 essentially every fundamental scientific theory has been changed significantly.[11]

In contrast, the physicist Steven Weinberg[12] points out that in the past hundred years not a single fundamental theory of physics has been refuted. These observations are not necessarily in conflict, as theories have been modified, but their reality basis has not been changed. Weinberg concludes, therefore, that science is moving closer to objective truth.

If we consider some findings of modern physics, however, it is rather easy to fall into a nihilistic depression. Consider the observation that sub-atomic matter is to some extent a function of the will of the experimenter and that it only tends to occur, or that chaos theory is unpredictable. More alarming and to the point, Bertrand Russell said, "The trouble with the world is that the stupid are cocksure and the intelligent full of doubt."[13] But it is this side of science, its uncertainty, that for many gives it its most intriguing character.

Because of the problems associated with validity and reach of knowledge, it may be perplexing that science possesses its current high level of credence. Empirical uncertainty, deductive uncertainty, lack of holistic consideration, evolution, uncertainty principles, necessity of viewing from the outside (Godel's Theorem), unpredictability of chaos theory, indeterminacy of quantum events, and human error all contribute to the difficulty in obtaining reliable knowledge. On the other hand, internal unity and coherence give science credibility, which allows it to make predictions with higher probability of accuracy than any other system.[14]

While the philosophers can continue the debate of knowledge validity, undoubtedly to our long-term benefit, scientists and technologists can suffice in the great merit of both successful prediction and technological achievement. As Bauer[15] explained, science helps keep authority honest as well. "Emperors and popes used to insist that people subscribe to lies about the earth, about the relationships between different sorts of people, and about a lot of other things."

Although the uncertainty of frontier science is real, the problem of validity is often exaggerated. As new principles are established, evaluation by an ever-increasing range of scientists can help to increase or decrease the validity of frontier knowledge. Overwhelmingly better than ignorance, approximate knowledge enables society to progress. Without a high degree of truth, prediction and technology would be far less successful, and progress in science would stagnate. Hypotheses, after extensive study and acceptance in the scientific community, become theory and textbook science. Largely true, textbook science probably will not undergo significant change.

Uncertainty in frontier science waves the red flag. It admonishes researchers to be ever vigilant and ever skeptical for even the most obvious and sacred tenet may need alteration or even total change to be brought a little closer to reality. Perhaps the most intriguing aspect of uncertainty in science is that it calls attention to a tremendous potential for creativity and discovery. It is not known if the potential for discovery is infinite, but it seems to be so immense that it might as well be. It is not like panning for gold in a depleted placer deposit; it is more like recovering a straw from an ever-renewing haystack—guarded by a mad bull! Israeli biologist Lee Segel[16] considers science to have a fractal structure [therefore, technology as well], such that there is no limit to things that can be investigated (see Chapter 4).

In the words of an incisive wit, "Science is continually making progress because it is never certain of its results."[17] Knowledge is dynamic and ever subject to change, and each change that gives a better approximation of reality represents a quantum jump via creativity. Thomas Huxley anticipated this thought when he said, "History warns us . . . that it is the customary fate of new truths to begin as heresies and to end as superstitions."[18]

The areas from which science receives its greatest sources of credibility are in successful prediction, repeatability, and technology. Although these consequences of good research do not impose epistemological verity, they are a representation of the value and of the high degree of workable ideas that can come from science. Continually being reconstituted, progress in science is marked by the ever-increasing reliability of knowledge. An asymptotic approach to truth, the process of science is the only reliable system for the evolution of knowledge.

Explained by Henry Bauer,[19] the constraints of reality have enabled an international consensus about many of the matters of science—in particular, textbook science. Consensus in science arises from what Bauer calls "reality therapy," the slow process of making one's beliefs fit observed reality. Other disciplines, Bauer observes, are in continuous dispute; and despite warfare and torture, politics and religion have not been able to achieve consensus. Society lives at the peak of materialism, which cannot last indefinitely. And then what? All philosophies, if they are to be viable, must continually evolve to accommodate inevitable change. The philosophy of science is continuously evolving and is generally designed to accommodate both change and consensus.

Observed by E.O. Wilson,[20] "It [science] is the accumulation of humanity's organized, objective knowledge, the first medium devised able to unite people everywhere in common understanding. It favors no tribe or religion. It is the base of a truly democratic and global culture."

## ENHANCEMENT OF THE SCIENTIFIC METHOD

Science is, indeed, a spectactular intellectual achievement, a complex system for achieving a vast amount of workably reliable knowledge that no other discipline can claim. Contended by Alan Cromer (Chapter 7), the greatest debt of gratitude is owed the ancient Greeks for this achievement. They firmly established the ideal of objectivity and other incipient stages of the methods of science. The Renaissance was a time for the expansion of science and technology and the renewed evolution of the scientific method. The current high success in science and technology, in addition to these earlier contributions, is the result of the development of multifarious variations of heuristic generated by creators since the Renaissance.

Contemporary science, therefore, cannot be accurately characterized by the scientific method. But it can be by a multitude of approaches that permit creativity and discovery to be far greater than if the classic ideal were practiced conservatively. In reality, therefore, innumerable variants of "scientific method" are utilized by scientists and technologists.

The pragmatic approach to creativity and discovery that is presented in Chapter 18, the thesis of this book, is a variant of the scientific method designed with the hope of improving the process of science and technology. It goes substantially beyond the scientific method and is generally a much closer fit with how the most successful contemporary scientists and technologists approach technical problems. Such a holistic system, approaching the unknown from many directions using idiosyncratic techniques, effectively appeals to creativity and an enhanced rate of knowledge growth.

A uniform, inflexible process of science, undoubtedly, would dangerously stagnate the growth of knowledge, and many fallacies would become chiseled in stone. The holistic approach to knowledge, along with the obligatory consensus for acceptance of new theory in the scientific community, enables a prolific development of new and reliable knowledge. Such an approach gives significant hope for the future of science—therefore, civilization.

## COMMERCIALIZATION OF DISCOVERY

Until discovery is verified and implemented, it can be considered little more than an intellectual curiosity—an exception being elegant theory. The definition of creativity generally demands implementation, which is essential to the demonstration of usefulness. Verification is commonly a long and arduous task, which may require as much effort as the original discovery. In technology, implementation, in effect, is commercialization.

Commercialization is beyond the scope of this book, but reduction to practice and sale of inventions is a subject about which many thoughtful and seemingly incisive tomes have been written. Only a few companies have become proficient at commercialization of new ideas. It is a process that is fraught with obstacles of which many are artifacts of management systems, many are deep-seated and psychological, and many are dependent on the idiosyncrasies of the marketplace. Perhaps the greatest weakness of industry, commercialization of new ideas is a process that deserves at least as much attention as discovery. Successful commercialization is an absolute necessity for the continued financial support of both basic and applied research.

A new model has been proposed for creativity and discovery, and its philosophy has been expounded from knowledge gain, through preparation, incubation, stimulation, illumination, and verification. It seems appropriate then to consider implementation of creativity and discovery in the last four chapters.

*Part III*

# Making Creativity and Discovery
# a Reality

*Chapter 18*

# The Environment and Actions That Stimulate Creativity and Discovery

The principles of creativity outlined in this book include:

- extensive, continuous learning,
- research for the generation of new, historical knowledge,
- broad dialectical interactions with knowledgeable people,
- use of both conventional and unconventional thought processes,
- holistic approaches to problem solving where possible,
- passionate perseverance, and
- an encouraging and supportive work environment.

These principles apply not only to creativity in science and technology but to all areas of human endeavor. They are keys to success in whatever career is chosen.

## THE CREATIVE PROCESS

In the creative process, scientists and technologists first build a platform of conventional knowledge. The size of this platform is critical to success, and critical mass is achieved only with the acquisition of an inordinate level of knowledge. This high level of knowing includes in-depth knowledge of a domain, and general knowledge over many domains.

Expansion of knowledge grows by way of diverse research across disciplinary lines, by the dialectic among diverse people, and by continuous mind experiments. Intrinsic motivation and passion for work are inseparable companions of the creative researcher. Publishing widely, the researcher builds the courage and the confidence to challenge conventionality.

In the view of Thomas Kuhn's normal science, the scientist clings to the conventional platform. The energy barrier between the conventional and the unconventional is enormous. Creative or revolutionary researchers take the giant plunge from this platform into heuristic and unconventionality. He or she has a mind-set to effect at least a ripple in the wisdom of the world. The irrational and the rational mix; reverie and dreams emerge as possibilities. Hopes of achievement become reality.

Establishing the platform of conventional knowledge generally follows an algorithmic path. Sequence and order are prime. The heuristic path is open-ended and many different approaches in time and space are pursued. It is this circuitous path that can lead, with the essential help of perseverance, to the unconventional. Called by existentialists the anxiety of nothingness,[1] the mental state in this venture into the unknown effects a probe into uncertainty where novelty resides.

As the creative process is conceived in this book, it begins with knowledge gain and, ideally, proceeds through preparation, incubation, stimulation, illumination, and verification. Knowledge gain is fundamental, not only to survival of life but to creativity. Preparation is the time of tackling a specific problem. This initial approach can be assisted by an informal algorithm. Using the scientific method in conjunction with breadth and depth of knowledge, the great power of the dialectic, a limited form of holism, and the mystique of unconventional thinking, creativity and discovery often are the products.

Incubation is a time for continuous reformulation, perhaps in the nonconscious mind, that often leads to inspiration and occasionally to *aha!*s. Coexistent with incubation, the processes of stimulation can further encourage creativity. These stimuli come under the headings of research, the shuttle effect, and thought processes.

Research is a primary source of mental stimulation. The constant effort to interpret and incorporate experimental observations often teases thought to go beyond the ordinary. It arouses the mind to be in a more acute state of awareness. Using the shuttle effect, different knowledge patterns from the dialectic are interacted synergistically. Novelty arises from the interaction of many knowledge patterns possessed by many different people in many locations, past and present. Conventional and unconventional thought are the mental artifacts that transform knowledge into holistic packets of novelty. Largely a result of unconventional thinking, novelty may arise from the most unexpected and seemingly irrational of mechanisms.

Although it is conceded generally that creativity in science and technology is heuristic and not algorithmic, this view should be modified as is outlined in the preceding paragraphs. To establish the platform of knowledge necessary to creativity, the path is largely algorithmic. At least in its early stages, research is generally algorithmic. To have a reasonable grasp of a discipline or a subject a rather high degree of knowledge organization is required.

A component of the scientific method, hypothesizing is often heuristic and unconventional, but the remainder of the steps generally are algorithmic. This is often true, even though different styles of research may take on some heuristic character and creativity may occur at any stage in the scientific process. Generally, quantum leaps in discovery do not arise until a broad knowledge base is established and the investigator has anguished and struggled to the point of frustration. From this point of departure springs the heuristic or the nonalgorithmic path to creativity.

Because the heuristic of creativity and discovery is the theme of this book, this summary chapter is devoted to highlighting those procedures most critical to the goal of discovery. These five points prescribe a preliminary approach to creativity in science and technology.

1. Cultivate a passionate immersion in your profession.
2. Carry out diverse research projects across disciplinary lines and maintain an international dialectic.
3. Cultivate an indelible hope of causing a ripple in the wisdom of the world.
4. Unshackle your mind of conditioned thought constraints.
5. Develop the confidence and the courage to defy convention.

## A PRAGMATIC APPROACH TO CREATIVITY AND DISCOVERY

Although there is much to be learned about how to achieve creativity, a pragmatic approach has been devised and is shown below. (The steps shown in the approach follow the model for creativity in Figure 6.1, and are published with minor modification, with the permission of Crisp Publications [Bundy, 1997, pp. 50–51].) These steps can be considered in addition to whatever variant of the scientific method the researcher may create. They are designed to preclude excessive reliance on the logical empiricism imposed by the scientific method. Such reliance generally preserves the status quo. For creativity and discovery, researchers transcend the conventional thinking of logical empiricism and plunge into the abyss of heuristic.

### Knowledge Gain

- Choose a work environment having a keen and broad-ranging intellectual spirit.
- As an ongoing process, cultivate a vast breadth of knowledge, particularly in the sciences and the arts. Carry out prolific diverse research projects that can be interrelated and potentially linked for problem solutions.

- Opposed to minute detail, concentrate on the most basic points of knowledge patterns.
- Through the process of knowledge gain and publication, develop the confidence and the courage to defy convention.
- Do not be afraid to cultivate intellectual unconventionality.

## Preparation

- Choose those problems of study for which you have or can cultivate intrinsic motivation. Choose those issues that are not fads, that may be considered too difficult by others, and that are anomalies.
- Create your own algorithmic approach to the initial stages of problem solution. Give special consideration to steps that will transcend conventional thinking.
- If appropriate to the problem, derive a mechanistic new product development schematic. From this derive an approximate new product formula and list research programs to address the weakest links in understanding.
- Make certain that the relevant fundamental science is understood before launching into targeted research.
- Continuously question assumptions.

## Incubation

- Carry out multiple tasks consisting largely of research projects.
- Take respites from the most refractory problems to allow incubation to proceed. This is accomplished partly by having multiple tasks and partly by restful, relaxing diversions.

## Stimulation

- Allow anomaly to drive your research.
- Be aware of the relative advantages of reductionism and holism. Practice holism where feasible to promote knowledge interaction and a greater potential for creativity.
- In the approach to problems generally, do not rely solely on the expertise of specialists. As much as possible, become the Renaissance man or woman of the company. For the academic scientist, learn, interact, and strive for connections with different disciplines.
- Cultivate "hands on" or Taoistic knowing in your approach to problem solution. For new product development, make technological market surveys.
- To avoid the paradigmatic mind-set, generate and test all feasible hypotheses. Be tenacious in attempting to find the most creative and useful hypothesis. Strive for elegant theory.
- To preclude the collapse of the Schrödinger wave function, do not focus on a hypothesis until all possibilities are considered.
- Satiate intuition and curiosity regarding all aspects of problems under study.

- Allow and perpetuate humor in your research effort.
- Promote diversity by exchange with global contacts, by giving papers at professional meetings, and travel for contact with diverse events.
- To assist the search for truth, attempt both to confirm and to falsify theory.
- Always view new knowledge in the sense of discovery—probe the impact that it may have on your knowledge. Ask what other questions new knowledge poses. What other research should be carried out? How can it be used to improve products or create new ones?
- Be aware of the power of the scientific method, but also know its limits and the importance of transcending conventional thinking.
- Cultivate many conventional and unconventional thought processes. Include verbal, spatial, and visual thought variations.
- By whatever means is effective for you, unburden and unshackle your mind of conditioned thought constraints. Tease the thought process into peak performance by purposely generating conflict and contradiction in perceptions. Think of similarities, opposites, and "what ifs." Create paradox, oxymorons, and reversals in logic. Visualize via *Anschauung*, *Anshaulichkeit*, homospatially, and by any other viable method.
- Be aware of the uncertainty of presuppositions, not only to help inhibit mind-sets but to be more alert to flaws in concepts and to be more receptive to change. As stated by Abraham Maslow, "Cultivate the humility of the empirical attitude."
- Be aware constantly and optimistically of the tremendous potential for discovery.

### Illumination

- Prepare company reports with the same diligence and thoroughness as manuscripts for publication.
- Be diligent in preparing papers for publication and for presentation at scientific and technological conferences. Strive for quality rather than quantity.

While it may not always be feasible or possible to follow all the steps, each suggests the ideal condition. The approach is pragmatic and inductive. Parameters outlined are those employed by the most successful creators. No substitute exists, however, for profound, abiding, and passionate interest.

Undoubtedly, other useful stimuli could be devised, but those listed are, perhaps, the most important. It is the persistent interaction of these many stimuli that occasionally produces novelty. As these stimuli are continuously and intensively pursued, the chances of creativity and discovery are enhanced. An active, abiding dialectic between all stimuli must exist for the probability of success to be at its peak. Creativity will emerge when a coalescence of stimuli produces a unique synergism that has utility.

If the path to novel ideas is thought of as a consequence of following each of these actions in sequence, creativity again takes on some algorithmic character. It is through the faithful execution of these steps in whatever order seems most appropriate, however, that the heuristic of inspiration, intuition, unconventional thinking, serendipity, visceral hypothesizing, and dreaming are activated.

These stimuli are tools for generating new ideas that will help creative exploration. Projection of new knowledge to concepts that are unique is the most basic tool of the creator. Much can be learned from art connoisseurs and their inspired interpretation of paintings, especially abstract. With the connoisseur's imagination, a seemingly vacuous painting is transformed into an intellectual treasure of ideas. This is in accord with Picasso's trenchment comment, "Art is a lie that helps us see the truth."[2]

Such a release of the imagination is precisely what creators seek in the study of natural phenomena—an intellectual treasure of ideas that will facilitate approaching truth by trying things that have never been tried before. Often making little difference how right or wrong the ideas are, they can open the door to many different approaches.

Unless the relative validity of new ideas is investigated, creativity will not flourish. New ideas frequently are shelved in favor of the pressure of daily routine—perhaps the most common reason for sparsity of discovery. So easily neglected, probing validity of new ideas is fundamental to tapping creative potential. It is the womb of creativity and the first stage of innovation.

Profound growth in understanding cannot occur without this process; it is basic to the shedding of fallacy and the evolution of new viable ideas. This process is nothing less than "research," which has gained a disturbingly high level of infamy in many industrial circles. Such an opinion often is justified when the research is not strategically oriented, and when new knowledge is not diligently probed for commercialization.

In industry, if new knowledge from research is always exhaustively analyzed for its relationship to commercial application, a surprising number of new, potential pathways to profit can be found. Commercialization of discovery is an essential source of wealth for the justification of research. Searching for ways to change knowledge into profit could be an approach to stimulate creative thinking in the academic researcher as well.

## THE ESSENTIAL INTERACTION BETWEEN INDUSTRIAL INNOVATION AND ACADEMIC BASIC RESEARCH

Business management often holds that research is a luxury that is unaffordable without first developing profitable products. It is not clear how they expect viable ideas to arise for new products. Seemingly they assume that sufficient knowledge exists, or that invention can be derived by the mythical "stroke of genius," or by serendipity.

Existing knowledge can sometimes be sufficient to develop new products, but it is the dynamics of knowledge promoted by research that is most effective in cultivating novelty. Occasionally, serendipity may lead to new products, but new knowledge gained through strategic research is a much more reliable and cost-effective route to novelty. Of subtle but great significance, it is through the gaining of new knowledge that serendipity is most likely to occur.

Strategic research and profitable new products are inextricably intertwined. The amount of research needed is in accord with the amount of new knowledge needed to achieve goals. When management wins in this conflict of philosophies, the status quo usually is maintained.

Innovation is the most basic driving force of successful industry and must be continuously promoted for general social wealth. By the steady support of academic, basic research and industrial, strategic research for idea generation, creativity and discovery can peak. Major breaks in carrying out this creative process subvert discovery and the source of wealth needed to maintain the research-discovery-innovation cycle (see Figure 18.1). Although often in subtle but important ways, academic research and industrial research thrive on each other's successes. The systems are not only cyclic but symbiotic. Biologist Lynn Margulis[3] believed that symbiosis has been the major innovator in the evolution of all nonbacterial organisms (as in the merger of microbe and animal cell or the merger of microbe and plant cell). Similarly, symbiosis has played a major role in the evolution of science and technology. Exemplified by X-ray diffraction in determining the structure of materials, many scientific revolutions are tool-driven, which makes technology essential to the maximum development of science. Concept-driven science may lead to new technology as Newtonian mechanics and relativity theories critical to the exploration of space. Science provides understanding and prediction of phenomena, essential to the continued advancement of technology.

New knowledge and theories from academe can lead to a better fundamental understanding of the universe, solutions to social problems, to new product concepts, and to strategic research for industry. Additionally, through new knowledge wealth can come to the academic institution by way of licenses for patents, grants, and indirectly through enhanced image.

To countervail the conservative approach of industry to research, the greater freedom of academe to do basic research is essential. Such freedom can lead to new ideas and new, viable approaches to problems that industry is unlikely to expose. Strategic research in industry can lead to innovation or to more basic research in academe. New product concepts sometimes generate new ideas for basic research.

The wealth generated from innovation may be a direct support for additional industrial research. Taxation of the resultant increase in social wealth can lead to larger university budgets and more government grants for support of fundamental research. This complex, social construct, cyclic

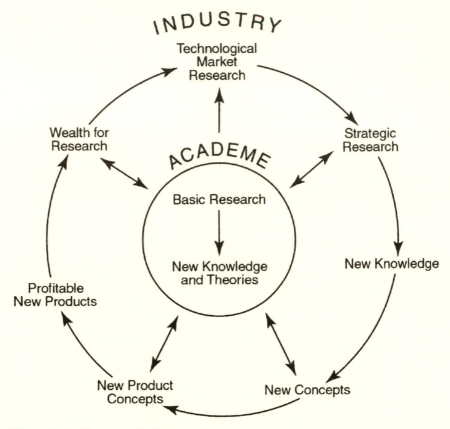

**Figure 18.1.** The research-discovery-innovation cycle.

and interdependent, is essential to the overall financial and technological well-being of society.

Without long-term support of industrial and academic research, the entire system is weakened. If new, strategic knowledge is not continuously generated, critical company problems that transcend conventional wisdom will likely languish amid vain attempts at resolution. And academic, basic research will flounder or even disappear in a less affluent society.

Emphasized by the late astronomer and biologist Carl Sagan,[4] the government has been urging the National Science Foundation to forego basic research and to support technology. Some members of Congress want to do away with the U.S. Geological Survey and critical environmental expenditures. The business of science is considered unimportant and is slighted in favor of expensive weapons of little need in the post-Soviet world. Such myopia is dangerous in a world where the science-technology interaction is critical to society's economic and social well-being.

Support of intellectual curiosity, frowned on in some circles, has led to the development of revolutionary technologies. Some of these are radio, radar, television, X rays, antibiotics, and methods to cure genetic diseases. Without fundamental science, technology would lose its major source of clout, and vice versa. The symbiosis between science and technology is the "invisible hand" of innovative industry and a thriving economy.

## AN APPROXIMATE ALGORITHM FOR NEW PRODUCTS AND NEW PROCESSES

Described by computer scientist Christopher Langton,[5] algorithms are expected to be precise and predictable. Surprisingly, he has found that in computers algorithms can lead to completely novel and unpredictable patterns. Here, algorithms can be just as turbulent as the outside world.

Because flexibility is encouraged and desirable, this protean character is even more true of informal algorithms. If followed rigidly, the scientific method usually preserves the status quo. With constructive modification it can become disarmingly creative. In this sense, the informal, general algorithm for new product and process development described below may be just as productive of creativity as Langton's computer algorithms.

Technological market surveys, mechanistic new product development schemes, the algorithm for initiation of problem study, and the stimuli for creativity can be thought of as parts of a rough algorithm for achieving novel results. The last part of the algorithm should include two stages for new product and new process development.

> *Stage I.*  Requires broad applied knowledge. This stage entails thorough probing of new knowledge to derive new research, product upgrades, new product concepts, or new process concepts.
>
> *Stage II.*  Through applied research, market research, process research, and costing, the new product concept is designed to achieve profit.

The first step in the general algorithm shown below, technological market surveys (Chapter 8) and mechanistic new product schemes (Chapter 9) are for new product and new process ideas. The initiation algorithm (Chapter 9) and the research stimuli in this chapter can be useful for both idea generation and intermediate development of new product and new process ideas. This step is essential for understanding mechanisms of the new product concept and for potential areas of use.

The two stages of new product study are for idea generation and for the final part of new product and new process development. Idea generation is common to all of the steps in the algorithm, which is useful for continually upgrading and expanding new product and new process goals. It is beyond knowing what all the caveats are that people follow to achieve their creative goals. Following diverse paths, people often achieve creative goals by idiosyncratic methods. As in Langton's computer algorithms, the approaches in the algorithm for new product and new process development, used as an open-ended process, may activate individual creativity.

| Technological | + | Initiation | + | Two Stages for | = | New Products |
| Market | | Algorithm and | | New Product | | and |
| Surveys | | Research | | Study | | New Processes |
| and | | Stimuli for | | | | |
| Mechanistic | | Creativity | | | | |
| New Product | | | | | | |
| Schemes | | | | | | |

Creativity can arise when there is a continuous, intensive interaction between the patterns of knowledge derived from these approaches. Straightforward, this informal algorithm is generally understood by technologists, but it is rarely practiced by them with the depth and consistency needed for success. Excessive unrelated duties and lack of management support for research are the most common obstacles to this creative pursuit.

The term research in the algorithm is meant to include empirical, hypothetical, literature, and dialectical activities (Chapter 11). Following the model for creativity (Part II), the initiation algorithm, and the environment and actions that stimulate creativity in this chapter, the researcher continuously enhances chances for discovery. Technological market research and applied research are essential for the change of knowledge into profit.

Although it is sometimes necessary to contract research in external laboratories, in-house research often is most effective. Researchers who gain new understanding have the most profound comprehension and emotional attachment to their newly acquired knowledge. They have the greatest interest in the fruit of their hard fought battle with the unknown. Others will be apt to have a superficial understanding of the new knowledge and often are afflicted with the NIH (not-invented-here) syndrome. Having both responsibilities, basic research and development of new product concepts, can promote the most effective interaction of different knowledge patterns, so critical to creativity.

## THE ULTIMATE GOAL: INNOVATION

For innovation, a visionary, charismatic, competent technical leader, and talented, knowledgeable, spirited technical staff are idealistic requirements, yet critical. The technical people are convinced of their mission to find new knowledge and to change it into profit. The leader facilitates both processes. This dual approach of discovery and commercialization is crucial.

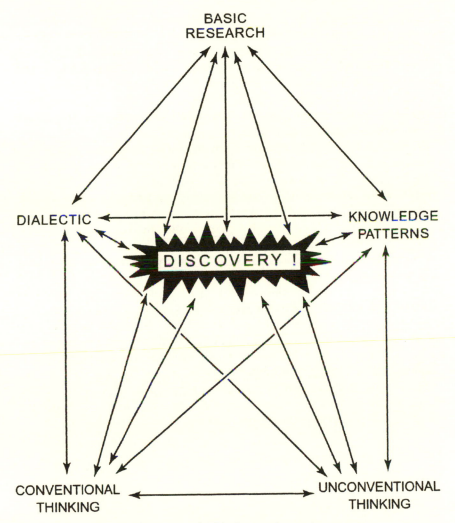

**Figure 18.2.** Discovery thrives in a highly interactive environment.

Some research people are averse to the "mundane" process of commercialization. Some may think that it is outside of their purview, or are fearful of the process. Others become so involved in their basic efforts that they lose contact with the need to apply. Without a dual quest to discover and apply, useful knowledge may never get into the hands of would-be entrepreneurs.

Following the devices described in this chapter, and others that you may develop, is a likely way to bypass the status quo and to find novelty. To have the talent of Einstein would help immeasurably, but passion and perseverance can displace the need for a great amount of talent. Passion and perseverance are the ultimate guides to novelty.

The raw truth is that there is nothing easy or magical about the discovery process. That's why many technology groups are not more innovative. Discovery requires extraordinarily hard work and the persistent interaction of a broad range of knowledge. Although the work is hard, if one begins to experience the emotional highs of even minor discovery, the process can become nearly exquisite pleasure.

Proprietary new products stem from discovery. Discovery arises most readily in a highly interactive environment as shown in Figure 18.2. Essentially dynamic, the creative process is continuously activated by intense interaction among research, diverse knowledge patterns and ways of thinking, and a continuous dialectic worldwide. These are powerful processes, a constant source of new energy that precludes the ultimate problem of entropy in a research laboratory.

The trove of creativity and discovery is potentially there for the individuals who want it almost as much as life itself. The beauty of the quest is that even if one fails to achieve the highest goal of discovery, the high probability is that the researcher will still be successful. Not only are high levels of scientific and technological knowledge usually in demand, it is enormously gratifying to be in command of a subject. The confidence and the prestige that such an achievement produces and the emotional high of discovery are well worth the costs.

The success of the science or technological part of a laboratory is usually strongly affected by the nature of the management. General management methods that promote discovery are outlined in the next chapter.

*Chapter 19*

# A Few Thoughts on the
# Management of Discovery

## INTRODUCTION

With suggested methods for the implementation of the best science and technology, Chapter 18 has been a review of the new model for creativity. Throughout the chapters that describe the new model, pathways to discovery have been analyzed by processes of science and technology. Management of technical groups plays an important role as well and is one of the most complex aspects of successful technology.

Today's competitive pressures for cost reduction can affect research and innovation. Industry trends are toward scaling back of research, emphasis on the short-term, and a tendency for market pull to suppress technology push.[1] Largely American,[2] this short-term orientation has additional life from restructuring, mergers, and takeovers. The resultant debt servicing and need to maximize cash flow take precedence over long-term investment. The atmosphere is risk averse with reduced technological capability. Not so dominated by short-term thinking and Wall Street pressures, companies formed in the last 20 years are the hope for the future of competitive America.

Although the destructive, short-term approach is not the practice of all companies, the growing competitive pressures of a global economy make giving new life to discovery and creativity critical to the well-being of industry. Scientists and technologists need to show, sell, and otherwise convince business management that invention is their richest and most ready source of vitality, growth, and profitability. With thoughtful incisive management and zero to modest budget increases, technology can invent lackluster industry into a competitive resurgence.

Many technology managers are vague about how to achieve a critical business goal—new products. This often leads to a haphazard approach and a failure to formulate viable new product concepts. Far too many new products fail, and the cost of failure can be inordinately high. Innovation failures, and innovation that is too slow, or not enough must bear considerable responsibility for low levels of competitiveness in industry.

The National Science Board Committee[3] surveyed R&D officials and published a report listing reasons believed to be the cause of recent erosion in U.S. technology leadership. General management practices and external financial pressures were listed as the two most important reasons for the decline. External financial pressures greatly affect management practices. Demands for substantial increases in profit each year and little understanding of the discovery process preclude the most effective long-term management practices.

Such observations wave the red flag signaling that changes in industry management practices for the achievement of innovation are essential to the U.S. economy. Practices that will enhance quality and quantity of discovery are needed. To address this need, eleven methods of discovery management that can be effective are listed in this chapter. There are other important principles that might be considered, but those presented are designed to impart a spirit of management that should embrace other important methods as well.

A primary tenet of management philosophy—that innovation is the most important goal of technology—is based on the industry axiom that the most successful companies are generally the most innovative. Otherwise cost reduction and increase in market share are the primary routes to increased profit. These latter two methods have limited utility whereas innovation has far greater potential.

Acceptance that innovation is the most important goal of technology means that the three most important functions of a technology group are (1) the optimization of creativity and discovery, (2) the generation of new product ideas, and (3) providing assistance for the commercialization of inventions.

## ELEVEN MANAGEMENT METHODS FOR DISCOVERY

The management of discovery can play a major role in bringing out the best in creative scientists and technologists. Eleven management methods described in this section are those that have been found to be the most successful in dealing with a wide range of disciplines and maverick personalities. It is not meant to be a definitive text on best practices but to highlight the most important aspects of discovery management.

1. *Through lab structure and management methods promote a highly interactive, knowledge-based system.*

A maxim of the creative process is that knowledge precedes novelty. Such that an anomaly will be recognized, even serendipity depends on sufficient understanding of the related discipline. Because invention arises from the interaction of different knowledge patterns, a major responsibility of the technology manager is to structure an manage the laboratory such that these diverse knowledge requirements are efficiently addressed and interacted.

The minimum knowledge requirements for each individual in an industrial research laboratory are shown in Figure 19.1 under knowledge gain and are described in Chapter 8. Researchers enhance their chances for discovery if they have the responsibility of diverse research projects covering these general subjects. Some gradational character of a broad range of projects can facilitate a more natural interaction. For best results, each project is of great interest to the individual, and the desire by the researcher to create and commercialize is insatiable.

These research programs can be set up as individual or group efforts, but overall it is helpful to have a cooperative effort to solve major problems. Approaching problems from as many different directions as possible can optimize chances for solution. The interaction between diverse approaches to problem solution is key to discovery.

Just as new knowledge derived from in-house research is mined thoroughly for potential utility, external research deserves the same treatment. Literature research is the most cost-effective way to enhance knowledge and to further the cause of innovation. Although invaluable, literature research does have its limits and cannot totally replace in-house, strategic research.

Periodic interactive sessions may be held to promote the benefits of dialectical research and to keep research spirit and direction vital, optimistic, and holistic. By way of appropriate rewards, the message can be clear that the success of the individual is as much dependent on cooperation with the group as it is on individual effort. If the leader of these sessions has sufficient research insight, the meetings can be kept lively and upbeat. Indeed, research spirit and morale can pivot around the quality of such meetings.

Progressive science and technology require the association of diverse professional people highly knowledgeable of the field and related fields. The dialectic between scientists and technologists that lead to invention precludes the viability of isolation. Richness of intellectual environment, availability of state of the art equipment, and access to abundant resources are important to the knowledge gain that will lead to invention.

The importance of the dialectic to creativity can be illustrated by a situation that occurred early in the history of the Ford Motor Company. Technology historian John Staudenmaier[4] described Henry Ford and his engineers between 1906 and 1914 as outstandingly innovative, creating perhaps the most successful technical design in American history. Designed with great efficiency to fit the needs of the time and to be sufficiently low cost for purchase by a broad range of people, the Model T was extraordinarily popular. To meet the tremendous demand, the moving assembly line enabling mass production was developed. Such innovation took place with outstanding and highly motivated engineers amid a system wide open to debate and risks.

The assembly line gave birth to onerous problems, particularly what the workers called "Forditis"—the consequence of the monotonous and nerve-racking effect of the moving line. This led to a turnover rate of 370%. With characteristic originality, Ford responded by shortening the workday and by doubling wages.

Emboldened by his great successes, he gradually attempted to control all aspects of the company. This was done by establishing a sociological department to control his workers, by vertically integrating the company, and by manipulation to become the sole owner of the Ford Motor Company. According to Staudenmaier, at this stage Ford became authoritarian and was not amenable to debate. He was drastically different and noncreative compared with what he was in the 1906 to 1914 period. His infatuation with his technological genius was in concert with his need to control.

Staudenmaier believed that such a plight can happen to any successful technologist. People cannot remain creative if they become so enamored with their creative ability that they forget to follow the most critical behavior that led them to their original success. People's ability to be creative is to a large extent a social covenant. An intense dialectic can enable a multiplicity of brains to merge and achieve what would be impossible or unlikely for the lone inventor.

Astutely observed by Staudenmaier, "Ford started out with a powerful conviction about what America wanted: the Model T. Then, having been so right, he forgot how to be wrong." Without debate, acceptance of error in ourselves and others, humor, hope, and imagination, the pathway to novelty disappears before the goal can be achieved.

Creativity is facilitated not only by an ongoing expansion of knowledge, but a continuous interaction of different knowledge patterns. While ideas are commonly profuse in research and development laboratories, frustration and futility in technologists often occur when they are being pressed for world-class ideas. This frustration usually stems from an inadequacy of conceptual base and a system that fails to promote extensive knowledge interaction.

2. *A technically competent, visionary leader working with highly talented scientists and engineers can enforce a judicious balance between time used for innovation and time used for other tasks.*

Successful technical laboratories seeking discovery are exciting, sexy places to work. Optimism, challenging goals, the exhilaration of problem solution, intellectually stimulating colleagues, and even minor discoveries ignite the imagination. Emotions become high pitched, ready to tackle every problem with a feverish drive to understand. Such an environment can be promoted by a strong, technically competent leader who can interact effectively with talented, technical people. He or she should have a contagious and visionary approach to the overall goal of the laboratory. Caught up in this emotional high, talented people are more apt to perform at levels of achievement heretofore unknown even to them. Always seeking new knowledge is their fuel for discovery and invention. Without such intensity, extraordinary achievements are not apt to occur.

Maintaining an empathy for technological needs is a critical aspect of good technology management. The player-coach method has great merit for this purpose. This way, technology managers maintain contact with research needs by conducting their own research project or projects, applied or basic, that relate to the needs of the group. They can follow through on their own ideas, and, thereby, grow in their understanding for assistance to the entire technology group. Their connection is then more than strictly managerial, but also directly linked by an empathy for the dialectic that must be promoted. This type of management potentially can have much greater meaning and credibility with the staff. It has greater potential for promoting goal achievement and morale, indeed, than much of the cumbersome baggage of modern business management.

The strength of the technology manager in asserting his or her leadership and technical competence is equally important. At the same time, all of the research staff can be participants in the decision-making process. Autocratic leadership notoriously disrupts egos and motivation. Freedom to question assumptions, to take chances, and to make mistakes gives researchers the leeway needed to achieve novelty. Job descriptions, other than the most general, restrict the broad activities essential to creativity. Organization charts, hierarchical and authoritarian management systems, and lack of tolerance for unique personalities and dress are generally anathema to talented, productive groups.

Protection from the "suits" was a major concern of the technical staff for the Manhattan Project. Administrative directives from other parts of the organization were major distractions and interfered with the openness needed for creativity.[5] Highly talented people are commonly nonconformists and averse to rules that interfere with free thought and action. While the group can be somewhat isolated to escape distractions, an open, nonsecretive company with free exchange of information can help give people the needed sense of participation and importance.

People who have demonstrated problem-solving and creative ability and have an abiding interest in challenging the leading edge of understanding are essential additions to effective discovery teams. Without talented, knowledgeable, and motivated people, no system of discovery or management is likely to be sufficiently productive to be cost-effective.

Such that they will feel uniquely driven, all staff understand that they were chosen because they are, or potentially can be, the best in their field. They understand that they will be working with other people who were chosen on a similar basis. Unless they are proficient at working with other talented people, the game can be lost to petty conflicts that will undermine the morale and cooperative spirit of the whole group. This is a critical point and one that often is not followed. No matter how talented technical people may be, if they cannot get along with other talented people, they can easily promote a zero-sum game.

A most difficult task of the technology manager is to find and hire these high quality scientists and technologists. In a spirited, research-based atmosphere where many external technical contacts have been cultivated, it is much easier to find and hire the best technical people. If the technical group becomes recognized for its excellence, even the best people will consider it an honor to join the group.

Without high quality talent that can work together in a highly spirited, goal-oriented atmosphere, it can be folly to spend lavishly on R&D. Short-term profit, reluctantly, might become a prime motivation. This situation may carry notable responsibility for the prevalent short-term financial orientation in the business world. When technology groups become more productive, business management becomes more supportive of research, and vice versa.

For the profit picture to be addressed, creativity, discovery, and support of commercialization of invention are primary concerns. In many industrial research laboratories an overwhelming amount of time is devoted to technical service. Although much of this effort is essential to good business management, more technical service is carried out commonly than is essential. This is true to a large extent because technical service addresses the short-term in the most reliable and discernible way. It satisfies the immediate needs of salesmen who may justifiably argue that maintenance or increase in sales may be the result. Any rational manager who is forced by policy to be concerned about quarterly earnings, given the choice, is likely to opt for technical service. New product concepts are often nebulous and much longer-term.

Additionally, excessive nondiscovery duties, as general paperwork, meetings, and administrative functions can easily absorb most of the working hours. Such activities preclude adequate time to achieve the most demanding of goals, discovery. In a similar vein, it is often the most competent researchers who acquire the greatest amount of administrative responsibility.

If technical service and other duties are allowed to preempt research and development, the company is inadvertently subverting its future. Optimization of efficiency and staffing is needed to do justice to both technical service and innovation. If the research manager takes a strong stand, other interfering duties often can be reduced to a reasonable level. To do so is not a luxury but an essential action for both laboratory morale and long-term company viability. Assuming that compensation is fairly distributed, the overwhelmingly important duties of technology managers are to participate in and promote discovery, invention, and commercialization.

Without the freedom to carry out projects necessary to invention, both motivation and invention will be suppressed. To the extent, therefore, that research and development are seriously preempted by other work, the technologists receive a negative message—that although innovation may be prized, the processes by which it is achieved are not understood well enough by management to be recognized and, therefore, prized as well. Unless this catch-22 is corrected, chances for innovation will be suppressed severely, and low morale will become a major laboratory problem.

3. *Promote the study of anomalies and the most creative solution of the puzzle, recognize that research failures are necessary stepping stones to success, and challenge all researchers to exceed their dreams of technical achievement.*

The choice of the problem to be tackled by researchers is a critical consideration where novelty is the goal. Luxury of choice is not always at hand, but the greatest chance for discovery occurs with anomalies that are bypassed by the majority. If the study of anomaly is rejected in favor of popular problems, those companies who promote such activity often will be spending most of their time attempting to catch up with the competition. Management can play a positive role in choosing the projects for study, making sure that they fit the idiosyncrasies of the researchers and that they are of deep concern to the research team. On the other hand, researchers are inspired if they are allowed the independence to follow their intuition and their curiosity, and to feel ownership and ultimate responsibility for their projects. The focus by the research team, ideally, is so great that the greatest reward will be the solution of the puzzle.

Therein resides one of the most difficult paradoxes of technology groups. Investigations by psychologists Teresa Amabile and Elizabeth Tighe[6] have shown that rewards and external constraints can affect creativity negatively. If the group feels overly pressured to produce, they are more apt to do what psychologists call "satisficing," or to do just enough to get by through the achievement of subgoals. By this means the motivation of the scientist or the technologist to receive the monetary reward, for example, can be made to exceed the motivation to solve the puzzle. This paradox brings into sharp focus the necessity of having talented staff and the critical role of management in bringing out creativity as opposed to "satisficing." Establishing a talented, spirited technology group having an exciting vision is far more effective than "fear and threat" management. It is one of the best ways to preclude "satisficing."

These observations fit the visceral feelings that many researchers have—

that MBOs (management by objectives), where bonuses and salary may be based on accomplishment of precise objectives within a time frame, are detrimental to creativity and discovery. Time frames are often necessary and certainly understandable but unless handled with great care they can lead to "satisficing" with consummate ease. In such an environment, all but minor risks are avoided, which precludes major acts of creativity.

Attempts to make discoveries or to invent are failures most of the time. The word "failure" is inappropriate as it is intrinsic to the creative process, and persistent effort powered by the lessons of failure is the most meaningful heuristic of discovery. Unless this sobering reality is understood and accepted by top management, the willingness of technologists to take risks, to tackle difficult problems, or to venture into the creative arena will lose in favor of resistance to change. Management has the burden of recognizing this onerous nature of research and of encouraging growth toward success by the lessons learned from each failure.

Fear of failure is anathema to invention. If creative researchers are to continue the innovative track with dedication, they need to receive considerable company support. As described in Chapter 8, management is often indirectly responsible for many of these failures by demanding targeted research without allowing for the acquisition of the underlying science needed to achieve the goal. Continuously striving for goals that are unattainable without the underlying science is demoralizing, contributing to low self-esteem.

Suppressed groups of people generally score lower on IQ tests than do nonsuppressed groups, strongly suggesting that low self-esteem is the intelligence detractor.[7] In Japan, the ethnic group known as the Burakumin are considered to be inferior to other Japanese. They score lower on IQ tests than do other Japanese, but when they move to California, where this low opinion is not held, their children score as well as other Japanese children. Similar observations have been made with blacks in America.

There may be an analogy here with technical groups who are demonized because of repeated failures to solve a company problem. This kind of demoralization can occur within any branch of the company. Tension and low self-esteem are not conducive to scoring high on tests, to solving problems, or to being creative. Assuming that the technical people have been hired because of demonstrated competence, that the researchers have the appropriate tools, and that management has not introduced too many obstacles to creativity, then the failures of the technology group are simply sources of knowledge for potential success.

A major problem for research in industry is the dynamic nature of the marketplace, frequently necessitating changes in projects. Frequent change in projects is a common source of morale slippage and can even lead to loss of valuable employees. Such occurrences point to the importance of a company strategic plan that clearly explains company objectives. This means the laboratory can establish a meaningful priority scheme that will be in concert with the rest of the company and will help to stabilize the system. Under these conditions most projects can be completed. If projects are changed frequently and rarely completed, the researchers develop a sense of futility and feelings of unimportance. Few people of substance will put up with such a demoralizing situation for long. Conversely, by completing projects technologists have a sense of achievement and are much more apt to believe that they are important cogs in the success of their companies. It does not require much stretch of the imagination to realize that those employees who believe they are contributing to the well-being of a company are generally the most loyal.

Challenged to become the best in their field, to make major discoveries, and to be the envy of the competition, the researchers may develop an obsessive drive to assuage their ego. By the same token, their interest in their projects may be peaked. Challenging the technologists as a group to achieve a common goal emphasizes the importance of intellectual cooperation, which can stimulate more open exchange of ideas. Ego excitation posed by challenge is often far more effective than bonuses in motivating people.

4. *Promote a mood of pristine honesty, a sense of freedom and openness to approach problems with wide-ranging hypotheses, and a desire by technologists to expostulate beyond the bounds of logical empiricism.*

Along with the responsibility of promoting diverse hypothesizing, the technology manager is confronted often with conflict between proponents of opposing hypotheses. The conflict that arises from these different approaches should be simply a quest for truth and not a contest that must be won. If one is not prepared for contrast in ideas, the resulting conflict can devastate egos and the spirit of cooperation. Without the excitement of contrasting ideas, however, opportunities for creative solutions will be buried under the overwhelming weight of mind-sets. Taken in the true spirit of scientific investigation, opposing hypotheses can be exciting, often generating an additional eclectic hypothesis of much greater merit. "Conflict is a fundamental necessity in the evolution of ideas."[8]

Technologists who participate in interactive sessions are commonly reluctant to be totally open in expressing their thoughts. Psychologist Abraham Maslow saw a connection between the approval and acceptance of our deeper selves and our ability to be creative.[9] In contrast to thought extroverts, average and neurotic people fear expressing their deeper thoughts lest others disapprove. As compensation, position, stature, and self-image in laboratories are based, largely, on knowledge scope and quality and on problem solution. How else can technologists be expected to behave? Indeed, the ability and courage to recognize openly knowledge deficiencies such that corrective action can be taken is an important characteristic of inventive technologists. Introspective perception and honesty in all aspects of science deserve cultivation and incentives in laboratories where creativity is prized.

Unwillingness to express ideas openly often takes a turn toward fear of usurpation and loss of credit. This kind of fear is generated most extensively in laboratories where individual effort is promoted to the exclusion of cooperation and is rewarded accordingly. The need for cooperation throughout the process of innovation is discussed in detail in Chapter 20. Laboratory structure, management direction, and rewards can be carefully geared toward the understanding that cooperation will give the greatest payoff.

The final phase of problem study is writing—a phase of study in which the researcher begins to see with greatest clarity the total picture and its potential significance. If researchers realize that their report will be scrutinized with respect to discovery, how this new knowledge can be interacted with existing information to effect invention, how, perhaps, their new knowledge disenfranchises former beliefs, and how the profit picture can be addressed directly or indirectly by their interpretations, extreme conservatism in interpretation may be precluded. Such an approach may avoid the strangling effect produced by over reliance on logical empiricism. This more liberal method of thoughtful, in-depth speculation offers greater opportunity for striking the mother lode of novelty.

5. *Support the needs of incubation—multiple tasks and intense study followed by a respite from the problem in question.*

No matter how intense or well-conceived a problem-solving effort, technologists may still fail to achieve their goal. Such failure need not be penalized, but valiant efforts, whatever the outcome, can be rewarded for a beneficial boost to the researcher's creativity. If after a Herculean effort failure persists, hope need not fade as the incubation stage of creativity necessarily becomes activated (Figure 19.1). It is a process that takes place, perhaps, in the nonconscious mind. Unexpected but viable new combinations of knowledge may be revealed by a seemingly spontaneous burst of illumination. This new understanding has been preceded, however, by a long period, perhaps years, of intense effort. The time required for creative cognition is indefinite, but the greater the intensity and breadth of study, the greater the chances that incubation will reveal creative ideas.

Incubation can be promoted in at least three ways: (1) long-term intense pursuit of understanding, (2) pursuing more than one project or having multiple tasks, and (3) stopping a project after intense effort, perhaps temporarily.[10, 11]

By virtue of temporarily shifting to a different task, solutions to refractory problems in the former project may incubate in the nonconscious mind. Additionally, clues to solution to problems encountered in the former task may arise from the study of a different problem.

6. *Promote diverse strategic research to address the weakest links in the understanding of critical problems.*

Invention and discovery occur most readily with a visionary, charismatic, competent technical leader and highly talented technical people interacting in a setting relatively free from distractions and steeped with mutually understood goals. Under these conditions the zeitgeist, the prevailing atmosphere, can become electric. Although it is this setting that provides the greatest stimulus for creativity and discovery, the processes of research, conventional and unconventional thinking, and the international dialectic are the mental tools for making discoveries.

Diverse strategic research is an essential parameter of any laboratory whose goal is creativity and discovery. The acquisition of new knowledge increases the probability of favorable knowledge interaction to achieve novelty. Furthermore, the new knowledge derived from research greatly increases the probability of discovery and commercialization outside the scope of the competition. Outlined by the algorithmic procedure in Chapter 9, knowledge deficiency that represents a weak link in the understanding of an important company objective can be the subject of a research project. This kind of research, strategic, is what management has the greatest obligation to promote, and whether it is basic or applied makes little difference. The primary objective is to gain the knowledge needed for strategic problem solving.

7. *Promote an atmosphere of wide-ranging thought processes, judiciously combining conventional and unconventional thinking.*

Specialized thought processes include conventional and unconventional (Figures 13.1 and 15.1), both of which should be firmly incorporated into each researcher's thought pattern. Conventional or scientific is the kind of thinking used in scientific method and is critical to reliable knowledge. Unconventional thinking is the primary conduit to creativity, but must finally be validated by conventional thinking.

Just how these kinds of thinking can be incorporated into one's thought repertoire is not cut and dried, but understanding the ramifications of conventional thought should be an individual responsibility. Practice in the utilization of known unconventional thought processes could be a group or an individual exercise. For example, metaphorical thinking would be easy to practice. Efforts could be made by each individual to understand their own thought processes, to cultivate the most viable methods, and to create new methods. Clear understanding of a broad range of methods of thinking and their use in a broad range of research are the best teachers. Perhaps the most neglected aspect of good research, understanding and cultivating viable thought procedures, conventional and unconventional, can be a productive way to stimulate new ideas.

8. *Assert the value of the shuttle effect stemming from presenting and*

*publishing research papers and from interacting with worldwide technical contacts.*

The shuttle effect, interaction of different disciplines, is a powerful tool in promoting discovery, as witness the Watson-Crick interaction leading to the discovery of the double helix structure of DNA (Chapter 11). Attendance at appropriate conferences, presenting and publishing research papers, and having dialogue with a broad range of international contacts are important activities for technologists attempting to be innovative.

Industry goes to great lengths to protect proprietary knowledge. Paradoxically, just as the impassioned secrecy of the alchemists held back the development of modern chemistry, secrecy in any area of science or technology will contribute to stagnation in the evolution of knowledge. Although many industry secrets need to be proprietary, many more are kept secret that are conventional wisdom among the competitors. The technology manager can differentiate this knowledge and promote the presentation and publication of papers and the technologists' interaction with diverse technical contacts. By this means the shuttle effect can be promoted.

9. *Reward all idea generation, and make certain that the most pertinent and potentially profitable ideas are expedited.*

A pleasant and jocular time in a laboratory accompanies a creation or a discovery, which is often alluded to as an *aha!*. Such that profit can be addressed expeditiously, technologists may set priorities on the most critical *aha!*s. Ordering of priority can be judged from the company strategic plan, the dynamics of customer needs, technical and logistical feasibility, and on economics.

*Aha!*s are the hallmarks of innovative laboratories. They are fundamental contributions, and some credit should be given to the contributing technologists at this development stage—for invention and for new knowledge. By the time that inventions are commercialized, many people will have become involved, and the significance of the original contributions can be lost in the complexity of the process. These early credits, however, do not absolve management from issuing further rewards for successful commercialization. Clearly there are other important laboratory achievements, but because *aha!*s are the incipient stages of innovation, they are most crucial.

In a review of a book on technology, Martin Gardner[12] deplored this very point. "Mathematicians and physicists scribble equations in their university labs or private studies, then years or even decades later up go the factories. Splitting the atom was implicit in relativity theory, yet Einstein is mentioned only as a signer of a famous letter urging research on the atom bomb." Although generally of less magnitude, such an event is not uncommon in industry.

Ideas that are irrelevant to the company strategic plan are unlikely to receive further attention and are generally culled and forgotten. If technologists are intimately familiar with company goals and have a general understanding of the functioning of all divisions, this demoralizing event may be precluded. By this means the ideas that are generated are more likely to be of immediate company significance. Lack of follow-through on pertinent ideas is an even greater source of demoralization and an effective terminator of idea generation. Often new idea confirmation is inefficiently pursued, and a common reason is the NIH (not-invented-here) syndrome. Pursuing the most viable new ideas, regardless of source, can lead to the most personal and company benefit. Few things are more demoralizing than to have new ideas demanded, and then to watch even the best and most novel concepts sublimate back to the place from where they came.

10. *Facilitate success of each technologist by promoting intrinsic motivation, by helping researchers to exert control over their future, and by working toward a cooperative spirit throughout the company.*

Perhaps the most important responsibility of technology managers is to facilitate the success of each member of their staffs. A critical way that success can be expedited is for the manager to be constantly alert to the organizational structure and the management methods that will lead most effectively to *aha!*'s. If other administrative duties preclude this kind of attention, then the interfering chores can be reconsidered for their necessity. If they are deemed necessary, a reexamination of commitment to innovation may be needed. The onus on technology managers is inordinately large, but, in fairness, they are also at the mercy of top management's perception of the mechanisms by which laboratories can achieve their goals. Nevertheless, the onus is still on technology managers to make their needs known, and to sell the power structure on their considered approach to innovation.

In the best technical groups the technology manager does whatever is necessary to intensify intrinsic interest, such as allowing freedom in effort, honoring fundamental achievements in science and technological novelty whether commercialized or not, by allowing and encouraging presentation of papers at international technical meetings, and by promoting external technical contacts. If accolades are restricted to those things that clearly increase profit, the progress to highly remunerative technology will be, at best, greatly inhibited.

Although great emphasis has been placed on reason to achieve technical goals, it is without meaning in the absence of motivation. While reason is the agent of problem solution, motivation directs our goals and facilitates decision making. An intense motivation of people is to control their environment and their future.[13] If people feel in control, their confidence and outlook on life are greatly enhanced; if people are not in control, they become passive and feel that all is hopeless. It is well documented in both animal and human research that such an aura can lead to motivational and cognitive deficits, reduced persistence, sadness, lowered self-esteem, and to serious health problems. Only those who believe that they have some level of control over their lives can rise above mediocrity and contribute to innovation.

Participatory management and personal selection of research projects within the limits of company strategy are two of the techniques for involving people in their environmental control. Open and honest discussions about their potential career paths within the company can be helpful. Involvement of people can be promoted by periodic meetings in which the financial health of the company, technological progress, and plans for the future are reviewed. Such a meeting provides an opportunity for explaining the role of each technologist in the game plan to answer questions and to address problems. Candid communication about all aspects of the company can aid technologists to think for themselves and to become an integral part of the solution to company problems. Some level of profit sharing can be a tremendous boost to the task of instilling feelings of importance and belonging.

The "us" against "them" syndrome seems to be inherent in the human psyche and can become a problem between company divisions. If there is a seamless web between company divisions, with extensive interaction and common goals, this problem can be reduced. Similarly, the research manager can be a promoter of understanding. By keeping the company appraised of progress toward new technology and how developments may promote the well-being of the company, people in other divisions will be less critical. Mystery promotes speculation, which is often an unfavorable judgment. This message by the research manager can be clear, incisive, honest, and believable. Maintaining the credibility of technology is a necessary component of the company-wide cooperation needed to achieve innovation.

To a considerable extent, then, the innovative potential of a technology group, aside from talent, depends on four points: (1) the strength of technology management and their ability to motivate people, (2) the understanding of the group on how to achieve and carry out discovery, (3) the commitment and empathy of top management for the needs of technology, (4) the ability of the technical group to maintain credibility with other company divisions.

11. *Sell the tenet to top management that all participants in creativity and discovery must be honored for the cooperative, creative process to flourish.*

Mentioned in a previous chapter,[14] the crux of the matter was concisely stated by Plato, "What is honored in a country will be cultivated there." Increasingly, proficient science and technology require a dialectic between experts of outstanding talent working as a team. Because rewards in laboratories are commonly directed exclusively toward primary inventors, a protective and secretive attitude may develop among some technologists. Invention and commercialization depend on cooperation as much as on

individual effort, and if credit is distributed unfairly, considerable antagonism can arise.

Great effort to reward all participants who contribute to creative results
can preclude morale slippage from unfair distribution of credit. "Satisficing" can be precluded by giving the greatest rewards to those people who
show the greatest creativity. To the extent that employees perceive and
accept this message, their amoeboid egos will embrace the creative company
spirit. Such people will be well on the way to becoming fiercely loyal with
an addictive desire to make even greater, creative contributions.

The philosophical belief in the exclusive contribution of competition
arose in the nineteenth century with the social Darwinists[15] who believed
that society is governed by the struggle for existence and the survival of
the fittest. This led to the notion that exploitation was natural, and,
therefore, justifiable. Overwhelming reliance on such a belief undermines
the importance of cooperation, which is an act of great moment to discovery and creativity. With great clarity, Warren Bennis, professor of business
administration at the University of Southern California and *Los Angeles
Times* staff writer Patricia Ward Biederman, in their book *Organizing Genius*,[16] show with several examples, such as Lockheed's skunk works and
the Manhattan Project at Los Alamos, how great achievements occur by
way of "Great Groups."

The background needed for major discoveries often requires far more
knowledge than any one person can possibly have. It is the collaborative
action of numerous talented people that leads to significant achievements.
Without cooperation, knowledge growth is suppressed. If all participants
believe that the company recognizes that they collectively have won the
struggle, the desire for cooperation and even greater discovery will only be
enhanced.

## VERIFICATION AND COMMERCIALIZATION

If verification and commercialization are added to the schematic for creativity (see Figure 19.1), the system is transformed into a schematic for
innovation. Verification is usually an arduous task; commercialization is
commonly intractable.

Successful innovation often requires strong sponsorship, preferably by
the president. Authority across divisional lines is usually a necessary component for the introduction of new concepts, simply because that is commonly the only way in which adequate cooperation can be achieved.
Sponsorship of great strength is critical in any company, without which the
self-interests of each division, understandably, will invariably come first.
The ideal situation would be if the interests of each division could have
greater commonality. MBOs (management by objectives) are constructed
commonly to be divisive, and there is great room for improvement in this

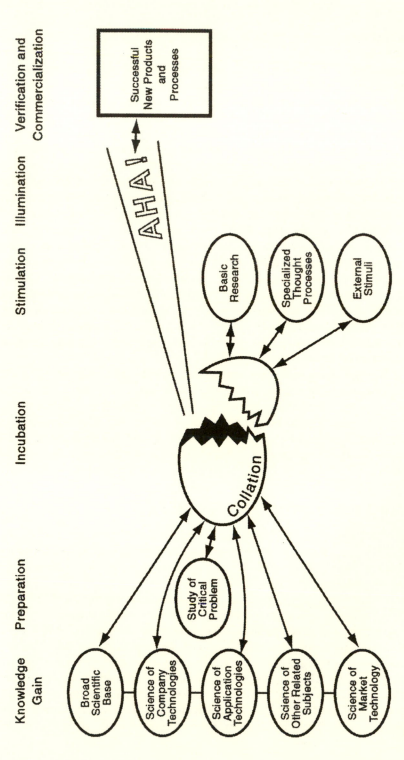

Figure 19.1. A schematic for innovation.

area. Such improvement could have greatest meaning in those companies that view innovation as their most important goal.

Translation of new ideas into profit is the source of wealth needed to support industrial research, and, indirectly, academic research as well. The fate of industrial research is largely at the mercy of an occasional commercial success; the frequency and extent of commercial successes are largely up to both technical and nontechnical management's understanding of the discovery process—such that inadvertent obstacles to innovation will not be created. In deference to commercial success of new technology, it is important that inventions be of high quality. This does not mean that every detail must be attended before commercialization, nor that risks should not be taken. Indeed, early introduction of new technologies is sometimes necessary to address competition adequately. These caveats, however, do not diminish the importance of high quality invention to successful commercialization. By virtue of following the eleven methods of discovery management and the algorithm for new product development earlier in this chapter, invention quality and quantity can be enhanced. By these methods, or with your creative modifications, the proficient management of technology should be simplified greatly.

The conflict between individualism and cooperation is often a sensitive issue, but social Darwinism has overemphasized the former. A discussion of this facet of social structure, as it occurs among technical people, is the topic of the next chapter.

*Chapter 20*

# The Social Structure of Innovation

Following the new model for creativity, researchers potentially can be highly successful in achieving discovery reducible to profit. Some mistaken notions have been purged and have been replaced with more reliable knowledge. Their approach to the solution of a problem likely has anastomosed, perhaps, in all conceivable directions, ultimately reaching a pathway to a creative solution. The preparation stage may have been inadequate to sever the Gordian knot, and incubation by way of the nonconscious may have intervened to effect great success. Management of research and development has been empathetic to the needs of creativity. Both individualism and cooperation probably have played roles in the discovery process.

## COOPERATION

Creation, whether it is of life or of ideas, requires high levels of cooperation and the merger of many different patterns of knowledge. The eleven principles of technology management, described in Chapter 19 and designed to promote creativity and discovery, are vitally dependent on cooperation, not only in the laboratory but in the entire company. Without cooperation the barriers to innovation can become overwhelming. Diverse philosophies, agendas, and idiosyncrasies preclude ideal levels of teamwork, but great effort can make the system work.

Innovation involves every function of a company including discovery of new ideas for profit, basic and applications research, process research, costing, procurement of raw materials, management, market research, manufacturing, sales, technical service, and public relations. Every division in the company usually has some input in new product development, along with significant influence on the spirit that keeps the process moving toward success. Sold on the idea that they too will reap some of the benefit from commercialization of discovery, each division in a company will be more cooperative.

In the United States where rugged individualism has received the greatest kudos, cooperation can be a difficult and unwanted idea. Technological sophistication has reached a level where a lone person is not likely to have the needed knowledge to achieve major discovery or invention. For such achievement, input from many people and diverse disciplines is important. Creativity is now recognized as a collective process based upon a wide range of contributions from both the past and the present.

When one individual bears the total responsibility for success or failure of a critical project, risk taking is deterred, and doing just enough to get by is often the result. Sharing of responsibility helps to establish a greater sense of adventure and less fear of failure. The group, ideally, is not bureaucratic, but collegial, and is structured according to expertise and role.[1]

Not inherently natural for people, cooperation stems from cultural conditioning. Our natural animal impulses and our need for social harmony are in continuous conflict. Recognition of this paradox was perhaps the most significant contribution to psychology by Sigmund Freud.[2] Natural selection, Darwin's mechanism for promoting evolution, has a singular goal—to promote those genes that favor survival and proliferation. As a consequence, *Homo sapiens* are held hostage to the trappings promoted by achieving these goals—that is, people are fundamentally libidinous, rapacious, and selfish, which perforce conflict with the civility needed for successful interaction with other human beings. Such civility entails cooperation, compromise, and restraint, which are generally essential to major innovation.

If competition was relied on solely as a strategy for economic progress, the great scientific and technological strides that are now enjoyed probably would not have occurred. Popular interpretation of Darwinian evolution led to the common belief that survival is always a vicious struggle among life forms. The philosopher Herbert Spencer coined the motto, "Survival of the fittest," which led late nineteenth-century entrepreneurs to justify ruthless labor practices. Social Darwinism, the application of this one-sided interpretation of natural selection to economic systems, results in survival of the fittest and disposal of the unfit.

Clearly, such an interpretation of Darwinian evolution has some merit, but cooperation has played an important role as well. This is exemplified by ecosystems where a homeostasis has been established among organisms. Symbiosis, a vital cooperation between certain organisms, has lead to new, more vigorous life forms. Cooperation between organisms evolves where such action promotes survival and reproduction. In both biological and cultural evolution, cooperation seems generally to arise from utilitarian schemes.

Cooperation is conditioned into the Japanese culture, which gives them a competitive edge. Recent research on this subject and discussed in this chapter may help in cultivating cooperation to further the process of innovation. Though banishment of individualism is not desirable nor the objective, refurbishing of the American psyche with a keen recognition of the importance of cooperation as well is essential to economic well-being. To initiate novelty, on the other hand, individualism is often needed to make the necessary break with the past and with peers. Thus, for best results there is a delicate balance between cooperation and individualism.

### Tit-for-Tat

Robert Axelrod, Professor of Political Science and Public Policy at the University of Michigan, in his book *The Evolution of Cooperation*[3] showed, by way of a computer game, how in a world of self-seeking egoists that cooperation can emerge. With emphasis on individualism in research, such environments decidedly consist of self-seeking egoists. The name of the game is the iterated prisoner's dilemma, in which players achieve mutual gains from cooperation. It also permits one player to exploit the other or for neither to cooperate. It is a game that shows how self-interest can be made to serve the greater good, and fits well with Adam Smith's concept of economic progress.

Axelrod described the general circumstance which gave rise to the prisoner's dilemma game. Two allies in a crime are apprehended and interrogated individually. If either defect, that individual may receive a lighter sentence whereas if both defect, the value of their confessions has less meaning. If the prisoners cooperate with each other and refuse to confess, they can be convicted only on a minor charge. Because they do not see much possibility of being in the same situation again soon, it is perceived by them that their biggest payoff will come by way of defection. Because they did not appreciate the nature of their dilemma, the prisoners took the path that led to the worst of possible payoffs.

Faced by everyone in social interactions and contracts, the prisoner's dilemma suggests that cheating is in each individual's self-interest. The dilemma suggests further that cooperation does not arise without some additional provocation, such as dictatorial enforcement. Repeated interaction between individuals, however, is the most effective way to promote cooperation. Knowing that one will have further contacts with another arouses an understanding that cooperation with that individual potentially can be the most profitable game to play.

Axelrod invited experts in game theory to submit programs to be applied to the prisoner's dilemma in a computer game contest. The simplest and most successful game submitted was Tit-for-tat. It is a strategy that starts with cooperation and all subsequent moves repeat what the opponent did on the previous move. The game is between two players. Both players must choose, independent of the other, whether to cooperate or defect. These choices result in one of four possibilities. If both cooperate, both receive a reward of three points. If one cooperates and the other defects, the cooperating player receives the sucker's payoff, zero points, and the defecting player, five points. If both defect, both receive one point. The greatest number of points generally is accumulated if both cooperate.

An interesting aspect of the prisoner's dilemma is that the players cannot get out of their dilemma by taking turns exploiting each other. It follows that an even chance of exploitation and being exploited produces fewer points than cooperation. Having played the game once, two egoists likely will choose defection, and each will get fewer points out of the game than had they cooperated. Cooperation is defeated if the game is played a known number of times and emerges only if the game is played indefinitely. Playing the game indefinitely refuted the long-held belief that defection is the most rational thing to do. Knowing that there will be a continuing interaction promotes cooperation, which will continue while this expectation of the future remains stable.

If the latter condition exists, cooperation develops in three stages. In the first stage cooperation is initiated, even in an environment of rampant defection, in small groups of individuals who use reciprocity to achieve cooperation. These individuals are never the first to defect. Cooperation will develop as long as some of their interactions are with each other. In the second stage, cooperation based on reciprocity can be stable in the midst of many other strategies. In the third stage, after the establishment of cooperation, the system will remain stable if it responds immediately to provocation.

The success of Tit-for-tat is accounted for by four qualities: being nice in the sense of never defecting first, being retaliatory, being forgiving, and being clear. By being nice, unnecessary trouble is precluded; retaliation discourages defection; forgiveness promotes cooperation; clarity allows the opponent to get the message without mistake. Furthermore, through cooperation, the payoff is greater for the opponent than from alternate systems, and neither side is outdone by an opponent. It is not a zero-sum game with a winner and a loser. All participants are winners. Cooperation evolves, then, by virtue of success and, perhaps, is assisted by less resentment stemming from envy.

Stability, besides the four qualities listed above, is paramount. Pointed out by Axelrod, in industry if a customer decides that one of its suppliers is in trouble and is no longer a stable source, all manners of defection, such as late payment or rejection of under-quality shipments, are frequent re-sults. The belief in a continuing stable relationship is the police officer of industrial ethics.

The strategy of Tit-for-tat seems to parallel the strategy that is most successful for innovation. Indeed, everyone in the company is made more successful, or at least more stable, by virtue of the cooperation that leads to innovation. For this system to work, the company is provocable in the sense that defection, undermining of the process of innovation, for exam-ple, is never tolerated. Job stability is necessary within a company to inhibit cutthroat tactics and for cooperation to prevail. By this long-term, multi-level bonding procedure, the company develops a familial character which greatly enhances the importance of future interactions. A company with such long-term history is prepared significantly better to be successful in handling complex problems than other less bonded companies.

The value of cooperation can be exemplified by symbiotic relationships in nature, such as between algae and fungus to form lichens, or the moiré phenomenon where different sound patterns interact to produce a new co-herent pattern. The interactions of different knowledge patterns to produce a creative concept, or of company divisions to transform an invention into a profitable new product, are the creative benefits that can transform a marginal company into one of stability or better. Cooperation is simply another example of the creative benefits of holistic approaches to problems.

Cooperation can be promoted by teaching people to care about others through reward and example. Axelrod emphasized that as opposed to the Golden Rule, defection can be impeded by immediate reciprocity—not turning the other cheek. It is by the agency of immediate reciprocity that exploitation strategies are suppressed.

Short-term financial orientation is another mechanism of instilling a sense of instability among employees. Milking the companies' resources, not do-ing long-term research for new products, and showing little concern for the well-being of employees are some of the negative activities of some com-panies that can effect strong feelings of insecurity. Morale of employees is a good measure of company stability.

Since Axelrod's book, other games have been developed that can defeat Tit-for-tat and are described by zoologist Matt Ridley.[4] Nevertheless, these alternate strategies still involve cooperation. It was found that serious weaknesses exist with Tit-for-tat. If one person defects for whatever reason, perhaps accidentally, recriminations become never ending. Zoologists are skeptical of Tit-for-tat because examples in nature are the exception rather than the rule, and this game theory seems to be most applicable to human beings. Finally, Tit-for-tat never wins in a single game played against a harsher strategy.

## Beyond Tit-for-Tat

Although originally believed to be evolutionarily stable, Tit-for-tat can be invaded by other newly developed, cooperative computer strategies. One such strategy is called Firm-but-fair. Favors are exchanged but on an alternating basis. It cooperates with cooperators even after a mutual defection, but punishes a sucker by further defection. This strategy continues to cooperate even after being a sucker. Such asynchrony makes generosity more rewarding than in other strategies.

The major problem in translating the lessons of prisoner's dilemma to company practice is that it is only a two-person game. In larger groups cooperation is not derived from reciprocal strategies alone. As explained by Ridley, the reason is that even rare defection cannot be tolerated in large groups. Unless punishment of the defector is expedited, people who defect and do not reciprocate will spread rapidly.

This flaw in dealing with large groups can potentially be handled by a moralistic strategy, which is to punish not only defectors but those who do not punish defectors. Emphasized by Ridley, this smacks of authoritarianism and reflects the power of fascist leaders. Inversely, company-wide rewards for helping to transform new ideas into profit could be of sufficient size to make defection an artifact of the past. Such is not an authoritarian strategy. Additionally, ostracism is a powerful tool for controlling defection, and this can be done by refusing to play with those who refuse to reciprocate or to play nice.

With these modifications to cooperative strategies, it seems that companies, assuming effective technology, could potentially be highly successful with innovation. This would entail a stable, long-term oriented company whose members reciprocate favors. Defection is not tolerated (with one exception) and is enforced by either removal or reprogramming of defectors. Significant rewards are given for diligent efforts to effect success of innovation.

Defection can originate from personality quirks and conflicts, hidden agendas, or from sincere, well-intentioned discord. Alternate, potentially more viable approaches to problems can become a formula for success. To maintain a stable system, however, lack of cooperation in the overall effort is not tolerated.

Greater commonality of company goals for each division of the company can help promote cooperation. The conflicts between the intense demands of daily production and the tenuous, interfering nature of new products inserted in an already busy production line are not readily resolved. Essential to the most effective new product development, well-equipped pilot plants often can be used to arbitrate this common problem.

Although conclusions drawn from computer games may not be fully congruent with industrial reality, they offer an intriguing rationale that deserves careful consideration. Not a solitary game, innovation is nonlinear and a holistic product of the interaction of the total company, not just some of its parts. Vigorous company cooperation and approaching problems with determination and optimism often give the necessary boost to successful innovation.

A kind of cultural learning that greatly increases chances of cooperation in large groups is conformism.[5] Among hunter-gatherers conformism must have been essential. It was their cohesiveness, largely gained through conformism, that enabled them to compete with other groups. If they conform to group practice, members gain greater acceptance as well. Conformity seems to be an adaptation that has become deeply ingrained in the human psyche. Ridley pointed out that people conform simply because everybody else is doing it. The ready following of Hitler is a prime example. In elections, many people vote for whoever is winning. Following tradition often makes sense, however, and it may reflect what many people have found correctly to be the most beneficent pathway. Against their own immediate self-interest, humans often cooperate by way of conformism, which seems to be instinctive.

A theory of why people are so strongly inclined to conform is known as the informational cascade. Behavior of large groups can be useful information and is often preferable to our own commonly flawed reasoning. By the same token, it is often wrong. Ridley gives the example of the fallacious belief that a religious idea is valid simply because people have been convinced of it for hundreds of years. It can be a matter of the blind following the blind perpetuated by the informational cascade. In contrast, self-interest generally wins over group interest. To the extent that cooperation and conformity occur, people participate for what they perceive as their overall self-interest. Cooperation, then, follows from expediency.

## INVIDUALISM

Conformity and creativity are unmistakably at odds, which reinforces the critical nature of flexible, unconventional thought processes. Tradition and conventional wisdom reflect conformity, which occasionally is nothing less than universal hallucination. Invention is a break with popular notions often held with emotional fervor. Nonconformity can lead to less social stability and even ostracism. A research team needs conformity for cooperation from which it sometimes defects to achieve novelty—a catch-22 that makes the process of innovation at once provocative and antagonizing.

Rational defection could be breaking with a hypothesis, a method of analysis, or a manufacturing process, among many potential conflicts. Perhaps the idea with which one is in conflict is staunchly and fervently held by the rest of the technology group. It can be an approach that even company members outside of technology may consider irrational. For invention to occur, however, some degree of rational defection is always necessary.

Although dissenters are following different pathways, it is the best practice for dissenters to be cooperative as well. Conflict arising from noncooperation often evolves into an insurmountable obstacle to innovative growth. It is from this complex of cooperation and rational defection that novelty can emerge most readily. Achieving such a delicate balance is not easy, but failure to do so can encourage the status quo.

Without some defection, however, consistency of thought would suffocate the process of invention and innovation. To make such a break requires courage and confidence in the potential benefit of an unpopular approach. Sometimes innovators even risk their loss of membership.

Research groups can be conditioned with the notion that carefully considered defection is occasionally essential for the group's success. Such a procedure is sometimes necessary to alter a dead-end paradigm that has prevented innovative progress. It is a process that differs drastically from our deeply ingrained adaptive character and makes creativity a tenuous and sometimes dangerous path to follow. For invention, acceptance of this dilemma by the individual researcher is essential, but it is preferable that the entire technology group be in concert with the necessity of rational defection. If it could be understood by the entire organization, in which conformity is often demanded, it would be a monumental achievement and a major move toward the company becoming innovatively exemplar.

The next chapter is a view of the current environment for creativity and discovery, some suggestions on the best environment and best company for innovation, and some speculations about the elusive future of industrial innovation and science.

*Chapter 21*

# The Elusive Future of the Technical, Creative Enterprise

To achieve such a high-minded goal as discovery, ideally a plethora of multidisciplinary knowledge has been continuously acquired in great depth for a single discipline and in great breadth for many disciplines. The preparation stage has been an approach to solving a problem from every conceivable direction. Incubation may have intervened to assist problem solution. The pragmatic approach to creativity in Chapter 18, idiosyncratic algorithms, technological market surveys, mechanistic new product schemes, and the new product algorithm have been followed leading to new knowledge, some of which is unique to the researchers. Intuition and curiosity have been explored when intrinsic motivation has rebelled against traditional pathways. Diversionary, the pathway to discovery has been a heuristic or open-ended approach that could not be achieved directly by any algorithm.

Transforming new knowledge to profit likely has led to many changes in the processing procedure and even product character to produce a unique and cost-effective way of addressing customer needs. Understanding the science and technology of the product and of the interactions with applications is a necessity for efficient process control, for dealing with customer problems with the new product, for product modification, or for other new product ideas.

The elusiveness of discovery is not simply of a technical nature. Methods of managing companies, managing research, managing the level of talent, and managing the social ripeness for inventions all play a part in the ultimate goal of profit.

## INDUSTRIAL INNOVATION

John Young,[1] president and chief executive officer of Hewlett-Packard, pointed out that the view of many leading economists is that the dominant force behind productivity growth is innovation. These economists have indicated that nearly 80% of U.S. productivity growth since the Great Depression of the 1930s has arisen from innovation. According to biologist Howard Bloom,[2] the strength of a country is directly related to its innovative growth. He attributes the fall of the British Empire to a failure to recognize three basic tenets:

1. Every technological breakthrough eventually grows old.
2. New inventions arrive to replace it.
3. The countries that dominate these new technologies often rule the world.

Young continued his exposition on innovation by explaining that our competitive position in the new global economy is being diminished by a low level of ability to commercialize invention. It is diminished further by our not making the necessary investments in research and training, and by our not giving the necessary credence and support to manufacturing.

Young pointed out that one reason U.S. manufacturers were unsuccessful in dominating the profits from their development of color television is that RCA and its licensees were not competitive at manufacturing. Constantly striving for incremental improvements, as do the Japanese, is essential to being competitive and can make the difference between success and failure. He believed that a persistent interaction throughout a company for an understanding of the best product design and for a common goal of innovation are primary pathways to discovery.

Inefficiency in commercializing new ideas in the United States is attributed by Young to the low status accorded manufacturing, and to a lack of teamwork between scientists, engineers, and managers. He indicated that evidence for a decline in U.S. competitiveness is ubiquitous as shown by trade deficits, slow productivity growth, stagnant real wages, and a declining share of real markets. Often allowing the Japanese to do the difficult but rewarding task of making a discovery pay high dividends, U.S. industry may need a change in outlook.

Aside from gaining support from management, a new understanding by scientists that it is prestigious and financially rewarding to translate discovery into commercial success could greatly aid productivity. If applied research could gain a level of prestige commensurate with basic research, it would become easier to attract the best talent. To accomplish this goal, it would be helpful if industry were to allow freedom for creative research. The greatest benefit might arise if scientists were to recognize that commercialization of new knowledge is the source of wealth for the continued pursuit of science.

Young's contentions concerning manufacturing skills were strongly reinforced by M.I.T. economist Lester Thurow.[3] In the late nineteenth and the twentieth centuries, countries that were highly endowed in natural resources had the greatest potential for being productive. Resources can now be moved at relatively low cost to wherever they are needed. Similarly, the new high-tech, brainpower industries can be located almost anyplace. For example, although devoid of iron and coal, Japan has the world's dominant steel industry. The world's capital market is now concentrated in New York, London, and Tokyo, which makes capital available almost anyplace in the world.

Comparative advantage is now confined to knowledge and skills, such that industries must locate where the brainpower is, or, at least, where it can be concentrated. Paradoxically, technology is at its peak of importance, but process technology has assumed greater importance than invention. Commercial exploitation of invention generally will gravitate to those countries where costs are lowest and appropriate knowledge and manufacturing skills can be concentrated. Many new technologies invented by Americans have been exploited commercially by the Japanese, as the video camera and recorder and the fax.

As Thurow describes the optimum system, "There must be a seamless web among invention, design, manufacturing, sales, logistics, and services that competitors cannot match." Skills permeate the organization, such that it can be the low-cost producer of the best product. Manufacturing skills are paramount.

To remain on top, a company needs to be dynamic, continually introducing new, more cost-effective products, always progressing faster than the competition. Organizing brainpower entails not only top research and development teams, but knowledgeable, skilled people throughout the organization who recognize the necessity of innovation and incremental product improvement. Continual creation to address rapid changes in the new global market, increasingly, are the critical components of successful companies. Those companies who have made the greatest gains in knowledge growth, derived to a large extent from strategic research and technological market surveys, will be in the best position to address changing needs rapidly.

Many practices of U.S. industry, education, and government unintentionally have introduced major obstacles to innovation. Otis Port,[4] an associate editor of *Business Week*, stated the problem in these terms: "After four decades of ebbing quality education, four decades of neglecting the factory, five decades of stroking consumption at the expense of savings, and seven decades of a parochial business outlook, America is now paying the piper."

Some strategies that Port listed for enhancing industrial innovation are the following:

1. Establish a permanent tax credit for U.S. research and development.
2. Increase tax credits for key-to-the-future technologies.
3. To overcome the enchantment with short-term returns, establish incentives for the long-term as a new tax category for long-term capital gains.
4. Further soften the antitrust laws to permit joint production.

Reasons listed by American managers for their lack of global competitiveness are lower labor costs overseas, unfair trade practices, and the ability of foreign competitors to raise capital at lower cost. Furthermore, within the United States, Wall Street quickly abandons companies at the first indication of softness in quarterly earnings. For some companies there is also contention with raiders or takeovers.[5]

After World War II, there was a major move in industry to diversify.[6] This was done in an effort to preclude excessive profit losses from business slumps in specific categories. Diversification reduced the familiarity that business managers could have with all of their business units. In response, business schools changed their management programs to a general formula such that executives supposedly could run any business. American industry is now permeated with managers that understand neither technology nor the underlying science. Even more serious, many do not have an empathy for the mechanisms of discovery. This means that they can and do inadvertently introduce obstacles to innovation.

Innovation does not always fit into the secret agenda of business managers as shown by a recent study.[7] Often managers provide rhetoric for the benefit of Wall Street that would imply a desire for innovation. But, in reality, they privately suppress new ideas. Overwhelmed with the daily problems of running a company, new ideas simply do not fit into an already overcrowded agenda. Failure in new product development can mean a failed career for some managers, who for that reason may not be willing to rock the boat. Risk aversion is strongly conditioned into many corporate cultures.

Richard Leet,[8] executive vice-president of Amoco and very much a realist, emphasized that many business managers are skeptical of the cost-effectiveness of research and development. Leading-edge technology may not be developed and commercialized during a career, and meanwhile managers can envision decreased profits. They are not motivated to sacrifice for a future they will not be part of. Making the issue even more difficult, equipment for research can be extremely expensive. Because of increased complexity, the solution of problems may require large teams rather than one individual.

The pressures of Wall Street promote the short-term, making harvesters out of companies rather than long-term builders. Intricate financial manipulations and merger mania are the rules of much of industry. This activity has made it painfully clear, as Leet explained, that "there is an element out there that don't give one damn about building enterprises for tomorrow." Leet called the bluff of critics, and pointed out that if they were to become a CEO of their company, they too would be tempted to give preference to the short-term. Clearly they would do so if they were concerned about their job stability.

With incisive candor, Leet made it clear that goals of modern business in the United States are the consequence of overwhelming and complex pressures. Business unit managers usually play an active role in managing certain aspects of research and development. They report to group vice-presidents who usually want short-term profits. The unit managers are gravely concerned about those projects that will not come to fruition for more than, perhaps, two years. Career paths of managers are largely dependent on their ability to increase company profit, which can be severely diminished by failed and expensive projects. They want to control such long-term projects, perhaps end them, recognizing that they desperately want to be promoted within a couple of years.

Given the general lack of understanding of the discovery process and the inadvertent obstacles imposed, it is understandable that many business managers take this position. Furthermore, unless a highly talented and spirited technology team has been developed, chances for innovation are severely hampered. Business managers, however, are often trapped in a complex system that demands short-term behavior. To bypass this obstacle requires courage on the part of managers, the following of the best procedures for achieving discovery, and setting an example through their successes. By following the best procedures for discovery, time frames can be compressed. In the new, dynamic global economy in which the rate of technological change is faster than ever and accelerating, high efficiency of technological innovation is essential.

## SCIENCE

Physicist John Ziman[9] alluded to Vannevar Bush's representation of science as an "endless frontier," which has been enlarged by analogy with the Koch curve (Chapter 4). This implies eternal opportunities for the determined scientist and technologist. Every discovery unveils innumerable new problems that beg for recognition and study. Current trends, however, show that there are limits to growth as imposed by tighter budgets. Ziman referred to this new stage of development in science and technology as "steady state." As he pointed out, a social attitude is developing by which the only acceptable case for expansion of science is the promise of a significant financial payoff or a solution to a critical social problem. Pursuing the traditional scientific enterprise of seeking truth for its own sake is becoming passé.

Outside the scientific community, impatience is growing, and the promise of long-term research is believed to have been oversold. Many politicians and business managers contend that better management practices would yield a better return. Although this generalization may have a degree of truth, the management practices that they often impose suppress creativity. Such management often entails algorithmic, highly restrictive, short-term targeted research with inadequate understanding of the underlying science, the shelving of anomalies, and the penalization of failure. This problem is complicated further by the unwillingness of some companies to pay the price for the best talent.

Such restrictive attitudes of the laity are understandable, yet destructive to the cause of discovery. The heuristic, unconventional nature of discovery abhors the algorithmic formula of management that the laity often dictates. But academic freedom, free exchange of ideas, and freedom to follow curiosity, intuition, and anomaly are essential nutrients of creativity and discovery. Unlimited funds are not available for every potentially viable research project, and some managerial restrictions must prevail. The essential point is that for discovery to prevail, high degrees of freedom are essential.

Strategic, basic research is essential to the long-term well-being of invention. Such high returns are demanded for capital investments over the short-term, however, that technology groups feel obligated to strive for innovations that will give the largest and quickest payoff. Often with reliance on serendipity alone, this inefficient approach is done despite inadequate knowledge to solve the problem and to innovate. Because the ultimate benefits that can be derived from basic research are generally not fully realized for unacceptably long periods, basic research has been stopped by many companies. The delay period for innovation is longer generally than Wall Street is willing to wait. This paradox, seeking short-term high returns without necessary knowledge from basic research, is a prime cause of the innovation slump that has existed in much of American industry for many years.

Basic research, by its very nature, generally necessitates long periods to reach maximum fruition and payoff. On the other hand, strategic basic research provides incremental bits of knowledge that are often essential to the development of new products. This new knowledge can lead to greater depth of thinking by the entire technical group and to new knowledge for the solution of other technical problems. This is usually true, even if the original objective is not achieved. Basic research done simply for the sake of new knowledge, distant from core company problems, can be reserved for academe. But the kind of basic research that is essential for innovation, and that generally is done most profitably in-house, is strategic research that can extract new knowledge for the solution of core company problems. Strategic research done in conjunction with targeted research often can resolve seemingly intractable development problems.

For example, let us ponder a relatively simple problem. Assume that a company goal is to develop a particulate mineral product, which provides gloss in paper coating significantly better than all commercially available products. A strategic, research pathway would be to determine all of the potential parameters of the mineral, natural or induced, and its interaction with various potential coating systems and their affect on coated paper gloss. The knowledge to be gained by this study is basic to problem solution. In such a problem, there are numerous parameters generally that are necessary for optimum understanding of gloss development. In this case, most parameters are usually understood at the outset of study by experienced researchers and through literature research for the fundamental bases of gloss. But careful, thorough research introducing new and novel parameters often will uncover previously unknown mechanisms that can lead to substantial benefit over conventional wisdom. By this means, a magic bullet for a unique method of improving coated paper gloss may make a dramatic appearance.

A few companies are doing outstanding jobs of innovating, and so the question arises, why not emulate success? To do so would require painful and major restructuring, which for many companies is an obstacle that will be avoided if possible.[10] Generally, each company has idiosyncratic needs, and what is good for one company may not be good for the other. Despite these objections, much can be learned from the practices of successful companies. Prime examples are Hewlett-Packard,[11] Merck,[12] and 3M.[13]

Research has lost credibility in many industries because of a poor track record arising from complex reasons.[14] Most companies have found that the risk of investing in original work, especially in mature industries, is unacceptably high. High return on investment requirements commonly discourage innovation. The more money management allots to research, the more control they exert, which leads to emphasis on predetermined research. Often this means targeted research without the requisite basic science. Such conflicts of time frame and mechanism generally lead to greatly reduced accomplishment.

## LESSONS TO HELP INDUSTRIAL INNOVATION

The United States can learn three lessons from Japan and Germany:[15] (1) long-term investments, (2) keen recognition of the importance of educating people, and (3) greater focus on incremental change. In those countries, technical people are prominent in the company hierarchy, as opposed to lawyers and financial managers in the United States.

Michael Wolff,[16] editor of *Research-Technology Management*, listed six guidelines for fostering breakthrough innovations as derived by Ketteringham and Nayak. John Ketteringham is senior vice-president of Arthur D. Little, Inc., and P. Ranganath Nayak is an Arthur D. Little colleague. Their guidelines were based upon twelve outstanding breakthroughs occurring in the last twenty years.

1. Make up your mind to invest a specific amount of money in the riskier long-term R&D.
2. Select those people for the long-term work who are most likely to be successful in breakthrough innovation.
3. Back the projects these people choose.
4. Make sure that the project draws upon the organization's technical strengths and addresses a problem customers care about.
5. Don't rely on market research.
6. Make sure that management joins the innovation team.

These guidelines have been designed for all, but especially for mature companies. The people chosen for working on these new ideas, ideally, have breadth and depth of experience and strong motivation to carry out their projects. To be successful, innovators interact with other corporate functions and with customers related to their project. If the information is transmitted to the innovator from the customer via market researchers, a great deal can be lost in visualization of new products.

Commercial success was not anticipated in these projects and was not expected until after the fact. Ketteringham, therefore, is definitive in his disparagement of prospective or targeted research: "The death of the breakthrough innovation is any attempt to do prospective research." Chemist Henry Bauer[17] alludes to Erwin Chargaff's observation that without the requisite understanding, goal-oriented research is analogous to alchemy. Relevant basic knowledge must exist for such a goal to be achieved, and the companies that waste their research budget on goal-oriented projects that are not knowledge-based are legion.

Alan Pearson,[18] director of the R&D research unit at the Manchester Business School in the United Kingdom, contended that technology managers should have management training that focuses on interpersonal skills and teamwork. Such training can be invaluable, but it would be even more beneficial if it were interlaced with management methods that promote discovery. Enough is known about the discovery process that an intelligent management system could be devised for technology managers (Chapter 18). In companies striving to be innovative, it is of overwhelming importance that all business managers gain insight into the potential mechanisms of discovery. This way, they can become highly effective team players and contributors to the innovative process.

Many technology managers are required by company policy or general practice to devote the major portion of their time to detailed paper work and prolific meetings. They are then chastised or worse for not promoting innovation. If both the short-term and the long-term are to be addressed with efficiency, technology managers need to manage discovery and incremental improvements in products, and promote commercialization. At least 80 percent of their time—perhaps more—is needed to achieve these goals. As opposed to detailed, nondiscovery types of management practices, employee morale is promoted overwhelmingly by success in their primary goals.

George Heilmeier,[19] Industrial Research Medalist for 1993, enumerated the characteristics of truly innovative companies. "They have leaders who know the business. They have close contact with the market at all levels. They have a very low incidence of NIH, the 'not-invented-here' syndrome. They minimize formal internal communication and rely heavily on informal or ad hoc communication. They have strong personal incentive systems. Their people are not afraid of failure; they take intelligent risks and try more things."

For creativity to proceed most effectively, the environment is culturally diverse, necessitating tolerant, unprejudiced attitudes. This is simply another method of diversifying the interaction of knowledge patterns which is complemented by the positive attitudes that are attendant with tolerance. Promotion of excessive competition between people is also a way of promoting conflict and ill will. Working toward a common goal can decrease hostility and increase cooperation.

Pursuing goals with high intensity, passion, and perseverance is a mechanism of maintaining control over our lives and of staying high on the pecking order. Our physical and mental health defects often arise from loss of control and descent from a preeminent position in the pecking order. For example, whereas high blood pressure may be related in part to stress, a common cause of low blood pressure is related to low social position. A study at the Centers for Disease Control showed that hope deprivation greatly increases one's likelihood of dying from heart disease.[20] Hope and control stimulate our hormones and increase the vitality of our immune systems. A rise in position of a superorganism, as a technology group or a company, arouses its people to exploration and adventure. A fall in position leads to conservative attitudes marked by unwillingness to take risks.[21] An appropriate and popular maxim is "If you snooze, you lose."[22]

## THE IDEAL ENVIRONMENT FOR INNOVATION

After the discussion of obstacles to creativity and discovery and potential remedies, it may be helpful to consider the ideal company in the ideal environment for the achievement of innovation. The ideal environment for an innovative company is Plato's world in which creativity and discovery are honored. Educated in science and technology, society has empathy for the power and limitations of these disciplines. The cyclic, interdependent nature of academic basic research and industrial strategic research are understood by the public. Researchers understand that wealth must be generated by innovation for the perpetuation of academic and industrial research. Education is geared to promote profound independent thinking and is a prized possession of people. Both science and technology are held in high esteem, and many of the brightest students seek careers in both areas.

Government and industry diligently cooperate to control and prevent the negative effects of technology. Whereas technology is a major factor in generating increased profits, social well-being is not neglected. Innovative companies thrive in this environment and are honored for their contributions to society and their restraint from harmful technologies. Incentives are provided by the government to promote long-term company goals and key future technologies. Similarly, the merger-mania and its ill-effects on the long-term are effectively discouraged.

To address the inordinately high cost of equipment and leading-edge research, the government has devised a mechanism to allow cooperation between companies, which promotes greater creativity. Providing that companies show ample evidence of long-term planning, Wall Street, convinced of the great value of long-term research, does not penalize reduction or lack of growth in short-term profits. Of great importance to new knowledge, agencies that fund research change their emphasis from projects that will give forseeable results to those that will be most apt to surprise.

## THE IDEAL COMPANY FOR INNOVATION

The ideal company has leaders who are not only technically competent but have a profound understanding of all aspects of the company. Such that obstacles are not established inadvertently, technical competence means an in-depth understanding of how discoveries are made and a working knowledge of the technologies involved. Innovation is a primary goal strongly supported by all managers. Such support goes beyond lip service and is exemplified by continuous supportive action. All members of the company are given incentives for assistance and promotion of the innovative process. Contradictions in goals between different members of the company are carefully avoided and innovation is forcefully characterized as a common goal. The entire company understands that although cooperation is critical, rational defection to achieve novelty is an ocassional event of a successful company. Promoted by education and on-site action, the basics of innovation become a mainstay of the company culture.

To preclude the suppression of creativity that generally comes with large size, the company is a business unit within a large conglomerate that has its own proficient technology group. Company goals are short-term to the extent needed for immediate healthy survival but are long-term otherwise. Annual profit plans are not devised for major increase in margin regardless of circumstances but are devised for change that is commensurate with future prospects. Long-term, strategic research is conducted continuously to enhance potential for highly profitable new products, which can not only extend the life of a company but may effect major increases in profit on a continuing basis.

By judicious concentration on the long-term, the short-term has become highly profitable. All divisions of the company are honored and held in high esteem. Research and development, operations, sales, accounting, marketing, and administration are all made to feel that they are enormously important and have prestigious positions in the company. Any group that feels unimportant will have less incentive and will become the weakest link in the chain leading to success. Although major innovation is an important goal, incremental improvement of existing products has a high priority as well. Highly skilled knowledgeable people, extensively coached in the necessity of broad company cooperation, permeate all divisions of the company.

Many technical people are included on the management team and help give the needed impetus for innovation. The technology manager has a broad in-depth background, has a spirited, contagious vision for technological achievement, and is familiar with the basic operation of all branches of the company. He or she has had training specifically directed toward the management of creativity and discovery and human relations. This manager interacts informally with all managers in the company and cooperation is understood to be paramount not only to company success but to individual success.

The technology staff is comprised of the best scientists and engineers; otherwise, technology expenditures with an eye toward innovation, other than for external image, are largely a waste. To build a superlative team, the company is willing to go beyond the norm in compensation and support of leading-edge research. The technology manager is geared primarily toward the promotion of creativity, discovery, incremental improvements, and the promotion of new product commercialization. Paperwork and meetings are minimized. To promote creativity and discovery, scientists and engineers have holistic responsibilities including strategic research, generation of new product ideas, incremental improvements of products, improvement of processes and development of new ones, and assistance in commercialization of new ideas. Culturally diverse and tolerant, the company is unafraid of intelligent risks, has overcome the NIH syndrome, and is willing to try many different things that may increase vitality.

The technology manager has developed, through experience, intensive study, and on-site investigation of systems used by the most innovative companies, a strong understanding and empathy for management methods to promote invention. He or she follows a close approximation of the eleven principles of discovery management described in Chapter 19, modified by the group's idiosyncratic needs to be creative. Each technologist enhances his or her creativity and potential for discovery by following most, if not all, of the stimuli for creativity listed in Chapter 12, again modified for individual needs.

By virtue of following these methods, the technology group's credibility, after a reasonable hiatus for knowledge gain, has been firmly established. All company managers, through required inculcation, understand the necessity of technology teams acquiring requisite basic science before pursuing related targeted research. Customer needs are monitored continuously and studied by the technology staff. The research effort is guided by the strategic plan, by the dynamics of customer needs, and by the anomalies observed in research projects.

Recognizing that success is dependent on the performance of all the staff, the technology manager consistently encourages and motivates each individual and facilitates the critical work of each. The entire company is informed of exceptional strides made by each technologist. Theoretically this company is highly successful, and whether youthful or "mature," is extraordinarily innovative. The entire company has acquired tremendous respect throughout the industry and among customers; such respect not only enlivens the company's innovative spirit but may attract new customers.

## CONCLUSION

Three basic parameters are indispensable to successful innovation:

1. *A strong, talented, visionary technical leader and talented researchers intrinsically motivated to discover and commercialize.* Management strives to find the best people and is willing to compensate accordingly. Having recognized its necessity for attracting and holding the best researchers and for successful targeted research, strategic basic research is promoted.

2. *A research group intimately familiar with mechanisms for generating technically viable and customer-oriented new product ideas.* Similarly, the group is fully indoctrinated with a broad range of research approaches that transcend conventionality. Researchers have the dual responsibility of discovery and generation of new product ideas from new knowledge where possible. They assist in commercialization of these new ideas. Targeted research is not expedited until there is a basic science understanding essential to goal achievement. Idiosyncratic techniques that help in discovery, even though unconventional, are supported by management.

3. *A company psyche empathetic to the current understanding of discovery mechanisms, to the process of innovation, and to the necessity of*

*interdivisional cooperation.* To preclude inadvertent obstacles, a company's support of technology and their design of management systems accommodate the subtle needs of creativity and discovery. By appropriate incentives for the innovative process, cooperation between all company divisions is facilitated.

With these three conditions met, a company has the greatest chance of gaining a handsome return on their research dollar, and of extending their vitality for an indefinite period. Unless they are equipped with a keen understanding of creativity in science and technology, technology groups, whose primary goal is innovation, are little more than luxurious decorations. This unfortunate circumstance is much too common and can create tension throughout a company.

Whether the concern is for life or for science and technology, evolution of these phenomena progress at an increasingly faster rate. The theoretical physicist Michio Kaku explains this phenomenon as follows:[23]

Although humans have existed on this planet for perhaps 2 million years, the rapid climb to modern civilization in the last 200 years was possible due to the fact that the growth of scientific knowledge is exponential; that is, its rate of expansion is proportional to how much is already known. The more we know, the faster we can know more. For example, we have amassed more knowledge since World War II than all the knowledge amassed in our 2 million–year evolution on this planet. In fact, the amount of knowledge that our scientists gain doubles approximately every 10 to 20 years.

Doubt is the subversive agent, the first critical step needed to eliminate ignorance. It is the opening for continuous improvement in understanding. The abstractness and remoteness of much of nature preclude giving definitive answers to great questions. Although it seems that our ignorance will never be totally eradicated, it is our responsibility to learn what we can for adjudication by the scientific method. Dogma, revelation, and authority are the enemies of the intellectual evolution of *Homo sapiens*.

By doubting, by debating, and by study, the well-being of people can be enhanced. That way credence and assistance will be given to the often illusive search for the good life. Making the most of life in the most rational, ethical, and humane way seems to be the most meaningful goal, or purpose, if you will, in this enigmatic, beautifully complex world. Purpose in this sense gives one something that can be grasped with a clear sense of reality.

To the extent that reasonably free rein is given to science and technology, ever more innovation will be generated to maintain a flourishing economy. In the words of computer and artificial life scientist Daniel Hillis,[24] "If I try to extrapolate the trends, to look at where technology's going sometime early in the next century, there comes a point where something incomprehensible will happen. Maybe it's the creation of intelligent machines. Maybe it's telecommunications merging us into a global organism."

To extend Hillis' optimism, if the superstring theory concerning the origin of the universe and the fundamental basis of matter and energy, proposed by some theoretical physicists, proves to be true and the necessary mathematics are discovered to solve the problem, then the unification of all of nature's forces into a single superforce may be accomplished.[25] The energy level needed to control ten-dimensional space, essential to the empirical demonstration of superstring theory, would be enormous—so large that, if possible, it will require centuries into the future before civilization can generate and control such astronomical feats of power.

The validation of superstring theory and the control of such levels of energy would enable people to change the structure of space. Exotic forms of matter could be produced. Conceivably, new worlds could be created with properties beyond present comprehension. Wormholes could be created and perhaps even the direction of time could be altered. Sometime in the distant future this seemingly wild speculation may be within the realm of possibility. If, indeed, such is possible, it seems reasonable to interpolate unimaginably exciting discoveries leading up to this ultimate achievement. The potential of science and technology, in this sense, is astronomical.

Alluded to in the introduction, science and technology may be confronted with Vannevar Bush's "endless frontier" of technical potential. Technology may be fractal in nature and its potential may correspond to the infinite length of the Koch curve (Chapter 4). Seemingly, with financial and moral support, science and technology will expand at an ever-increasing rate. To maintain a vital world, all of this can be done in the context of extending natural resources and preserving the quality of the environment. Although survival is a game of trade-offs, technological growth long-term will be meaningful only if it is done with concern for the whole of nature. This would entail a full realization of the interdependency of lifeforms and that maintenance of maximum biological diversity in all ecosystems is intertwined with the long-term well-being of people.

For the reason that human nature cannot be changed, zoologist Matt Ridley[26] discredits the notion of ecological virtue. Here game theory and the most propitious solution to the prisoner's dilemma become critical (Chapter 20). The dominance of self-interest, perhaps, can be made to work with strategies of cooperation for the general good. Cooperative strategies from game theory may help solve this conundrum by concealing innate selfishness and groupishness in systems where cooperation will evolve.

The future of the technical, creative enterprise is uncertain and is greatly dependent on a general social empathy for the cyclic and interdependent nature of innovation and its importance to wealth. If academic basic research and industrial strategic research are supported consistently, innovation will continuously invigorate our economy. If business management and technology management philosophies evolve to effect greater efficiency of innovation, the future of civilization can be full of hope. A major effort can be made to educate society on the nature of science and technology, and how these disciplines play a vital role in our economic and social well-being. To effect these goals, a climate for discovery and invention can be continuously cultivated. Consilience among all branches of learning could be a critical aid to cultural and technical detente, and to the enhancement of innovation.

Although these comments smack of scientism (in essence, the belief that the establishment of truth must finally be reduced to rationalism), all answers to the world's problems will not be forthcoming by the methods of science. Indeed, science probably will not penetrate all of the secrets of the universe. But the nature of the world is such that there is no other method to enhance knowledge in a reliable fashion.

Consilience, viewed by E.O. Wilson as a "seamless web of cause and effect"[27] across the ever-expanding sea of learning, would be a task of monumental proportion. He sees the ultimate form of consilience to be the reduction of all learning to the laws of physics. At the least, the interaction of all knowledge patterns seems to hold the greatest promise for growth in understanding and resolution of social problems. Consilience is accepted by the neurosciences and evolutionary biology, which Wilson sees as bridges to the humanities and the social sciences. All branches of learning may eventually be embroidered in holistic explanations for the maximum growth of knowledge and for the most proficient interplay of people world-wide.

Such consilient learning could be of great benefit to companies as well in all aspects of their operations. Undoubtedly, sufficient industrial experimentation and thought will continue to take place such that more and more viable solutions to company vitality will evolve. With its intensive competition, the new global economy has stimulated a great deal of thought about new potential pathways to increased competitiveness. Those companies that resist constructive change to vitalize the innovative process will obsolesce. Although the United States will continue to find ways to increase productivity, it is doubtful that it will do so with a momentous flare without a revolution in the way innovation is supported and expedited.

# Notes

**PREFACE**

1. Snow, 1959.

**CHAPTER 1**

1. May, 1976, p. 27.
2. Russell, 1989, p. 13.
3. Csikszentmihályi, 1990b, pp. 162–164.
4. Wilson, 1998.
5. Bundy, 1997.

**CHAPTER 2**

1. Otis, 1990, p. 208.
2. Mesthene, 1990, p. 80.
3. May, 1976, p. 137.
4. Gregory, 1981, p. 38.
5. Editors, *The Smithsonian Book of Invention*, 1978, p. 13.
6. Beniger, 1990, p. 54.
7. Eklund, 1978, pp. 72–81.
8. Asimov, 1997, p. 103.
9. Allman, 1994, pp. 186–200.
10. Pfeiffer, 1982, pp. 226–252.
11. Ridley, 1997, p. 69.
12. Barrow, 1995, p. 66.
13. Dabbs and Dabbs, 2000, pp. 194–195.
14. Dawkins, 1998, pp. 294–307.

15. Diamond, 1999, pp. 239–264.
16. White, 1978, pp. 64–71.
17. Diamond, 1999, pp. 11–417.
18. Temple, 1986, p. 9.
19. Slobodkin, 1992, pp. 127–128.
20. Wilson, 1998, pp. 30–31.
21. Burke, 1995, p. 68.
22. Ibid., p. 102.
23. Shlain, 1991, pp. 29–30.
24. Rothman and Sudarshan, 1998, pp. 87–88.
25. Bloom, 1995, pp. 307–308.
26. Stevens, 1999, pp. 44–47.
27. Burke, 1995, pp. 157–161.
28. Kauffman, 1995, p. 13.
29. Ibid., p. 208.
30. Burke, 1995, pp. 18–22.
31. Shlain, 1991, pp. 40–41.
32. Pacey, 1992, p. 29.
33. Ibid., pp. 29–75.
34. Shlain, 1991, pp. 52–53.
35. White, 1978, pp. 64–71.
36. Ibid.
37. Dyson, 1999, p. 60.

## CHAPTER 3

1. Shlain, 1991, p. 292.
2. Diamond, 1999, pp. 258–260.
3. Dibner, 1978, p. 125.
4. Pacey, 1992, pp. 56–57.
5. Shlain, 1991, p. 57.
6. Pacey, 1992, p. 57.
7. Dibner, 1978, p. 128.
8. Forman, 1978, p. 139.
9. Pacey, 1992, pp. 80–81.
10. Wilson, 1998, p. 48.
11. Barrow, 1998, p. 85.
12. Calne, 1999, p. 52.
13. Asimov, 1997, pp. 98–99.
14. Pacey, 1992, p. 94.
15. Wilson, 1998, pp. 14–45.
16. Pacey, 1992, p. 131.
17. Ibid., pp. 185–187.
18. Russell, 1989, pp. 264–266.
19. Marx, 1990, pp. 5–7.
20. Russell, 1989, p. 232.
21. Marx, 1990, pp. 7–10.

22. Florman, 1976, p. 80.
23. Ibid., pp. 99–101.
24. Morrison, 1990, p. 17.
25. Drucker, 1990, p. 160.
26. Florman, 1976, p. 23.
27. Wilson, 1999, pp. 347–349.
28. Price, 1978, p. 189.
29. Ziman, 1994, p. 78.
30. Pacey, 1992, p. 242.
31. Price, 1986, p. 190.
32. Ibid., p. 190.
33. Wright, 1992, p. x.
34. Beniger, 1990, pp. 51–76.
35. Mesthene, 1990, pp. 77–93.

## CHAPTER 4

1. Slobodkin, 1992, pp. 116–117.
2. Ziman, 1991, p. 3.
3. Cromer, 1993, p. 38.
4. Kauffman, 1993, pp. 76–77.
5. Cohen, 1978, p. 85.
6. Seitz, 1992, p. 3.
7. Miller, 1996, p. ix.
8. Seitz, pp. 7–16.
9. Casti, 1994, pp. 4–9.
10. Boden, 1990, p. 239.
11. Casti, 1990, p. 29.
12. Barrow, 1998, pp. 1–26.
13. Dupré, 1993, pp. 11–14.
14. Gazzaniga, 1992, p. 95.
15. Pagels, 1994, p. 94.
16. Hofstadter, 1979, pp. 15–19.
17. Casti, 1994, pp. 18–19.
18. Barrow, 1998, p. 220.
19. Smolin, 1997, pp. 18–23.
20. Dawkins, 1998, pp. 20–21.
21. Hawking, 1993, p. ix.
22. Atkins, 1995, p. 125–130.
23. Casti, 1989, pp. 12–13.
24. Bauer, 1994, p. 125.
25. Post, 1978, p. 24.
26. Diamond, 1999, p. 244.
27. Burke, 1995, pp. 7–9.
28. Gleick, 1988, pp. 98–100.
29. Root-Bernstein, 1989c, pp. 43–50.
30. Asimov, 1997, p. 103.

## CHAPTER 5

1. Wills, 1998, pp. 1–13, 230–240.
2. Dyson, 1999, pp. 108–109.
3. Amabile and Tighe, 1993, p. 9.
4. Miller, 1996, p. 335.
5. Gardner, 1993b, pp. 37–39, 42–43.
6. Bateson, 1979, pp. 44–45.
7. Restak, 1993, p. 169.
8. Goleman, Kaufman, and Ray, 1993, pp. 172–173.
9. Ibid., p. 120.
10. Siler, 1992, pp. 128–129.
11. Calne, 1999, pp. 193–195, 241.
12. Gardner, 1993a, p. 131.
13. Boden, 1991, p. 221.
14. Koestler, 1964, p. 102.
15. Gardner, 1993a, pp. 8–9.
16. Cszentmihályi, 1990a, pp. 190–212.
17. Gruber, 1989, pp. 3–24.
18. Albert and Runco, 1990, pp. 255–269.
19. Harrington, 1990, pp. 143–169.
20. Coveney and Highfield, 1991, p. 188.
21. Amabile and Tighe, 1993, pp. 7–27.
22. Slobodkin, 1992, pp. 4–5.
23. Cohen, 1977, p. 14.
24. Csikszentmihályi, 1990a, pp. 190–212.
25. Schwartz, 1992, p. xvii.
26. Cohen, 1977, p. 148.

## CHAPTER 6

1. Simonton, 1993, pp. 176–201.
2. Penrose, 1989, p. 226.
3. Edelman, 1992, pp. 10, 199.
4. Stenger, 1995, pp. 132–134.
5. Coveney and Highfield, 1991, p. 116.
6. Zohar, 1993, pp. 202–218.
7. Asimov, 1997, p. 166.
8. Rothman and Sudarshan, 1998, pp. 179–180.
9. Pagels, 1994, p. 137.
10. Harth, 1993, pp. 144–148.
11. Prigogine and Stengers, 1984, p. 141.
12. Lewin, 1992, p. 149.
13. Stenger, 1995, pp. 260–286.
14. Kauffman, 1995, pp. 26–29.
15. Cohen, 1977, pp. 35–36.
16. Boden, 1991, pp. 19–21.
17. Amabile and Tighe, 1993, pp. 7–27.

# CHAPTER 7

1. Prochnow, 1982, p. 105.
2. Gardner and Reese, 1975, p. 63.
3. Plotkin, 1994, pp. 125–134.
4. Penrose, 1995, p. 22.
5. Plotkin, 1994, p. 49.
6. Ibid., pp. 134–178.
7. Donald, 1991, pp. 9–14.
8. Plotkin, 1994, p. 162.
9. Dyson, 1999, p. 7.
10. Cromer, 1993, p. vii.
11. Judson, 1987, pp. 239–240.
12. Wolpert, 1993, pp. 15–16.
13. Cromer, 1993, pp. 28–30.
14. Sagan, 1995, pp. 312–317.

# CHAPTER 8

1. Editor, *Skeptical Inquirer*, 2001, pp. 12–15.
2. Sagan, 1995, p. 311.
3. Ibid., p. 4.
4. Editor, *Skeptical Inquirer*, 2001, p. 12.
5. Barrow, 1995, pp. 44–45.
6. Margolis, 1987, pp. 37–48.
7. de Bono, 1992, pp. 28–29.
8. Amabile, 1990, p. 82.
9. Asimov, 1997, p. 89.
10. Lewin, 1992, p. 118.
11. Maslow, 1966, pp. 45–65.
12. Ibid., pp. 95–101.
13. Wilson, 1998, p. 117.
14. Edelman, 1992, pp. 79–80.
15. Harth, 1993, pp. 70–73.
16. Gazzaniga, 1992, pp. 121–133.
17. Langton, 1996, p. 349.
18. Ridley, 1999, pp. 151–152.
19. Tweney, 1989, pp. 91–106.
20. Gruber, 1989, p. 12.
21. Wolff, 1981, pp. 29–31.
22. Root-Bernstein, 1989b, p. 37.
23. Schwartz, 1992, pp. 130–131.
24. Coveney and Highfield, 1991, p. 168.
25. Atkins, 1995, p. 127.
26. Asimov, 1997, pp. 9–10.
27. Bloor, 1991, pp. 31–33.
28. Wright, 1998.

29. Cromer, 1997, p. 7.
30. Sternberg, 1988, pp. 9–10.
31. Calvin, 1991, p. 12.
32. Restak, Richard, 1991, pp. 18–19.
33. Wills, 1998, pp. 247–249.
34. Edelman, 1992, p. 17.
35. Klivington, 1989, p. 174.
36. Wright, 1998, pp. 58–61.
37. Wills, 1998, pp. 256–257.
38. Ridley, 1999, pp. 82–85.
39. Johnson, 1992, pp. 168–172.
40. Maturana and Varela, 1992, pp. 166–171.
41. Restak, 1991, pp. 138–141.
42. Slobodkin, 1992, pp. 42–43.
43. Sternberg, 1988, pp. 83–90.
44. Boden, 1991, pp. 24–25.
45. Benardete, 1961, p. 40.
46. Rothenberg, 1990, p. 160.
47. Russell, 1989, pp. 52–53.

## CHAPTER 9

1. Oliver, 1991, pp. 32–33.
2. Gould, 1996, p. 62.
3. Bateson, 1979, pp. 84–85.
4. Adams, 1974, pp. 113–125.
5. Wolff, 1987, pp. 35–36.
6. Bennis and Biederman, 1997, pp. 117–141.
7. Souder, 1987, pp. 13–17.
8. de Bono, 1992, pp. 145–150.
9. Restak, 1991, pp. 36–39.
10. de Bono, 1992, pp. 237–295.
11. Bransford and Stein, 1984, pp. 20–41.
12. Diebold, 1990, p. 21.
13. Dyson, 1999, pp. 105–106.

## CHAPTER 10

1. Rothenberg, 1990, pp. 48–51.
2. Boden, 1991, pp. 244–245.
3. Weisberg, 1993, p. 54.
4. Miller, 1996, p. 334.
5. Stenger, 1995, p. 288.
6. Humphrey, 1996, p. 201.
7. Cohen, 1977, pp. 93–94.
8. Ibid., 1977, pp. 97–100.
9. Wilson, 1998, p. 77.

10. Rothenberg, 1990, pp. 49–56.
11. Restak, 1991, p. 153.
12. Adams, 1986, p. 14.
13. Margolis, 1987, pp. 188–195.
14. Russell, 1989, p. 18.
15. Gleick, 1988, p. 35.
16. Restak, 1991, pp. 105–106.
17. Coveney and Highfield, 1991, pp. 25–26.
18. Smolin, 1997, p. 144.
19. Koestler, 1964, pp. 317–319.
20. Root-Bernstein, 1989b, pp. 36–41.

## CHAPTER 11

1. May, 1976, pp. 149–169.
2. Wright, 1994, p. 319.
3. West, 1991, pp. 185–186.
4. Gardner and Reese, 1975, p. 149.
5. Ziman, 1994, p. 30.
6. Scolnick, 1990, pp. 21–25.
7. Ziman, 1994, p. 31.
8. Humes, 1975, p. 8.
9. Ibid., p. 50.
10. Koestler, 1964, pp. 33–45.
11. Root-Bernstein, 1988, pp. 26–34.
12. Stephan and Levin, 1992, pp. 105–106.
13. Judson, 1987, pp. 239–240.
14. Leebaert and Dickinson, 1991, pp. 293–295.

## CHAPTER 12

1. Cromer, 1993, p. 27.
2. Feynman, 1999, p. 112.
3. Sternberg, 1988, pp. 40–41.
4. Root-Bernstein, 1988, pp. 26–34.
5. Weisberg, 1993, p. 28.
6. Gardner and Reese, 1975, p. 197.
7. Kosko, 1993, p. 40.
8. Plotkin, 1994, pp. 190–193.
9. Wolpert, 1993, pp. xi–xii.
10. Cohen, 1978, p. 23.
11. Slobodkin, 1992, pp. 114–138.
12. Bauer, 1994, pp. 46, 91.
13. Asimov, 1997, p. 8.
14. Casti, 1990, p. 31.
15. Johnson, 1992, p. 165.
16. Ornstein and Ehrlich, 1990, pp. 207–208.

17. Ibid., p. 31.
18. Margolis, 1987, p. 33.
19. Restak, 1991, pp. 51–57.
20. Wilson, 1998, p. 106.
21. Cromer, 1993, p. 137.
22. Dupré, 1993, pp. 1–2.
23. Brown, 1979, p. 108.
24. Weisberg, 1993, pp. 51–52.
25. Hawking, 1993, pp. 42–43.
26. Bauer, 1994, p. 31.
27. Hawking, 1993, pp. 42–44.
28. Tarnas, 1991, p. 27.
29. Ziman, 1978, p. 76.
30. Weisberg, 1993, pp. 18–21.
31. Cohen, 1978, p. 123.
32. Bronowski, 1978a, pp. 50–51.
33. Dupré, 1993, p. 131.

## CHAPTER 13

1. Van Doren, 1991, pp. 31–34.
2. Gardner and Reese, 1975, p. 195.
3. Russell, 1989, p. 16.
4. Wolpert, 1993, p. 54.
5. Bauer, 1994, p. 52.
6. Gardner, 1993a, p. 10.
7. Bennis and Biederman, 1997, p. 122.
8. Barrow, 1998, p. 97.
9. Bloom, 1995, pp. 57–58.
10. Wilson, 1999, pp. 5–6.
11. Brown, 1979, pp. 132–137.
12. Cohen, 1978, pp. 84–85.
13. Bruner, 1979, p. 7.
14. Wilson, 1998, p. 137.
15. Bauer, 1994, p. 43.
16. Friedman, 1999, pp. 180–184.
17. Barrow, 1998, p. 116.
18. Russell, 1990, pp. 75–81.
19. Piatelli-Palmarini, 1994, pp. 38–39.
20. Rothman and Sudarshan, 1998, p. 37.
21. Tarnas, 1991, p. 112.
22. Gillispie, 1990, pp. 74–82.
23. Johnson, 1992, pp. 217–218.
24. Cohen, 1978, p. 139.
25. Kaku, 1994, pp. 327–328.
26. Johnson, 1991, pp. 112–113.
27. Salmon, 1979, p. 11.

28. Plotkin, 1994, pp. 16–19.
29. Bloor, 1991, p. 32.
30. Dormann, 1987, p. 170.
31. Metcalf, 1987, p. 143.
32. Salmon, 1979, p. 18.
33. Casti, 1989, pp. 32–35.
34. Gazzaniga, 1992, p. 136.
35. Casti, 1989, p. 30.
36. Ibid., 1989, pp. 48–50.
37. Otis, 1990, p. 15.
38. Plotkin, 1994, pp. 16–19.
39. Ibid., pp. 243–245.
40. Russell, 1989, p. 266.
41. Plotkin, 1994, p. 237.
42. Casti, 1989, p. 61.
43. Poundstone, 1988, pp. 15–16.

## CHAPTER 14

1. Siler, 1990.
2. Miller, 1996, p. 35.
3. Wolpert, 1993, p. 92.
4. Russell, 1989, p. 277.
5. Kuhn, 1970, pp. 43–51.
6. De Mey, 1992, p. 85.
7. Casti, 1989, p. 39.
8. Dyson, 1999, pp. 14–15.
9. Bloor, 1991, pp. 26–27.
10. Bauer, 1994, p. 76.
11. Margolis, 1987, pp. 188–250.
12. Brown, 1979, pp. 11–112.
13. Kuhn, 1970, pp. 23–24.
14. Root-Bernstein, 1989c, pp. 43–50.
15. Miller, 1996, p. 228.
16. Brown, 1979, pp. 136–137.
17. Cromer, 1993, p. 6.
18. Weisberg, 1993, pp. 21–22.
19. Holyoak, 1990, pp. 134–135.
20. Keegan, 1989, pp. 107–125.
21. Eldredge and Gould, 1972.
22. Wilson, 1999, pp. 88–89.
23. Weisberg, 1993, pp. 105–113.
24. Mayer, 1992, p. 22.
25. Ibid., pp. 98–99.
26. Ibid., pp. 101–102.
27. Churchland and Churchland, 1995, pp. 64–68.

## CHAPTER 15

1. Bloom, 1995, p. 118.
2. Penrose, 1989, pp. 423–425.
3. Bloom, 2000, p. 52.
4. Russell, 1989, p. 247.
5. Penrose, Roger, 1995, p. 17.
6. Capra, 1988, pp. 77–78.
7. Bronowski, 1978a, pp. 67–89.
8. Ziman, 1994, pp. 22–23.
9. Russell, 1989, p. 253.
10. Bohm and Peat, 1987, pp. 68–72.
11. Gregory, 1981, p. 86.
12. Horgan, 1995, p. 189.
13. Siler, 1992, pp. 59–60.
14. Smolin, 1997, pp. 33–34.
15. Weiner, 1999, p. 216.
16. Ornstein and Ehrlich, 1990, pp. 234–265.
17. Kaku, 1997, pp. 9–12.
18. Friedman, 1999, p. 15.
19. Wilson, 1998, pp. 8–13, 266.
20. Smolin, 1997, pp. 152–156.
21. Weisberg, 1993, pp. 10–11.
22. Morris, 1993, pp. 130–148.
23. Ruse, 1999, pp. 74–75.
24. Riordan and Schramm, 1991, pp. 138–142.
25. Kaku, 1994, pp. 179–185.
26. Edelman, 1992, pp. 75–77.
27. Kosko, 1993.
28. Shlain, 1991, pp. 239–242.
29. Gardner, 1996b, pp. 155–163.
30. Barrow, 1998, pp. 195–197.

## CHAPTER 16

1. de Bono, 1968.
2. Sternberg, 1988, p. 91.
3. Ibid., pp. 89–90.
4. Mayer, 1992, pp. 57–62.
5. Conrath, 1985, pp. 6–10.
6. Breton and Gold, 1987, pp. 9–12.
7. Holyoak, 1990, p. 120.
8. Rothenberg, 1990, pp. 23–25.
9. Pagels, 1994, pp. 36–40.
10. Green, 1999, pp. 56–58.
11. Gardner and Reese, 1975, p. 69.
12. Adams, 1974, pp. 98–105.

13. Harth, 1993, p. 57.
14. Restak, 1984, p. 197.
15. Ziman, 1994, p. 114.
16. Plotkin, 1994, p. 189.
17. Harth, 1993, p. 87.
18. Restak, 1991, pp. 172–174.
19. Miller, 1996, p. 45.
20. Ibid., p. 34.
21. Ibid., pp. 247–249.
22. Pagels, 1994, pp. 51–52.
23. Ibid., pp. 84–94.
24. Miller, 1989, p. 248.
25. Slobodkin, 1992, pp. 20–22.
26. Maslow, 1966, pp. 11–12.
27. Ziman, 1994, pp. 42–43.
28. Rothenberg, 1990, pp. 25–41.
29. Osowkski, 1989, pp. 127–145.
30. Rothenberg, 1990, pp. 31–35.
31. Miller, 1989, p. 219.
32. Restak, 1984, pp. 239–240.
33. Shlain, 1991, p. 399.
34. Ibid., p. 402.
35. Klivington, 1989, pp. 45–46.
36. Dabbs and Dabbs, 2000, pp. 42–43.
37. Klivington, 1989, pp. 54–55.
38. West, 1991, pp. 14–15.
39. Ibid., p. 26.
40. Adams, 1974, pp. 98–99.
41. Koestler, 1964, p. 45.
42. Goleman, Kaufman, and Ray, 1993, p. 174.

## CHAPTER 17

1. Judson, 1987, pp. 209–210.
2. Horgan, 1995, p. 88.
3. Root-Bernstein, 1989c, pp. 43–50.
4. Goleman, Kaufman, and Ray, 1993, pp. 125–126.
5. Root-Bernstein, 1989c, p. 133.
6. Gardner, 1993b, pp. 31–33.
7. Holmes, 1989, p. 55.
8. Gruber, 1989, pp. 10–11.
9. Koestler, 1964, pp. 108–109.
10. Johnson, 1992, pp. 12–13.
11. Bronowski, 1978a, p. 56.
12. Gardner, 1996b, p. 256.
13. Otis, 1990, p. 57.
14. Bronowski, 1978b, p. 131.

15. Bauer, 1994, pp. 134–135.
16. Horgan, 1995, p. 238.
17. Cohen, 1978, p. 126.
18. Gardner and Reese, 1975, p. 199.
19. Bauer, 1994, p. 146.
20. Wilson, 1998, p. 246.

## CHAPTER 18

1. May, 1976, p. 2.
2. Dormann, 1987, p. 16.
3. Margulis, 1996, p. 134.
4. Sagan, 1995, pp. 396–398.
5. Brockman, 1996, p. 347.

## CHAPTER 19

1. Perel, 1990, pp. 7–9.
2. Hoeg, 1990, pp. 7–8.
3. National Science Board Committee, 1991, pp. 36–42.
4. Staudenmaier, 1994, pp. 34–44.
5. Bennis and Biederman, 1997, p. 22.
6. Amabile and Tighe, 1993, pp. 7–27.
7. Wright, 1998, pp. 195–196.
8. Holton, 1988, pp. 408–413.
9. Maslow, 1966, pp. 48–49.
10. Root-Bernstein, 1989b, pp. 36–41.
11. Shapero, 1986, pp. 25–30.
12. Gardner, 1996b, p. 194.
13. Gazzaniga, 1992, pp. 184–186.
14. Cohen, 1977, p. 91.
15. Capra, 1982, pp. 44–45.
16. Bennis and Biederman, 1977.

## CHAPTER 20

1. Bennis and Biederman, 1977, p. 104.
2. Wright, 1994, p. 321.
3. Axelrod, 1984, pp. 1–215.
4. Ridley, 1997, pp. 69–84.
5. Ibid., pp. 177–186.

## CHAPTER 21

1. Young, 1990, pp. 299–310.
2. Bloom, 1995, p. 276.

3. Thurow, 1996, pp. 16–18.
4. Port, 1989b, pp. 170–173.
5. Mitchell, 1989, pp. 106–118.
6. Port, 1989a, pp. 14–18.
7. Kozlov, 1989, p. 18.
8. Leet, 1991, pp. 15–17.
9. Ziman, 1994, p. 79.
10. Port, 1989a, p. 18.
11. Barnholt, 1997, pp. 12–16.
12. Weber, 1989, p. 120.
13. Mitchell, 1989, p. 121.
14. Highman and de Limur, 1981, pp. 8–11.
15. Chen, 1990, pp. 76–78.
16. Wolff, 1988, pp. 8–9.
17. Bauer, 1994, p. 121.
18. Pearson, 1993, pp. 45–51.
19. Heilmeier, 1993, pp. 27–32.
20. Bloom, 1995, p. 121.
21. Ibid., p. 299.
22. Ibid., pp. 310–326.
23. Kaku, 1994, p. 274.
24. Hillis, 1996, pp. 385–386.
25. Kaku, 1994, pp. 273–274.
26. Ridley, 1997, pp. 224–230.
27. Wilson, 1998, pp. 266–268.

# Bibliography

Adams, James L. 1974. *Conceptual Blockbusting: A Guide to Better Ideas*. San Francisco: W.H. Freeman and Company.

———. 1986. *The Care and Feeding of Ideas: A Guide to Encouraging Creativity*. Reading, MA: Addison-Wesley Publishing Company.

Albert, Robert S., and Runco, Mark A. 1990. Observations, Conclusions, and Gaps. In *Theories of Creativity*, edited by Mark A. Runco and Robert S. Albert. Newbury Park, CA: Sage Publications, pp. 255–269.

Allman, William F. 1994. *The Stone Age Present: How Evolution Has Shaped Modern Life—from Sex, Violence, and Language to Emotions, Morals, and Communities*. New York: Simon & Schuster.

Amabile, Teres M. 1990. Within You, Without You: The Social Psychology of Creativity and Beyond. In *Theories of Creativity*, edited by Mark A. Runco and Robert S. Albert. Newbury Park, CA: Sage Publications, pp. 61–91.

———, and Tighe, Elizabeth. 1993. Questions of Creativity. In *Creativity*, edited by John Brockman. New York: Simon & Schuster, pp. 7–27.

Asimov, Isaac. 1997. *The Roving Mind*. Amherst, MA: Prometheus Books.

Atkins, P.W. 1995. The Limitless Power of Science. In *Nature's Imagination: The Frontiers of Scientific Vision*, edited by John Cornwell. Oxford: Oxford University Press, pp. 122–132.

Axelrod, Robert. 1984. *The Evolution of Cooperation*. New York: Basic Books.

Barnholt, Edward W. 1997. Fostering Business Growth with Breakthrough Innovation. *Research Management* (March–April), pp. 12–13.

Barrow, John D. 1995. *The Artful Universe: The Cosmic Source of Human Creativity*. Boston: Back Bay Books/Little, Brown, and Company.

———. 1998. *Impossibility: The Limits of Science and the Science of Limits*. Oxford: Oxford University Press.

Bass, Thomas A. 1994. *Reinventing the Future: Conversations with the World's Leading Scientists*. Reading, MA: Addison-Wesley Publishing Company.

Bateson, Gregory. 1979. *Mind and Nature: A Necessary Unity*. New York: Bantam Books.

Bauer, Henry H. 1994. *Scientific Literacy and the Myth of the Scientific Method*. Urbana: University of Illinois Press.

Benardete, Doris. 1961. *Mark Twain: Wit and Wisecracks*. Mount Vernon, NY: The Peter Pauper Press.

Beniger, James R. 1990. The Control Revolution. In *Technology and the Future*, edited by Albert H. Teich. New York: St. Martin's Press, pp. 51–76.

Bennis, Warren, and Biederman, Patricia Ward. 1997. *Organizing Genius: The Secrets of Creative Collaboration*. Reading, MA: Addison-Wesley Publishing Company.

Bloom, Howard. 1995. *The Lucifer Principle: A Scientific Expedition into the Forces of History*. New York: The Atlantic Monthly Press.

———. 2000. *Global Brain: The Evolution of Mass Mind from the Big Bang to the 21st Century*. New York: John Wiley & Sons.

Bloor, David, 1991. *Knowledge and Social Imagery*. Chicago: University of Chicago Press.

Boden, Margaret A. 1991. *The Creative Mind: Myths and Mechanisms*. New York: Basic Books.

Bohm, David, and Peat, David F. 1987. *Science, Order, and Creativity*. New York: Bantam Books.

Bransford, John D., and Stein, Barry S. 1984. *The Ideal Problem Solver: A Guide for Improving Thinking, Learning, and Creativity*. New York: W.H. Freeman and Company.

Breton, Ernest J., and Gold, Raelene J. 1987. Cultivating Invention. *Research Management* (September–October), pp. 9–12.

Brockman, John. 1996. *The Third Culture*. New York: Simon & Schuster.

Bronowski, Jacob. 1978a. *The Origins of Knowledge and Imagination*. New Haven, CT: Yale University Press.

———. 1978b. *The Common Sense of Science*. Cambridge, MA: Harvard University Press.

Brown, Harold I. 1979. *Perception, Theory, and Commitment: The New Philosophy of Science*. Chicago: University of Chicago Press.

Brown, Lester R., Flavin, Christopher, and Wolf, Edward C. 1990. Earth's Vital Signs. In *Technology and the Future*, edited by Albert H. Teich. New York: St. Martin's Press, pp. 139–152.

Bruner, Jerome. 1979. *On Knowing: Essays for the Left Hand*. Cambridge, MA: Belknap Press of Harvard University Press.

Bundy, Wayne M. 1997. *The Art of Discovery: Fueling Innovation for Company Growth*. Menlo Park, CA: Crisp Publications.

Burke, James. 1995. *Connections*. Boston: Little, Brown and Company.

Calne, Donald B. 1999. *Within Reason: Rationality and Human Behavior*. New York: Pantheon Books.

Calvin, William H. 1991. *The Ascent of Mind: Ice Age Climates and the Evolution of Intelligence*. New York: Bantam Books.

Capra, Fritjof. 1988. *The Turning Point: Science, Society, and the Rising Culture*. Toronto: Bantam Books.

Casti, John L. 1989. *Paradigms Lost: Images of Man in the Mirror of Science*. New York: William Morrow and Company.

———. 1990. *Searching for Certainty: What Scientists Can Know about the Future*. New York: William Morrow and Company.

———. 1994. *Complexification: Explaining a Paradoxical World through the Science of Surprise*. New York: HarperCollins.

Chen, Katherine T. 1990. Contrasting Strategies Are Pursued by Big Three Economic Powerhouses. *IEEE Spectrum* (October), pp. 76–78.

Churchland, Paul M., and Churchland, Patricia S. 1995. Intertheoretic Reduction: A Neuroscientist's Field Guide. In *Nature's Imagination: The Frontiers of Scientific Vision*, edited by John Cornwell. Oxford: Oxford University Press, pp. 64–77.

Cohen, Daniel. 1977. *Creativity: What Is It?* New York: M. Evans and Company.

Cohen, Morris R. 1978. *Reason and Nature: An Essay on the Meaning of Scientific Method*. New York: Dover Publications.

Conrath, Jerry. 1985. The Imagination Harvest: Training People to Solve Problems Creatively. *Supervisory Management* (September), pp. 6–10.

Coveney, Peter, and Highfield, Roger. 1991. *The Arrow of Time: A Voyage through Science to Solve Times's Greatest Mystery*. New York: Fawcett Columbine.

Cromer, Alan. 1993. *Uncommon Sense: The Heretical Nature of Science*. New York: Oxford University Press.

———. 1997. *Connected Knowledge: Science, Philosophy, and Education*. New York: Oxford University Press.

Csikszentmihályi, Mihályi. 1990a. The Domain of Creativity. In *Theories of Creativity*, edited by Mark A. Runco and Robert S. Albert. Newbury Park, CA: Sage Publications, pp. 190–212.

———. 1990b. *Flow: The Psychology of Optimal Experience*. New York: Harper & Row.

Dabbs, James McBride, and Dabbs, Mary Godwin. 2000. *Heroes, Rogues, and Lovers: Testosterone and Behavior*. New York: McGraw-Hill.

Dawkins, Richard. 1998. *Unweaving the Rainbow: Science, Delusion, and the Appetite for Wonder*. Boston: Houghton Mifflin Company.

de Bono, Edward. 1968. *New Think: The Use of Lateral Thinking in the Generation of New Ideas*. New York: Basic Books.

———. 1992. *Serious Creativity: Using the Power of Lateral Thinking to Create New Ideas*. New York: HarperBusiness.

De Mey, Marc. 1992. *The Cognitive Paradigm*. Chicago: University of Chicago Press.

Diamond, Jared. 1999. *Guns, Germs, and Steel: The Fates of Human Societies*. New York: W.W. Norton & Company.

Dibner, Bern. 1978. Merchants of Light. In *The Smithsonian Book of Invention*. New York: Simon & Schuster, pp. 124–131.

Diebold, John. 1990. *The Innovators: The Discoveries, Inventions, and Breakthroughs of Our Time*. New York: Truman Talley Books.

Donald, Merlin. 1991. *Origins of the Modern Mind: Three Stages in the Evolution of Culture and Cognition*. Cambridge, MA: Harvard University Press.

Dormann, Henry O. 1987. *The Speaker's Book of Quotations*. New York: Fawcett Columbine.

Drucker, Peter F. 1990. New Technology: Predicting Its Impact. In *Technology and the Future*, edited by Albert H. Teich. New York: St. Martin's Press, pp. 159–163.

Dupré, John. 1993. *The Disorder of Things: Metaphysical Foundations of the Disunity of Science*. Cambridge, MA: Harvard University Press.

Dyson, Freeman. 1995. The Scientist as Rebel. In *Nature's Imagination: The Frontiers of Scientific Vision*, edited by John Cornwell. Oxford: Oxford University Press, pp. 1–11.

———. 1999. *The Sun, the Genome, and the Internet: Tools of Scientific Revolutions*. New York: The New York Public Library and Oxford University Press.

Edelman, Gerald M. 1992. *Bright Air, Brilliant Fire: On the Matter of Mind*. New York: Basic Books.

Editor. 2001. Science Indicators 2000: Belief in the Paranormal or Pseudoscience. *Skeptical Inquirer*, No. 1 (January–February), pp. 12–15.

Editors. 1978. *The Smithsonian Book of Invention*. New York: W.W. Norton & Company.

Eklund, Jon B. 1978. From the Artisan's Hand. In *The Smithsonian Book of Invention*. New York: W.W. Norton & Company, pp. 72–81.

Eldredge, Niles, and Gould, Stephen Jay. 1972. Punctuated Equilibria: An Alternative to Phyletic Gradualism. In *Models in Paleobiology*, edited by T.J.M. Schopf. San Francisco: Freeman Cooper, pp. 82–115.

Feynman, Richard P. 1999. *The Pleasure of Finding Things Out: The Best Works of Richard P. Feynman*. Cambridge, MA: Perseus Books.

Florman, Samuel C. 1976. *The Existential Pleasures of Engineering*. New York: St. Martin's Press.

Forman, Paul. 1978. The Atom Smashers. In *The Smithsonian Book of Invention*. New York: W.W. Norton & Company, pp. 132–139.

Foster, Richard. 1986. *Innovation: The Attacker's Advantage*. New York: Summit Books.

Friedman, Thomas L. 1999. *The Lexus and the Olive Tree: Understanding Globalization*. New York: Farrar, Straus, Giroux.

Gardner, Howard. 1993a. *Creating Minds: An Anatomy of Creativity Seen through the Lives of Freud, Einstein, Picasso, Stravinsky, Eliot, Graham, and Gandhi*. New York: Basic Books.

———. 1993b. Seven Creators of the Modern Era. In *Creativity*, edited by John Brockman. New York: Simon & Schuster, pp. 28–47.

Gardner, John W., and Reese, Francesca Gardner. 1975. *Quotations of Wit and Wisdom: Know or Listen to Those Who Know*. New York: W.W. Norton & Company.

Gardner, Martin. 1996a. *The Night Is Large*. New York: St. Martin's Press.

———. 1996b. *Weird Water and Fuzzy Logic*. Amherst, MA: Prometheus Books.

Gazzaniga, Michael S. 1992. *Nature's Mind: The Biological Roots of Thinking, Emotions, Sexuality, Language, and Intelligence*. New York: Basic Books.

Gillispie, Charles Coulston. 1990. *The Edge of Objectivity: An Essay in the History of Scientific Ideas*. Princeton, NJ: Princeton University Press.

Gleick, James. 1988. *Chaos: Making a New Science*. New York: Viking.

Goleman, Daniel, Kaufman, Paul, and Ray, Michael. 1993. *The Creative Spirit.* New York: Plume.

Gould, Stephen Jay. 1996. The Pattern of Life's History. In *The Third Culture,* edited by John Brockman. New York: Simon & Schuster, pp. 51–73.

Greene, Brian. 1999. *The Elegant Universe: Superstrings, Hidden Dimensions, and the Quest for the Ultimate Theory.* New York: W.W. Norton & Company.

Gregory, Richard L. 1981. *Mind in Science: A History of Explanations in Psychology and Physics.* Cambridge: Cambridge University Press.

Gruber, Howard E. 1989. The Evolving Systems Approach to Creative Work. In *Creative People at Work: Twelve Cognitive Case Studies,* edited by Doris B. Wallace and Howard E. Gruber. New York: Oxford University Press, pp. 3–24.

———. 1993. Aspects of Scientific Discovery: Aesthetics and Cognition. In *Creativity,* edited by John Brockman. New York: Simon & Schuster, pp. 48–74.

Harrington, David M. 1990. Ecology and Culture. In *Theories of Creativity,* edited by Mark A. Runco and Robert S. Albert. Newbury Park, CA: Sage Publications, pp. 143–169.

Harth, Eric. 1993. *The Creative Loop: How the Brain Makes a Mind.* Reading, MA: Addison-Wesley Publishing Company.

Hawking, Stephen. 1993. *Black Holes and Baby Universes and Other Essays.* New York: Bantam Books.

Heilmeier, George. 1993. Room for Whom at the Top? Promoting Technical Literacy in the Executive Suite. *Research-Technology Management* (November–December), pp. 27–32.

Highman, Arthur, and de Limur, Charles. 1981. Research and Development Is Generally a Good Investment—Myth or Reality? *Research Management* (May), pp. 8–11.

Hillis, W. Daniel. 1996. Close to the Singularity. In *The Third Culture,* edited by John Brockman. New York: Simon & Schuster, pp. 379–397.

Hoeg, Donald F. 1990. Recapturing Yankee Ingenuity. *Research-Technology Management* (May–June), pp. 7–8.

Hofstadter, Douglas R. 1979. *Gödel, Escher, Bach: An Eternal Golden Braid.* New York: Basic Books.

Holmes, Frederic L. 1989. Antoine Lovoisier and Hans Krebs: Two Styles of Scientific Creativity. In *Creative People at Work: Twelve Cognitive Case Studies,* edited by Doris B. Wallace and Howard E. Gruber. New York: Oxford University Press, pp. 44–68.

Holton, Gerald. 1988. *Thematic Origins of Scientific Thought: Kepler to Einstein.* Cambridge, MA: Harvard University Press.

Holyoak, Keith J. 1990. Problem Solving. In *Thinking: An Invitation to Cognitive Science,* edited by Daniel N. Osherson and Edward E. Smith. Cambridge, MA: The MIT Press, pp. 117–146.

Horgan, John. 1995. *The End of Science: Facing the Limits of Knowledge in the Twilight of the Scientific Age.* Reading, MA: Addison-Wesley Publishing Company.

Humes, James C. 1975. *Podium Humor: A Raconteur's Treasury of Witty and Humorous Stories.* New York: Harper & Row.

Humphrey, Nicholas. 1996. The Thick Moment. In *Third Culture*, edited by John Brockman. New York: Simon & Schuster, pp. 198–208.

Johnson, George. 1992. *In the Palaces of the Memory: How We Build the Worlds inside Our Heads*. New York: Vintage Books.

Judson, Horace Freeland. 1987. *The Search for Solutions*. Baltimore, MD: The Johns Hopkins University Press.

Kaku, Michio. 1994. *Hyperspace: A Scientific Odyssey through Parallel Universes, Time Warps, and the 10th Dimension*. New York: Anchor Books.

———. 1997. *Visions: How Science Will Revolutionize the 21st Century*. New York: Anchor Books.

Kauffman, Stuart A. 1993. The Sciences of Complexity and "Origins of Order." In *Creativity*, edited by John Brockman. New York: Simon & Schuster, pp. 75–107.

———. 1995. *At Home in the Universe: The Search for the Laws of Self-Organization*. New York: Oxford University Press.

Keegan, Robert T. 1989. How Charles Darwin Became a Psychologist. In *Creative People at Work: Twelve Cognitive Case Studies*, edited by Doris B. Wallace and Howard E. Gruber. New York: Oxford University Press, pp. 107–125.

Klivington, Kenneth. 1989. *The Science of Mind*. Cambridge, MA: The MIT Press.

Koestler, Arthur. 1964. *The Act of Creation*. London: Arkana.

Kosko, Bart. 1993. *Fuzzy Thinking: The New Science of Fuzzy Logic*. New York: Hyperion.

Kozlov, Alex. 1989. Competitive Edge: Breaking the Cycle that Stifles Innovation. *Psychology Today* (October), p. 18.

Kuhn, Thomas S. 1970. *The Structure of Scientific Revolutions*. Chicago: University of Chicago Press.

Langton, Christopher G. 1996. A Dynamical Pattern. In *The Third Culture*, edited by John Brockman. New York: Simon & Schuster, pp. 244–358.

Leebaert, Derek, and Dickinson, Timothy. 1991. A World to Understand: Technology and the Awakening of Human Possibility. In *Technology 2001: The Future of Computing and Communications*, edited by Derek Leebaert. Cambridge, MA: The MIT Press, pp. 293–321.

Leet, Richard H. 1991. How Top Management Sees R&D. *Research-Technology Management* (January–February), pp. 15–17.

Lewin, Roger. 1992. *Complexity: Life at the Edge of Chaos*. New York: Collier Books.

Lovelock, James. 1991. *Healing Gaia: Practical Medicine for the Planet*. New York: Harmony Books.

Margolis, Howard. 1987. *Patterns, Thinking, and Cognition: A Theory of Judgement*. Chicago: University of Chicago Press.

Margulis, Lynn. 1996. Gaia Is a Tough Bitch. In *The Third Culture*, edited by John Brockman. New York: Simon & Schuster, pp. 129–146.

Marx, Leo. 1990. Does Improved Technology Mean Progress? In *Technology and the Future*, edited by Albert H. Teich. New York: St. Martin's Press, pp. 3–14.

Maslow, Abraham H. 1966. *The Psychology of Science: A Reconnaissance*. South Bend, IN: Gateway Editions, Ltd.

Maturana, Humberto R., and Varela, Francisco J. 1992. *The Tree of Knowledge: The Biological Roots of Human Understanding.* Boston: Shambala.

May, Rollo. 1976. *The Courage to Create.* New York: Bantam Books.

Mayer, Richard E. 1992. *Thinking, Problem Solving, Cognition.* New York: W.H. Freeman and Company.

Medawar, Peter. 1991. *The Threat and the Glory: Reflections on Science and Scientists.* Oxford: Oxford University Press.

Mesthene, Emmanuel G. 1990. The Role of Technology in Society. In *Technology and the Future*, edited by Albert H. Teich. New York: St. Martin's Press, pp. 77–99.

Metcalf, Fred. 1987. *The Penguin Dictionary of Modern Quotations.* London: Penguin Books.

Miller, Arthur I. 1989. Imagery and Intuition in Creative Scientific Thinking: Albert Einstein's Invention of the Special Theory of Relativity. In *Creative People at Work: Twelve Cognitive Case Studies*, edited by Doris B. Wallace and Howard E. Gruber. New York: Oxford University Press, pp. 171–185.

———. 1996. *Insights of Genius: Imagery and Creativity in Science and Art.* New York: Copernicus.

Mitchell, Russell. 1989. Nurturing Those Ideas. *Business Week* (special bonus issue), pp. 106–118.

———. Mining the Work Force for Ideas. *Business Week* (special bonus issue), p. 121.

Morris, Richard. 1993. Inventing the Universe. In *Creativity*, edited by John Brockman. New York: Simon & Schuster, pp. 130–148.

Morrison, Robert S. 1990. Visions. In *Technology and the Future*, edited by Albert H. Teich. New York: St. Martin's Press, pp. 15–38.

National Science Board Committee. 1991. Why U.S. Technology Leadership Is Eroding. *Research-Technology Management* (January–February), pp. 36–42.

Needham, Cynthia, Hoagland, Mahlon, McPherson, Kenneth, and Dodson, Bert. 2000. *Intimate Strangers: Unseen Life on Earth.* Washington, DC: ASM Press.

Norman, Donald A. 1993. *Things That Make Us Smart: Defending Human Attributes in the Age of the Machine.* Reading, MA: Addison-Wesley Publishing Company.

Oliver, Jack E. 1991. *The Incomplete Guide to the Art of Discovery.* New York: Columbia University Press.

Ornstein, Robert, and Ehrlich, Paul. 1990. *New World, New Mind: Moving toward Conscious Evolution.* New York: Simon & Schuster.

Osowkski, Jeffrey V. 1989. Ensembles of Metaphor in the Psychology of William James. In *Creative People at Work: Twelve Cognitive Case Studies*, edited by Doris B. Wallace and Howard E. Gruber. New York: Oxford University Press, pp. 126–145.

Otis, Harry B. 1990. *Simple Truths: The Best of the Cockle Bur.* Kansas City, MO: Andrews and McMeel.

Pacey, Arnold. 1992. *The Maze of Ingenuity: Ideas and Idealism in the Development of Technology.* Cambridge, MA: The MIT Press.

Pagels, Heinz R. 1994. *The Cosmic Code: Quantum Physics as the Language of Nature.* London: Penguin Books.

Pearson, Alan W. 1993. Management Development for Scientists and Engineers. *Research-Technology Management* (January–February), pp. 45–51.

Pendleton, Winston K. 1984. *Speaker's Handbook of Successful Openers and Closers*. Englewood Cliffs, NJ: Prentice-Hall.

Penrose, Roger. 1989. *The Emperor's New Mind: Concerning Computers, Minds, and the Laws of Physics*. Oxford: Oxford University Press.

———. 1995. Must Mathematical Physics Be Reductionist? In *Nature's Imagination: The Frontiers of Scientific Vision*, edited by John Cornwell. Oxford: Oxford University Press, pp. 12–26.

Perel, Mel. 1990. Discontinuities and Challenges in the Management of Technology. *Research-Technology Management* (July–August), pp. 7–9.

Pfeiffer, John E. 1982. *The Creative Explosion: An Inquiry into the Origins of Art and Religion*. Ithaca, NY: Cornell University Press, 1982.

Piatelli-Palmarini, Massimo. 1994. *Inevitable Illusions: How Mistakes of Reason Rule Our Minds*. New York: John Wiley & Sons.

Pinker, Steven. 1997. *How the Mind Works*. New York: W.W. Norton & Company.

Plotkin, Henry. 1994. *Darwin Machines and the Nature of Knowledge*. Cambridge, MA: Harvard University Press.

Port, Otis. 1989a. Back to Basics. *Business Week* (special bonus issue), pp. 14–18.

———. 1989b. Innovation in America. *Business Week* (special bonus issue), pp. 170–173.

Post, Robert C. 1978. The American Genius. In *The Smithsonian Book of Invention*. New York: W.W. Norton & Company, pp. 22–31.

Poundstone, William. 1988. *Labyrinths of Reason: Paradox, Puzzles and the Frailty of Knowledge*. New York: Anchor Books.

Price, Derek de Solla. 1986. The Evolution of Invention. In *The Smithsonian Book of Invention*. New York: Simon & Schuster, pp. 184–191.

Prigogine, Ilya, and Stengers, Isabelle. 1984. *Order Out of Chaos: Man's New Dialogue with Nature*. New York: Bantam Books.

Prochnow, Herbert V. 1982. *Toastmaster's Quips and Stories: And How to Use Them*. New York: Sterling Publishing Company.

Restak, Richard. 1984. *The Brain*. Toronto: Bantam Books.

———. 1991. *The Brain Has a Mind of Its Own: Insights from a Practicing Neurologist*. New York: Crown Trade Paperbacks.

———. 1993. The Creative Brain. In *Creativity*, edited by John Brockman. New York: Simon & Schuster, pp. 164–165.

Ridley, Matt. 1997. *The Origins of Virtue: Human Instincts and the Evolution of Cooperation*. New York: Viking.

———. 1999. *Genome: The Autobiography of a Species in 23 Chapters*. New York: HarperCollins.

Riordan, Michael, and Schramm, David N. 1991. *The Shadows of Creation: Dark Matter and the Structure of the Universe*. New York: W.H. Freeman and Company.

Root-Bernstein, Robert S. 1988. Setting the Stage for Discovery. *The Sciences* (May–June), pp. 26–34.

———. 1989a. *Discovering: Inventing and Solving Problems at the Frontiers of Scientific Knowledge*. Cambridge, MA: Harvard University Press.

————. 1989b. Strategies of Research. *Research-Technology Management* (May–June), pp. 36–41.

————. 1989c. Who Discovers and Invents. *Research-Technology Management* (January–February), pp. 43–50.

Rothenberg, Albert. 1990. *Creativity and Madness: New Findings and Old Stereotypes.* Baltimore, MD: The Johns Hopkins University Press.

Rothman, Tony, and Sudarshan, George. 1998. *Doubt and Certainty.* Reading, MA: Perseus Books.

Ruse, Michael. 1999. *Mystery of Mysteries: Is Evolution a Social Construction?* Cambridge, MA: Harvard University Press.

Russell, Bertrand. 1989. *Wisdom of the West.* London: Bloomsbury Books.

————. 1997. *Religion and Science.* New York: Oxford University Press.

Sagan, Carl. 1995. *The Demon-Haunted World: Science as a Candle in the Dark.* New York: Random House.

————. 1997. *Billions and Billions: Thoughts on Life and Death at the Brink of the Millennium.* New York: Random House.

Salmon, Wesley C. 1979. *The Foundation of Scientific Inference.* Pittsburgh: University of Pittsburgh Press.

Schwartz, Joseph. 1992. *The Creative Moment.* New York: HarperCollins.

Scolnick, Edward M. 1990. Basic Research and Its Impact on R&D. *Research-Technology Management* (November–December), pp. 21–25.

Searle, John. 1984. *Minds, Brains, and Science.* Cambridge, MA: Harvard University Press.

Seitz, Frederick. 1992. *The Science Matrix: The Journeys, Travails, Triumphs.* New York: Springer-Verlag.

Shapero, Albert. 1986. Creativity and Idea Management: Managing Creative Professionals. Selected papers from *Research Management* (1981–1986), pp. 25–30.

Shlain, Leonard. 1991. *Art & Physics: Parallel Visions in Space, Time and Light.* New York: William Morrow.

Siler, Todd. 1992. *Breaking the Mind Barrier: The Artscience of Neurocosmology.* New York: Simon & Schuster.

Simonton, Dean Keith. 1993. Genius and Chance: A Darwinian Perspective. In *Creativity*, edited by John Brockman. New York: Simon & Schuster, pp. 176–201.

Slobodkin, Lawrence B. 1992. *Simplicity and Complexity in Games of the Intellect.* Cambridge, MA: Harvard University Press.

Smolin, Lee. 1997. *The Life of the Cosmos.* New York: Oxford University Press.

Snow, C.P. 1959. *Two Cultures and the Scientific Revolution.* Cambridge: Cambridge University Press.

Souder, W.E. 1987. Stimulating and Managing Ideas. *Research-Technology Management* (May–June), pp. 13–17.

Staudenmaier, John M. 1994. Henry Ford's Big Flaw. *American Heritage of Invention and Technology* 10, pp. 34–42.

Stenger, Victor J. 1995. *The Unconscious Quantum: Metaphysics in Modern Physics and Cosmology.* Amherst, MA: Prometheus Books.

Stephan, Paula, and Levin, Sharon. 1992. *Striking the Mother Lode in Science: The Importance of Age, Place, and Time.* New York: Oxford University Press.

Sternberg, Robert J. 1988. *The Triarchic Mind: A New Theory of Human Intelligence.* New York: Viking.

Stevens, William K. 1999. *The Change in the Weather: People, Weather and the Science of Climate.* New York: Delacorte Press.

Tarnas, Richard. 1991. *The Passion of the Western Mind: Understanding the Ideas That Have Shaped Our World View.* New York: Ballantine Books.

Temple, Robert. 1986. *The Genius of China: 3,000 Years of Science, Discovery, and Invention.* New York: Simon & Schuster.

Thurow, Lester C. 1996. *The Future of Capitalism: How Today's Economic Forces Shape Tomorrow's World.* New York: William Morrow and Company.

Tweney, Ryan D. 1989. Fields of Enterprise: On Michael Faraday's Thought. In *Creative People at Work: Twelve Cognitive Case Studies,* edited by Doris B. Wallace and Howard E. Gruber. New York: Oxford University Press, pp. 91–106.

Weber, Joseph. 1989. A Culture That Just Keeps Dishing Up Success. *Business Week* (special bonus issue), p. 120.

Weiner, Jonathan. 1999. *Time, Love, Memory: A Great Biologist in His Quest for the Origins of Behavior.* New York: Vintage Books.

Weisberg, Robert W. 1993. *Creativity: Beyond the Myth of Genius.* New York: W.H. Freeman and Company.

West, Thomas G. 1991. *In the Mind's Eye: Visual Thinkers, Gifted People with Learning Difficulties, Computer Images, and the Ironies of Creativity.* Buffalo, NY: Prometheus Books.

White, Lynn, Jr. 1978. The Flowering of Medieval Invention. In *The Smithsonian Book of Invention.* New York: Simon and Schuster, pp. 64–71.

Wills, Christopher. 1998. *Children of Prometheus: The Accelerating Pace of Human Evolution.* Reading, MA: Perseus Books.

Wilson, Edward O. 1998. *Consilience: The Unity of Knowledge.* New York: Alfred A. Knopf.

———. 1999. *The Diversity of Life.* New York: W.W. Norton & Company.

Wolff, Michael. 1978. What Do We Really Know about Managing R&D? A Talk with Edwin P. Roberts. *Research Management* (November), pp. 6–11.

———. 1981. The Why, When and How of Directed Basic Research. *Research Management* (May), pp. 29–31.

———. 1987. To Innovate Faster, Try the Skunk Works. *Research-Technology Management* (September–October), pp. 35–36.

———. 1988. Fostering Breakthrough Innovations. *Research-Technology Management* (November–December), pp. 8–9.

Wolpert, Lewis. 1993. *The Unnatural Nature of Science.* Cambridge, MA: Harvard University Press.

Wright, Robert. 1994. *The Moral Animal: Evolutionary Psychology and Everyday Life.* New York: Vintage Books.

Wright, Will. 1992. *Wild Knowledge: Science, Language, and Social Life in a Fragile Environment.* Minneapolis: University of Minnesota Press.

Wright, William. 1998. *Born That Way: Genes, Behavior, Personality.* New York: Alfred A. Knopf.

Young, John A. 1990. Technology and Competitiveness: A Key to the Economic

Future of the United States. In *Technology and the Future*, edited by Albert H. Teich. New York: St. Martin's Press, pp. 299–310.

Ziman, John. 1991. *Reliable Knowledge: An Exploration of the Grounds for Belief in Science*. Cambridge: Cambridge University Press.

———. 1994. *Prometheus Bound: Science in a Dynamic Steady State*. Cambridge: Cambridge University Press.

Zohar, Danah. 1993. Creativity and the Quantum Self. In *Creativity*, edited by John Brockman. New York: Simon & Schuster, pp. 202–218.

# Index

## About the Author

WAYNE M. BUNDY holds a doctorate in geology and specialized in clay minerology and geochemistry until his retirement. He has worked for the New Mexico Bureau of Mines, the Indiana Geological Survey, and as Vice President of Technology for the Georgia Kaolin Co. He has published articles in the journals of his field and holds nine U.S. patents. This is the second of his two recent books on the topic of innovation and creativity.